T0212490

Lecture Notes in Computer Science 9764

Commenced Publication in 1973
Founding and Former Series Editors:
Gerhard Goos, Juris Hartmanis, and Jan van Leeuwen

More information about this series at http://www.springer.com/series/7408

Andrzej Wąsowski · Henrik Lönn (Eds.)

Modelling Foundations and Applications

12th European Conference, ECMFA 2016
Held as Part of STAF 2016
Vienna, Austria, July 6–7, 2016
Proceedings

 Springer

Editors
Andrzej Wąsowski
IT University of Copenhagen
Copenhagen
Denmark

Henrik Lönn
Volvo Group Trucks Technology
Gothenburg
Sweden

ISSN 0302-9743   ISSN 1611-3349   (electronic)
Lecture Notes in Computer Science
ISBN 978-3-319-42060-8   ISBN 978-3-319-42061-5   (eBook)
DOI 10.1007/978-3-319-42061-5

Library of Congress Control Number: 2016943463

LNCS Sublibrary: SL2 – Programming and Software Engineering

Printed on acid-free paper

This Springer imprint is published by Springer Nature
The registered company is Springer International Publishing AG Switzerland

Foreword

Software Technologies: Applications and Foundations (STAF) is a federation of leading conferences on software technologies. It provides a loose umbrella organization with a Steering Committee that ensures continuity. The STAF federated event takes place annually. The participating conferences may vary from year to year, but all focus on foundational and practical advances in software technology. The conferences address all aspects of software technology, from object-oriented design, testing, mathematical approaches to modeling and verification, transformation, model-driven engineering, aspect-oriented techniques, and tools.

STAF 2016 took place at TU Wien, Austria, during July 4–8, 2016, and hosted the five conferences ECMFA 2016, ICGT 2016, ICMT 2016, SEFM 2016, and TAP 2016, the transformation tool contest TTC 2016, eight workshops, a doctoral symposium, and a projects showcase event. STAF 2016 featured eight internationally renowned keynote speakers, and welcomed participants from around the world.

The STAF 2016 Organizing Committee thanks (a) all participants for submitting to and attending the event, (b) the program chairs and Steering Committee members of the individual conferences and satellite events for their hard work, (c) the keynote speakers for their thoughtful, insightful, and inspiring talks, and (d) TU Wien, the city of Vienna, and all sponsors for their support. A special thank you goes to the members of the Business Informatics Group, coping with all the foreseen and unforeseen work (as usual ☺)!

July 2016   Gerti Kappel

Preface

The European Conference on Modelling Foundations and Applications (ECMFA) is dedicated to advancing the state of knowledge and fostering the industrial application of model-based engineering (MBE) and related methods. By model-based engineering we understand an approach to the design, analysis, and development of software and systems that relies on exploiting high-level models and computer-based automation to achieve significant boosts in both productivity and quality.

The 12th edition of ECMFA was held during July 6–7, 2016, in Vienna as part of the Software Technologies: Applications and Foundations (STAF) federation of conferences. The Program Committee received 47 submissions. Each submission was reviewed by at least three Program Committee members. The committee decided to accept 16 papers, 12 papers for the Foundations Track and four papers for the Applications Track, resulting in an overall acceptance rate of 34 %. Papers on a wide range of MBE aspects were accepted, including topics such as foundations for modeling semantics, model management and evolution, model transformation, modeling tools, and model-driven engineering in neurorobotics.

We thank Krzysztof Czarnecki and Stefan Voget for interesting talks on the use of MDE in the automotive domain and other areas of embedded systems engineering. Furthermore, we are grateful to all the Program Committee members and all additional reviewers for providing their expertise and quality while reviewing the submitted papers. Their helpful and constructive feedback is most appreciated. We thank the STAF organization for providing an excellent framework in which ECMFA can continue to exist. Last but certainly not least, we thank all authors who submitted papers to ECMFA 2016, contributing to this important research area.

July 2016

Andrzej Wąsowski
Henrik Lönn

Organization

Program Committee

Andreas Abele	Robert Bosch GmbH
Shaukat Ali	Simula Research Laboratory, Norway
Behzad Bordbar	University of Birmingham, UK
Goetz Botterweck	Lero, University of Limerick, Ireland
Marco Brambilla	Politecnico di Milano, Italy
Ruth Breu	University of Innsbruck, Austria
Jean-Michel Bruel	IRIT, France
Jordi Cabot	ICREA - UOC (Internet Interdisciplinary Institute), Spain
Marsha Chechik	University of Toronto, Ontario, Canada
Federico Ciccozzi	Mälardalen University, Sweden
Benoit Combemale	IRISA, Université de Rennes 1, France
Nancy Day	University of Waterloo, Canada
Juergen Dingel	Queen's University, Canada
Maged Elaasar	JPL, USA
Sebastien Gerard	CEA, LIST, France
Sudipto Ghosh	Colorado State University, USA
Martin Gogolla	University of Bremen, Germany
Jeff Gray	University of Alabama, USA
Esther Guerra	Universidad Autónoma de Madrid, Spain
Oystein Haugen	Østfold University College, Norway
Regina Hebig	Chalmers — Gothenburg University, Sweden
Thomas Hildebrandt	IT University of Copenhagen, Denmark
Ekkart Kindler	Technical University of Denmark
Dimitris Kolovos	University of York, UK
Thomas Kuehne	Victoria University of Wellington, New Zealand
Vinay Kulkarni	Tata Consultancy Services, India
Philip Langer	EclipseSource, Austria
Roberto Erick Lopez-Herrejon	Institute for Systems Engineering and Automation, Johannes Kepler University, Austria
Ralf Lämmel	Universität Koblenz-Landau, Germany
Henrik Lönn	Volvo, Sweden
Shahar Maoz	Tel Aviv University, Israel
Ileana Ober	IRIT - Université de Toulouse, France
Rolf-Helge Pfeiffer	DMI, Denmark
Daniel Ratiu	Siemens Corporate Technology, Munich, Germany
Charles Rivet	Zeligsoft, Canada
Bernhard Rumpe	RWTH Aachen University, Germany

Houari Sahraoui	DIRO, Université De Montréal, Canada
Rick Salay	University of Toronto, Canada
Ina Schaefer	Technische Universität Braunschweig, Germany
Bernhard Schaetz	TU München, Germany
Andy Schürr	TU Darmstadt, Germany
Michal Smialek	Warsaw University of Technology, Poland
Perdita Stevens	University of Edinburgh, UK
Harald Störrle	Danmarks Tekniske Universitet, Denmark
Gabriele Taentzer	Philipps-Universität Marburg, Germany
Ramin Tavakoli Kolagari	Nuremberg Institute of Technology, Germany
Francois Terrier	CEA, LIST, France
Juha-Pekka Tolvanen	MetaCase, Finland
Antonio Vallecillo	Universidad de Málaga, Spain
Mark Van Den Brand	Eindhoven University of Technology, The Netherlands
Hans Vangheluwe	University of Antwerp, Belgium and McGill University, Canada
Daniel Varro	Budapest University of Technology and Economics, Hungary
Stefan Voget	Continental Automotive GmbH
Andrzej Wąsowski	IT University of Copenhagen, Denmark
Manuel Wimmer	Business Informatics Group, Vienna University of Technology, Austria
Steffen Zschaler	King's College London, UK

Additional Reviewers

Babur, Önder	Heinz, Marcel
Baller, Hauke	Hili, Nicolas
Bayha, Andreas	Härtel, Johannes
Berardinelli, Luca	Jäger, Alexandra
Bergmayr, Alexander	Karsten, Sohr
Bucaioni, Alessio	Kelter, Udo
Bürdek, Johannes	Kluge, Roland
Canovas Izquierdo, Javier Luis	Kowal, Matthias
Clarisó, Robert	Kulcsár, Géza
Corley, Jonathan	Kusmenko, Evgeny
Debreceni, Csaba	Martínez, Salvador
Degueule, Thomas	Mayerhofer, Tanja
Disenfeld, Cynthia	McKinna, James
Doan, Khanh-Hoang	Mengerink, Josh
Garcia-Dominguez, Antonio	Morelli, Matteo
Gönczy, László	Nguyen, Phu
Haeusler, Martin	Salay, Rick

Seidl, Christoph
Selim, Gehan
Strüber, Daniel
Sutii, Ana-Maria
Tzoref-Brill, Rachel

Wang, Shuai
Weckesser, Markus
Wei, Ran
Whiteside, Iain

Keynotes

A Model-Based Driver's License
for Self-Driving Cars:
Challenges and Future Directions

Krzysztof Czarnecki

University of Waterloo, Canada
czarnec@gsd.uwaterloo.ca

Abstract. Vehicles with limited self-driving capabilities are already on the market and some car makers have promised products capable of autonomous driving in an urban setting in 2020. Self-driving cars will eventually completely transform the automotive industry, replacing private car ownership by service-based products such as robotic cabs. The deployment of large-scale self-driving vehicle fleets will reduce the number of crashes and crash severity, reduce emissions, allow commuters to use their time more effectively, and free up spaces occupied by parked cars. The engineering of self-driving cars requires sophisticated models of the environment and the electronic driver system in order to develop the necessary perception and motion planning and control functions. While current self-driving technologies have improved immensely in recent years, a major challenge is assuring the safe operation of an autonomous vehicle in all traffic situations and all road conditions. I will present a reference architecture for self-driving cars and use it to describe the types of models used in engineering of such systems. I will then focus on the challenges of assuring model-based engineering of self-driving cars. I will close by outlining promising directions to address these challenges.

Usage of Domain Specific Modeling Languages in the Automotive Industry

Stefan Voget

Continental Automotive GmbH
stefan.voget@continental-corporation.com

Abstract. Before the introduction of model based engineering, the answer for the language question within the automotive industry was simple: use C. The idea of model based engineering is to shift the complexity out of a textual representation of the code (the source code in C) to a model. Here, the question about language comes up again. This time, it revolves around the decision which language to use to represent the model. Today, the answer is not that simple anymore. Within the automotive industry nearly each project uses it's own representation. Often the representation is determined by the architectural tool used in the project. To become independent from these "tool languages", more and more domain specific modeling languages come up, most of which end up as project specific modeling languages, i.e. specific languages used only in a very dedicated context. In the keynote I will present a motivation for the definition and usage of domain specific modeling languages by using two examples. The first example integrates the development lifecycle of a SW developer with the one of a responsible for functional safety. The second example describes a unified approach for the configuration of different software platforms. Both examples and their motivations are quite different from each other, but show the needs for comprehensive common languages and the importance of model to model transformations to interact between them.

Contents

Experience Reports and Case Studies

Variability and Uncertainty

Multi- and Many Models

Hierarchical Clustering of Metamodels for Comparative Analysis and Visualization

Önder Babur[1]([⊠]), Loek Cleophas[1,2], and Mark van den Brand[1]

[1] Eindhoven University of Technology, 5600 MB Eindhoven, The Netherlands
{O.Babur,L.G.W.A.Cleophas,M.G.J.v.d.Brand}@tue.nl
[2] Stellenbosch University, Matieland 7602, South Africa

Abstract. Many applications in Model-Driven Engineering involve processing multiple models or metamodels. A good example is the comparison and merging of metamodel variants into a common metamodel in domain model recovery. Although there are many sophisticated techniques to process the input dataset, little attention has been given to the initial data analysis, visualization and filtering activities. These are hard to ignore especially in the case of a large dataset, possibly with outliers and sub-groupings. In this paper we present a generic approach for metamodel comparison, analysis and visualization as an exploratory first step for domain model recovery. We propose representing metamodels in a vector space model, and applying hierarchical clustering techniques to compare and visualize them as a tree structure. We demonstrate our approach on two Ecore datasets: a collection of 50 state machine metamodels extracted from GitHub as top search results; and ~100 metamodels from 16 different domains, obtained from AtlanMod Metamodel Zoo.

Keywords: Model-Driven Engineering · Model comparison · Vector space model · R · Hierarchical clustering

1 Introduction

Model-Driven Engineering (MDE) promotes the use of models and metamodels as first-class artefacts to tackle the complexity of software systems [15]. As MDE is applied for larger problems, the complexity, size and variety of models increase. With respect to model size, the issue of scalability has been pointed out by Kolovos et al. [15]. However, scalability with respect to model variety and multiplicity (i.e. dealing with a large number of different models) is also an important issue, and has been diagnosed by Klint et al. as an interesting aspect to explore [14]. There are many approaches to fundamental operations such as model comparison [25] and matching [16]; applied to problems such as model merging [8], versioning [3] and clone detection [9]; however those mainly focus

---

The research leading to these results has been funded by EU programme FP7-NMP-2013-SMALL-7 under grant agreement number 604279 (MMP).

A. Wąsowski and H. Lönn (Eds.): ECMFA 2016, LNCS 9764, pp. 3–18, 2016.
DOI: 10.1007/978-3-319-42061-5_1

on pairwise and 'deep' comparison of models to achieve high accuracy for a very small number of models. [23] further discusses the inadequacy of pairwise comparison for multiple models and proposes an N-way model merging algorithm.

Indeed, many problems in MDE involve processing a potentially large number of models. Some good examples are domain model recovery from several candidate (meta-)models [14], metamodel recovery [13] and family mining for Software Product Lines (SPL) from model variants [11]. A further problem can be given in the context of our ongoing project for a flexible multiphysics engineering simulation framework, where the domain contains an overwhelming number of tools [5], making it difficult to extend manual model extraction efforts such as in [6] to cover the whole domain.

We are interested in the case where a common (meta-)model is reverse engineered out of several candidate (meta-)models. For this paper we focus particularly on metamodel comparison and clustering; however our techniques are generic and thus applicable for the general model comparison and clustering problems. In essence, we treat metamodels as instances of the meta-metamodel. Having said that, the rest of the paper uses this convention. We argue that, as the number and variety of input metamodels gets larger, the initial data analysis and preprocessing step gets more and more relevant and necessary. This in turn calls for a need to inspect the dataset for an overview, identify potential relations between them such as proximities, cluster formations, outliers, etc. This information can be used potentially for filtering noisy data, for grouping metamodels, or even for determining the order of processing for a pairwise metamodel merging or SPL generation algorithm (see [23] for a discussion on how pairwise comparison order affects the outcome of merging multiple models).

In this paper, we present a continuation of our previous study [4]. We propose hierarchical clustering for comparative analysis and visualization of the dataset as a first explorative step in domain model recovery. We apply techniques from the Information Retrieval (IR) and unsupervised machine learning domains in the MDE context. In IR, a vector space model (VSM) is used to represent text documents, with vector elements corresponding to word occurrence (incidence) or frequency. We borrow this concept to represent metamodels as vectors of the unigrams from metamodel element identifiers. We apply an array of NLP techniques and weighting schemes to further improve the VSM and reduce the metamodel comparison problem into distance calculation between points in the vector space. We then use the R statistical software [20] to hierarchically cluster, analyse and visualize the dataset as a hierarchical structure. We demonstrate our approach on two Ecore datasets: a collection of 50 state machine metamodels extracted from GitHub as top search results, and ~100 metamodels from 16 different domains, obtained from AtlanMod Metamodel Zoo.

Objectives. The purpose of this study is to answer the following questions:

- **RQ1.** How can we represent metamodels for large-scale comparative analysis?
- **RQ2.** How can we analyse, compare and visualize a large set of metamodels?

2   Preliminaries: Information Retrieval and Clustering

Information Retrieval [19] has a long history of developments in dealing with effectively indexing, analyzing and searching various forms of content including natural language text documents. As a first step for document retrieval in general, documents are collected and indexed via some unit of representation. Index construction can be implemented using models ranging from boolean indices to complex neural networks. One such model is the vector space model (VSM) with the following major components:

- A vector representation of (binary) occurrence of the vocabulary in a document, named *term incidence*;
- Optionally *zones* (e.g. 'author' or 'title' zones separate from the text bodies),
- Optionally weighting schemes to be used as multipliers such as:
  - *inverse document frequency (idf)* (see Sect. 3.1) to increase the discriminative effect of rare words,
  - zone weights, e.g. higher for important zones,
- Optionally Natural Language processing (NLP) techniques such as:
  - methods for handling compound terms, e.g. tokenization or multi-word similarity measures,
  - methods for detecting synonyms, hyponyms, and semantically related words, e.g. use of a stemmer or WordNet[1].

The VSM allows transforming each document into an n-dimensional vector, thus resulting in an $m \times n$ matrix where m is the number of documents and n is the size of the vocabulary.

Once the VSM is constructed, the similarity of documents can be defined as the distance between these vectors. There exist several distance a.k.a. similarity measures, such as Euclidian, Cosine or Manhattan, to be chosen considering the underlying problem domain and dataset. VSM with a selected distance measure is the prerequisite for identifying similar groups of documents in the vector space. This unsupervised machine learning technique is called clustering. Among many different clustering methods [12,19], there is a major distinction between flat clustering and hierarchical clustering. Flat clustering needs a pre-specified number of clusters and results in a flat assignment of each document into one cluster. Hierarchical clustering, on the other hand, does not require a pre-specified number of clusters, and outputs a hierarchy of proximities; it thus is more flexible and informative than flat clustering. Specifically, hierarchical agglomerative clustering (HAC) outputs a nested tree structure called *dendrogram*, which is suitable for visualization and manual inspection. As can be seen in Fig. 3, the leaves of the dendrogram represent data points, and each merge is represented by a horizontal line. The height of the merge point corresponds to the distance (inverse similarity) of the data points and/or subclusters.

The HAC algorithm calculates the pairwise distances of all the points in the dataset. In a bottom-up manner, it starts with each data point in a separate

---

[1] https://wordnet.princeton.edu/.

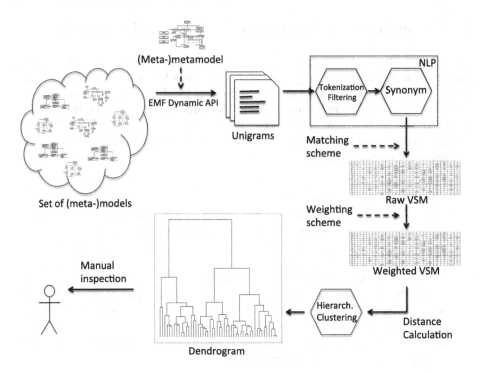

Fig. 1. Overview of our approach.

cluster and recursively merges similar points/clusters into bigger clusters. There is a further parameter for HAC for determining how this merge is decided with respect to the inter-cluster distance: single-link assumes cluster distance is the maximum similarity of any individual points in two clusters, while complete and average-link are the correspondingly minimum and average similarity.

3   Method for Metamodel Clustering

In this section, we elaborate our approach on a small example. The method is based on that in [4], extended with various features. We put emphasis on NLP aspects and real datasets, and as a result choose to use unigrams (item 2(a) below) rather than bigrams (sequence of two related unigrams, e.g. a class X with its attribute Y). The readers are referred to Sect. 5.1 for a short discussion on this choice. An overview of our approach is given in Fig. 1 with the main steps as:

1. Obtaining input dataset
   (a) Obtaining a set of metamodels with the same type, e.g. Ecore metamodels in our case, to be analyzed,
2. Creating VSM representation

    (a) Generating the unigram vocabulary (i.e. the element identifiers) from the input metamodels and the unigram types (similar to zones in IR) from the meta-metamodel (the generic Ecore meta-metamodel in our case, rather than lower level domain-specific ones),

    (b) Expanding the unigrams with tokenization, and then filtering e.g. stop-words,

    (c) Detecting synonyms and relatedness amongst tokens,

    (d) Utilizing a synonym and type matching mechanism/threshold,

    (e) Utilizing an idf and type-based weighting scheme,

    (f) Calculating the term incidence matrix,

3. Clustering

    (a) Picking a distance measure and calculating the vector distances,

    (b) Applying hierarchical clustering over the VSM,

    (c) Visualizing the resulting dendrogram for manual inspection.

A Small Example Dataset. Here we introduce a small dataset of Ecore-based metamodels. In contrast to [4], we build this work directly on Ecore, though we extract a subset of the metamodel elements (see Sect. 3.1). Here we gather 4 metamodels related to state machines, selected from our first case study (Sect. 4.1). The dataset, depicted in Fig. 2, consists of two plain finite state machine (FSM) metamodels; one hierarchical FSM metamodel (the latter has the package name FSM though); and one data flow metamodel.

3.1   Representation as VSM

Generating the unigram vocabulary. From the input metamodels and Ecore meta-metamodel, we construct a typed unigram vocabulary. We adopt a *bag of words* representation for the vocabulary, where each item in the vocabulary is considered individually, discarding the context and order. The type information comes from Ecore ENamedElements, i.e. identifiers: we get the set {**EPackage, EDataType, EClass, EAttribute, EReference, EEnum, EEnumLiteral** and **EDataType**}. Next, we use the EMF Reflexive API (in Java) to recursively go over all the content for each metamodel element to extract the union of unigrams. The first metamodel in Fig. 2 would yield **Metamodel 1 = {FSM(EPackage), StateMachine(EClass), transitions(EReference), states(EReference), name(EAttribute), ... }**. Note that several parts of Ecore are deliberately not included in the unigram generation such as EAnnotations and OCL constraints. These are negligible in our case studies, might require further techniques, and are left as future work.

Vocabulary expansion with tokenization, and then filtering. As identifiers in the metamodels typically are compound names (similar to source code identifiers), we apply tokenization and turn compound names into their tokens to include the vocabulary. We use the Identifier Name Tokenization Tool[2] for implementing this

---

[2] https://github.com/sjbutler/intt

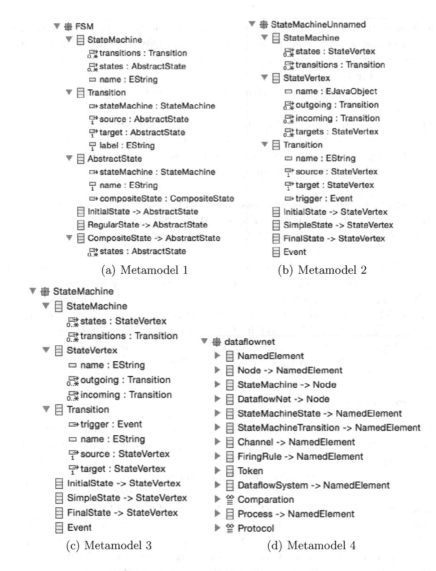

(a) Metamodel 1　　　　(b) Metamodel 2

(c) Metamodel 3　　　　(d) Metamodel 4

Fig. 2. Example dataset.

functionality. The types of the original identifiers are retained in the tokens. The expansion of **StateMachine(EClass)** for instance would yield **State(EClass)** and **Machine(EClass)** unigrams. Afterwards we apply a set of filters for the tokens: removal of stop words such as *'of'* and *'from'*, removal of overly short tokens (< 3 characters) and ones consisting of only digits. Note that having done this tokenization step, we use term and token interchangeably for this paper. It is also noteworthy to mention that tokenization reduces the vector space for large datasets significantly: e.g. from 7507 to 5842 for case study 2 (Sect. 4.2).

This contributes to the scalability of the approach with respect to the growing size of the dataset.

NLP techniques for synonym and relatedness detection. For the synonym and relatedness detection, we use another array of techniques after normalizing all the tokens into lower case. First of all, we use a Porter Stemmer (Java implementation[3]) for comparing word stems (e.g. *'located', 'location'* and *'locations'* have the common stem *'locat'* and therefore are considered synonyms. Next we measure the normalized Levenshtein distances of the tokens, and consider close words (< 0.1 difference) as synonyms. This allows for approximate string matching, tackling e.g. small typos. Finally, tokens which have a WordNet[4] WuP similarity score above a certain threshold (0.8 for the examples here) are considered synonyms. We use the WS4J Java library[5] for this calculation.

Unigram matching scheme. We further use a type matching and synonym matching scheme. When comparing two typed unigrams, we add a reducing multiplier of 0.5 for non-exact type matches and use the similarity score as a reducing multiplier for synonym matching. As an example a typed unigram **name(EAttribute)** would yield 1 when matched against itself, while yielding $0.5 * 0.88 = 0.44$ against **label(EReference)**, where 0.88 is the WordNet WuP similarity score of *'name'* and *'label'*. As mentioned before, a detailed evaluation of different values and parameter settings is out of scope for this paper and left as future work.

Idf and type weighting scheme. The similarity calculation described above gives a score in the range $[0, 1]$ for each metamodel-token pair. On top of this, we apply a weighting scheme on the term incidence matrix, which includes two multipliers: an inverse document frequency (idf) and a type (zone) weight. The idf of a term t is used to assign greater weight to rare terms across metamodels. Idf as the normalized log is defined as:

$$idf(t) = log_{10}\left(1 + \frac{\text{\# total metamodels}}{\text{\# metamodels with the term t}}\right) \qquad (1)$$

Furthermore, a type weight is given to the unigrams representing their semantic importance. We use a similar scheme as in [4], this time for all the Ecore ENamedElements listed above. We claim, for instance, that classes are semantically more important than attributes, thus deserve a greater weight. We have used this experimental scheme for this paper:

$$typeWeight(t, w) : \{\text{EPackage} \rightarrow 1.0, \text{EDataType} \rightarrow 0.2, \text{EClass} \rightarrow 1.0,$$
$$\text{EReference} \rightarrow 0.5, \text{EAttribute} \rightarrow 0.3, \text{EEnum} \rightarrow 1.0,$$
$$\text{EEnumLiteral} \rightarrow 1.0, \text{EOperation} \rightarrow 0.5, \text{EParameter} \rightarrow 0.1\}$$

---

[3] http://tartarus.org/martin/PorterStemmer/.
[4] https://wordnet.princeton.edu/.
[5] https://github.com/coriane/ws4j.

A part of the resulting matrix where all the preprocessing steps above have been done, and the term incidences have been multiplied by idf and weights, is given in Table 1.

Table 1. Idf and type weighted term incidence matrix.

Metamodel	FSM	State	Machine	source	label	Initial	Channels	...
M1	0.35	0.15	0.15	0.09	0.05	0.15	0	...
M2	0	0.15	0.15	0.09	0.05	0.15	0	...
M3	0	0.15	0.15	0.09	0.04	0.15	0	...
M4	0	0.15	0.15	0	0.04	0.15	0.18	...

3.2 Clustering

Picking a distance measure and calculating the distance matrix. As the next step of our approach, we reduce the metamodel similarity problem into a distance measurement of the corresponding vector representations of metamodels. We had previously suggested to pick Manhattan distance [4]. In common natural language text retrieval problems however, cosine distance is used most frequently. Based on the empirical comparisons between the two and the fact that cosine distance is a length normalized metric in the range [0, 1] (while Manhattan is not), we choose to use cosine distance for our current work. A quantitative evaluation of the various framework parameters such as distance measure and their effect on clustering is left as future work. p and q being two vectors of n dimensions, cosine distance is defined as:

$$cosineDistance(p, q) = 1 - \frac{p \cdot q}{\| p \| \| q \|} = 1 - \frac{\sum_{i=1}^{n} p_i q_i}{\sqrt{\sum_{i=1}^{n} p_i^2} \sqrt{\sum_{i=1}^{n} q_i^2}}. \qquad (2)$$

To be used by the hierarchical clustering, we calculate the pairwise distance matrix of all the models. The distance matrix for the example dataset is given in Table 2. We use the lsa package in R for this computation [27].

Hierarchical clustering and visualization. We apply agglomerative hierarchical clustering over the VSM to obtain a dendrogram visualization. We used the hclust function in the stats package [20] with average linkage to compute the dendrogram. The interpretation of this diagram depicted in Fig. 3 is as follows: the red and green dotted line at heights 0.3 and 0.6 (manually inserted by us) denote horizontal cuts in the dendrogram. Metamodel 4, which stays far above the cut, can be considered as a clear outlier. Depending on the requirements and interpretation of the user, Metamodels 1–3 can be considered to be in one single cluster (i.e. dendrogram cut at height = 0.6) or just Metamodels 2 and 3 (i.e. cut at height = 0.3).

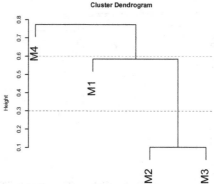

Table 2. Pairwise distance matrix.

	M1	M2	M3
M2	0.61		
M3	0.56	0.10	
M4	0.72	0.81	0.79

Fig. 3. Dendrogram of the examples. (Color figure online)

4 Case Studies

We introduce two case studies to demonstrate the feasibility of our approach.

4.1 Case Study 1 - GitHub Search Results

Dataset design. For this case study, we searched GitHub[6] on 11.02.2016 for Ecore metamodels using the search terms *'state machine extension:ecore'* and extracted the top 50 results out of 1089 (code) results in total, sorted by *Best Match* criteria. The search facility of GitHub has an internal mechanism for indexing and retrieving relevant text files. Although the intention of this search is to obtain various types of state machine metamodels, we expect to get a heterogeneous dataset, and apply clustering to give an overview of the results.

Objectives. This case study aims to demonstrate the applicability of our approach in a large dataset of a single domain (i.e. state machines), with possible duplicates, outliers, and subdomains. We are eventually interested in large (i.e. > 3 data points) groups of closely similar (e.g. cosine distance < 0.8) metamodels and wish to exclude the outliers. The fact that the we obtain metamodels through searching in GitHub also leads to a secondary objective of metamodel searching and exploration (e.g. for reuse, in the sense of traversing a repository/search results and finding the desired metamodels).

Results. Figure 4 shows the resulting dendrogram. We have visually identified and labelled the clusters from 1 to 5. Cluster 1 composes of two very similar (distance < 0.1) groups of duplicate metamodels (distance = 0) as basic FSMs with states, transitions and associations. In Cluster 2, there are two groups of UML-labelled metamodels with controller elements, triggers, etc. Cluster 3 has metamodels with specializations such as initial and final states, while Cluster 4

---

[6] https://github.com.

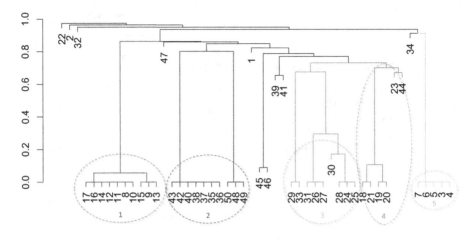

Fig. 4. Dendrogram of the first dataset.

has hierarchical state machines with composite states (Metamodel 23 is a false positive: it is labelled NHSM - *non*-hierarchical and is yet put in this cluster). Cluster 5 has duplicate metamodels labelled as AUIML with agents, messages, etc. and is clearly separate from the rest of the clusters. Outliers include a metamodel with identifiers in French (22), a train behaviour metamodel (2), the dataflow metamodel as given in the example dataset (34) and so on. The models 45, 46, 39 and 41 are deliberately not considered as a cluster due to the requirements we set above regarding cluster size and maximum distance.

4.2 Case Study 2 - AtlanMod Metamodel Zoo

Dataset design. For this case study, we used a subset of the Ecore metamodels in the AtlanMod Ecore Metamodel Zoo[7]. The Zoo is a collaborative open repository of metamodels in various formalisms including Ecore, intended to be used as experimental material by the MDE community. The repository itself has a wide range of metamodels from different domains; e.g. huge metamodels for programming languages or small class diagram examples for specific problems. We manually selected a subset of 107 metamodels, from 16 different domains. The domain labels are mostly retained as labelled in the repository. Table 3 depicts the domain decomposition. The cell below each domain shows the total number of metamodels in that domain, and the corresponding identifiers used in the resulting dendrogram in Fig. 5.

Objectives. This case study aims to demonstrate the applicability of our approach in a large dataset of multiple domains and subdomains. The domains are chosen to be in a wide range, hence the clustering is meant to show the groups

---

[7] http://web.emn.fr/x-info/atlanmod/index.php?title=Ecore.

Table 3. Number of metamodels in each domain in case study 2

Bibliography	Conference	Business process	Bug tracker	Multi-agent	ADL
8(1–8)	14(9–22)	6(23–28)	3(29–31)	2(32–33)	15(34–48)
Build Tool	Data Warehouse	Database	Office	Performance	SBVR
5(49–53)	6(54–59)	5(60–64)	10(65–74)	3(75–77)	4(78–81)
Soft. Process	State Machine	Petri Net	Use Case	Total	
3(82–84)	8(85–92)	11(93–103)	4(104–107)	107	

and subgroups in the dataset in a bird's eye point of view. The fact that the metamodels reside in a well-known repository also leads to a side-objective of model repository management and exploration.

Results. Figure 5 shows the resulting dendrogram. We have visually identified and labelled the clusters from 1 to 16. Let us summarize a part of this dendrogram. Cluster 1 (multi-agent) is recognizable as a separate small cluster from the rest of the dataset. Clusters 2 (petri nets) and 3 (state machines) reside as sibling branches. Similarly, clusters 4 (bibliography) and 5 (conference) are clearly detectable as sibling clusters. Cluster 6 and to some extent 8 are a mixture of individual metamodels from different domains, therefore are erroneous according to our initial categorization. Cluster 7 is of build tools. Cluster 9 (database) is in close proximity to the big cluster 10 (office), the latter of which can be decomposed into two subclusters (left subtree as Word, and right as Excel). Clusters 11–16 correspond to various remaining domains with varying percentages of false positives.

As an external measure of cluster validity, we employ the $F_{0.5}$ measure. Given k as the cluster labels found by our algorithm, l as the reference cluster labels and *cluster pairs* as the pairs of data points in the same cluster, $F_{0.5}$ can be defined as:

$$F_{0.5}(k, l) = \frac{1.25 * Precision(k, l) * Recall(k, l)}{0.25 * Precision(k, l) + Recall(k, l)} \tag{3}$$

$$Precision(k, l) = \frac{|\text{ cluster pairs in } k \cap \text{cluster pairs in } l|}{|\text{ cluster pairs in } k|} \tag{4}$$

$$Recall(k, l) = \frac{|\text{ cluster pairs in } k \cap \text{cluster pairs in } l|}{|\text{ cluster pairs in } l|} \tag{5}$$

The reason for selecting this measure is that the F_β measure is more common than e.g. purity or the Rand index in the software engineering community, and that we value precision higher than recall; hence the $F_{0.5}$ variant. According to this formula, and using the R package `clusteval` [21] for the co-membership table computation, we obtain an $F_{0.5}$ score of 0.73 for our manual clustering.

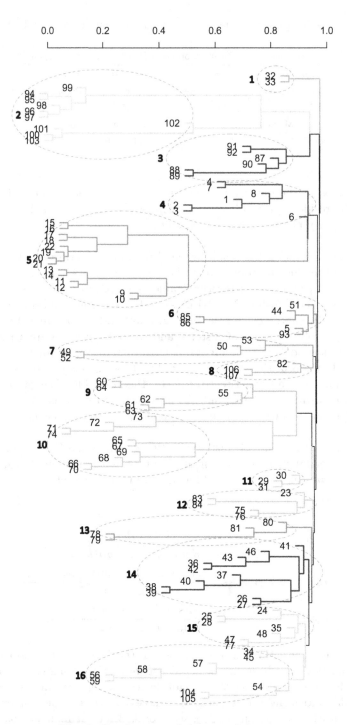

Fig. 5. Dendrogram of the second dataset.

5 Discussion

This paper improves our previous work in [4] considerably, in terms of NLP features and case studies on real datasets. Based on the two case studies, we confirm our previous claim that a statistical perspective on the comparative analysis and visualization of large datasets seems promising. We make a step towards the handling of large datasets. Using VSM allows a uniform representation of metamodels for statistical analysis, while the accompanying idf and type-based weighting scheme yields a suitable scaling in the vector space (**RQ1**). Using a distance measure and hierarchical clustering over VSM, many characteristics and relations among the metamodels, such as clusters, subclusters and outliers, can be analyzed and visualized via a dendrogram (**RQ2**).

Particularly for the first case study, it is clearly noticeable that there are distinct outliers and groupings in the search results. This information can be used for instance by a domain model recovery tool to improve the quality of the domain model. Furthermore, the model search functionality, either in GitHub or a specialized model search engine such as [18], can improve the navigation or precision of the search results. The second case study, on the other hand, deals with a heterogeneous set of domains and allows identifying domains, subdomains and also the proximities between related ones. We achieve a $F_{0.5}$ score of 0.73 from our manual clustering, which can be considered quite high for such a heterogeneous dataset. This grouping information can be used for domain model recovery as well as model repository management scenarios.

An advantage of our approach is the scalability and tool support. The algorithm complexities range from linear (e.g. VSM construction) to polynomial (hierarchical clustering) with respect to the size of the dataset and of the metamodels in it. Indeed this technique, and more advanced versions thereof, have already been in widespread use in IR for document retrieval and clustering of large collections of data. Moreover, R provides a plethora of efficient and flexible statistical libraries for analysis. (Meta-)metamodel-based construction of the unigram vocabulary and tokenization provides a good amount of reduction in vector space, improving over basic IR indexing. Finally we would like to repeat and emphasize that, although we used the term 'metamodel' clustering throughout the paper (because of the datasets we chose), we regard the metamodels as instances of the Ecore meta-metamodel, thus simply as models. Thus we deal with the generic problem of model comparison and clustering.

5.1 Threats to Validity

There are several threats to validity for this study. First of all, the NLP techniques employed might not be accurate enough and need to be improved with features such as context-sensitivity and a domain-specific thesaurus. The fact that we regard metamodel identifiers as bag of words and unigrams, thus ignoring structural relations such as containment and inheritance and semantics, could reduce the accuracy and applicability of our approach in some scenarios. Ignoring the multiplicities and modifiers (e.g. abstract) of model elements also might lead to a similar shortcoming. Furthermore, the datasets we used are assembled by us; actual datasets that are used in domain model recovery or SPL extraction should be investigated to compare the results. The visualization and manual inspection approach could limit our approach (as it is now) for larger datasets (e.g. > 1000 items) and further reduction and visualization techniques might be needed. Last but not the least, the quantitative comparison of the accuracy of different combinations of parameters/components in virtually every step of our approach, and automation of this process would relieve the user from the effort of trial-and-error exploration of the parameters.

6 Related Work

Only a few model comparison techniques consider the multiplicity of input models without doing pairwise comparisons, such as N-way merging based on weighted set packing [23]. Feature model extraction [24] and concept mining [1] use NLP to cluster features/concepts. Another technique proposes building domain ontologies as the intersection of graphs of APIs [22], but does not focus on the statistical dimension of problem. Metamodel recovery [13] is another approach which assumes a once existing (but somehow lost) metamodel, and does not hold for our scenario. A technique similar to ours is applied specifically for business process models using process footprints [10], and thus lacks the genericness of our approach. Note that a thorough literature study beyond the technological space of MDE, for instance regarding data schema matching and ontology matching/alignment, is out of scope for this paper and is therefore omitted.

Clustering is considered in the software engineering community mostly within a single body of code [17] or model [26]. A related technique uses clustering for the visualization of Simulink model clones according to the percentage differences and patterns among clones [2]. A very recent approach, which we encountered after publishing our early work, is presented by Basciani et al. [7]. They share most of our objectives, though focusing on repository management. Moreover they use cosine distance of term vectors representing models and HAC for visualization of metamodel repositories. However, they do not report in detail the NLP techniques (e.g. synonym checking) or IR techniques (e.g. weighting) they use. It is left as future work to compare their approach with ours.

7 Conclusion and Future Work

In this paper, we have presented a new perspective on the N-way comparison and analysis of models as a first step in domain model recovery. We have proposed a generic approach using the IR techniques VSM and tf-idf enhanced with NLP techniques to uniformly represent multiple metamodels, and apply hierarchical clustering for comparative analysis and visualization of a large dataset. We demonstrated our approach on two real datasets; one of top search results from GitHub and another from the AtlanMod Metamodel Zoo. The results, both qualitatively for both case studies and quantitatively for the second case study, indicate that our generic and scalable approach is a promising first step for analysing large datasets of models or metamodels.

As future work, we definitely wish to address the points listed as threats to validity. Most notably, the efficiency of different parameters and components of our approach such as various weighting and idf schemes, distance measures and clustering algorithms can be quantitatively evaluated and compared. Another crucial improvement is to incorporate into the analysis both structure and context information (either as n-grams, or tree/graphs) as well as semantics of the metamodel elements. Furthermore, one could investigate the application of our approach for different formalisms such as UML models, and different problems such as model versioning, model merging and model clone or pattern detection.

References

1. Abebe, S.L., Tonella, P.: Natural language parsing of program element names for concept extraction. In: 2010 IEEE 18th International Conference on Program Comprehension (ICPC), pp. 156–159. IEEE (2010)
2. Alalfi, M.H., Cordy, J.R., Dean, T.R.: Analysis and clustering of model clones: an automotive industrial experience. In: 2014 Software Evolution Week-IEEE Conference on Software Maintenance, Reengineeringand Reverse Engineering (CSMR-WCRE), pp. 375–378. IEEE (2014)
3. Altmanninger, K., Seidl, M., Wimmer, M.: A survey on model versioning approaches. Int. J. Web Inf. Syst. **5**(3), 271–304 (2009)
4. Babur, Ö., Cleophas, L., Verhoeff, T., van den Brand, M.: Towards statistical comparison and analysis of models. In: Proceedings of the 4th International Conference on Model-Driven Engineering and Software Development, pp. 361–367 (2016)
5. Babur, Ö., Smilauer, V., Verhoeff, T., van den Brand, M.: Multiphysics and multiscale software frameworks: an annotated bibliography. Technical report 15-01, Dept. of Mathematics and Computer Science, Technische Universiteit Eindhoven, Eindhoven (2015)
6. Babur, Ö., Smilauer, V., Verhoeff, T., van den Brand, M.: A survey of open source multiphysics frameworks in engineering. Procedia Comput. Sci. **51**, 1088–1097 (2015)
7. Basciani, F., Di Rocco, J., Di Ruscio, D., Iovino, L., Pierantonio, A.: Automated clustering of metamodel repositories. In: Nurcan, S., Soffer, P., Bajec, M., Eder, J. (eds.) CAiSE 2016. LNCS, vol. 9694, pp. 342–358. Springer, Heidelberg (2016). doi:10.1007/978-3-319-39696-5_21
8. Brunet, G., Chechik, M., Easterbrook, S., Nejati, S., Niu, N., Sabetzadeh, M.: A manifesto for model merging. In: Proceedings of the 2006 International Workshop on Global Integrated Model Management, pp. 5–12. ACM (2006)
9. Deissenboeck, F., Hummel, B., Juergens, E., Pfaehler, M., Schaetz, B.: Model clone detection in practice. In: Proceedings of the 4th International Workshop on Software Clones, pp. 57–64. ACM (2010)
10. Dijkman, R., Dumas, M., van Dongen, B., Käärik, R., Mendling, J.: Similarity of business process models: metrics and evaluation. Inf. Syst. **36**(2), 498–516 (2011)

11. Holthusen, S., Wille, D., Legat, C., Beddig, S., Schaefer, I., Vogel-Heuser, B.: Family model mining for function block diagrams in automation software. In: Proceedings of the 18th International Software Product Line Conference: Companion Volume for Workshops, Demonstrations and Tools, vol. 2, pp. 36–43. ACM (2014)
12. Jain, A.K., Dubes, R.C.: Algorithms for Clustering Data. Prentice-Hall Inc., Englewood Cliffs (1988)
13. Javed, F., Mernik, M., Gray, J., Bryant, B.R.: Mars: a metamodel recovery system using grammar inference. Inf. Softw. Tech. **50**(9), 948–968 (2008)
14. Klint, P., Landman, D., Vinju, J.: Exploring the limits of domain model recovery. In: 2013 29th IEEE International Conference on Software Maintenance (ICSM), pp. 120–129. IEEE (2013)
15. Kolovos, D.S., Rose, L.M., Matragkas, N., Paige, R.F., Guerra, E., Cuadrado, J.S., De Lara, J., Ráth, I., Varró, D., Tisi, M., Cabot, J.: A research roadmap towards achieving scalability in model driven engineering. In: Proceedings of the Workshop on Scalability in Model Driven Engineering, BigMDE 2013, pp. 2:1–2:10. ACM, New York (2013). http://doi.acm.org/10.1145/2487766.2487768
16. Kolovos, D.S., Ruscio, D.D., Pierantonio, A., Paige, R.F.: Different models for model matching: an analysis of approaches to support model differencing. In: ICSE Workshop on Comparison and Versioning of Software Models, 2009. pp. 1–6. IEEE (2009)
17. Kuhn, A., Ducasse, S., Gírba, T.: Semantic clustering: identifying topics in source code. Inf. Softw. Technol. **49**(3), 230–243 (2007)
18. Lucrédio, D., de M. Fortes, R.P.: Moogle: a metamodel-based model search engine. Softw. Syst. Model. **11**(2), 183–208 (2012)
19. Manning, C.D., Raghavan, P., Schütze, H., et al.: Introduction to Information Retrieval, vol. 1. Cambridge University Press, Cambridge (2008)
20. R Core Team: R: A Language and Environment for Statistical Computing. R Foundation for Statistical Computing, Vienna, Austria (2014). http://www.R-project.org/
21. Ramey, J.A.: clusteval: Evaluation of Clustering Algorithms (2012). http://CRAN.R-project.org/package=clusteval, r package version 0.1
22. Ratiu, D., Feilkas, M., Jürjens, J.: Extracting domain ontologies from domain specific apis. In: 12th European Conference on Software Maintenance and Reengineering, 2008, CSMR 2008, pp. 203–212. IEEE (2008)
23. Rubin, J., Chechik, M.: N-way model merging. In: Proceedings of the 2013 9th Joint Meeting on Foundations of Software Engineering, pp. 301–311. ACM (2013)
24. She, S., Lotufo, R., Berger, T., Wøsowski, A., Czarnecki, K.: Reverse engineering feature models. In: 2011 33rd International Conference on Software Engineering (ICSE), pp. 461–470. IEEE (2011)
25. Stephan, M., Cordy, J.R.: A survey of model comparison approaches and applications. In: Modelsward, pp. 265–277 (2013)
26. Strüber, D., Selter, M., Taentzer, G.: Tool support for clustering large meta-models. In: Proceedings of the Workshop on Scalability in Model Driven Engineering, p. 7. ACM (2013)
27. Wild, F.: LSA: Latent Semantic Analysis (2015). http://CRAN.R-project.org/package=lsa, r package version 0.73.1

Advanced Local Checking of Global Consistency in Heterogeneous Multimodeling

Harald König[1]([✉]) and Zinovy Diskin[2,3]

[1] University of Applied Sciences, FHDW Hannover, Hanover, Germany
harald.koenig@fhdw.de
[2] NECSIS, McMaster University, Hamilton, Canada
[3] Generative Software Development Lab, University of Waterloo, Waterloo, Canada
zdiskin@uwaterloo.ca

Abstract. Software design requires deployment of interdependent models conforming to different metamodels. This set of models is called a *multimodel*, and it must satisfy a set of *global* constraints regulating interaction of the multimodel components. A straightforward approach to global consistency checking would require merging component metamodels modulo their overlap, adding, perhaps, new global constraints to this merge, merging component models modulo their overlap, and checking the latter merge against the constraints in the former one. Being a natural *definition* for global consistency, these steps can not be used algorithmically because of two major practical drawbacks: they involve costly (meta)model matching to specify overlaps, and require building big and unfeasible merged metamodels and models.

The present paper makes two contributions. First, it presents a new algorithm to check each global constraint individually, and *as local as possible*, i.e., only using those (meta)model elements that affect the validity of the constraint. Second, it develops a mathematical foundation that allows us to formally prove that this individual local consistency checking is sound and complete w.r.t. the definition of global consistency.

1 Introduction

Modeling a complex system normally results in a *multimodel*, i.e., a set of heterogenous models each one conforming to its own metamodel. A fundamental fact about multimodeling is that the merge of legal local models can result in a model violating global constraints declared in the integrated metamodel. This can be easily observed even for the simple homogeneous case, when all local models, and hence their merge, are instances of the same metamodel. For example, suppose that the metamodel of a domain says that persons in the domain are uniquely identified by their names, i.e., attribute 'name' is a key to class 'Person'. Then the merge of two perfectly legal local instances can violate the

This work is supported by the Automotive Partnership Canada via the Network on Engineering Complex Software Intensive Systems (NECSIS).

A. Wąsowski and H. Lönn (Eds.): ECMFA 2016, LNCS 9764, pp. 19–35, 2016.
DOI: 10.1007/978-3-319-42061-5_2

constraint, if there are different persons with the same name but they do not appear in the same instance.

Heterogeneous multimodeling expands the issue of global consistency enormously. For example, consider a metamodel M_1 that extends the class Person above with attribute 'birthdate', and a metamodel M_2 that extends 'Person' with reference 'drives' to class 'Car' owning attribute 'carType'. Suppose that the domain is subject to the constraint that persons with age under 25 only drive sporty cars. This *global* constraint cannot be declared in either of the metamodels (the first one knows nothing about cars, the second one does not know ages of persons), yet checking its validity for a multimodel (A_1, A_2) with $A_{1,2}$ being legal instances of $M_{1,2}$ is important. A more complex example is consistency between a UML sequence diagram specifying collaborative behavior, and a statechart specifying a state machine protocol for that behavior. An obvious consistency requirement that traces specified by the sequence diagram should be allowed by the statechart is again global and cannot be declared in either of the local metamodels. Following [6], we call such requirements *inter-metamodel constraints*.

A straightforward approach to global consistency checking would require merging component metamodels M_i modulo their overlap (class 'Person' with attribute 'name' in the example above), adding, perhaps, new global constraints to this merge ('young persons drive sporty cars'), merging component models A_i modulo their overlap, and checking the model merge A_+ against the constraints over the metamodel merge M_+. In fact, this specification can be regarded as a *definition* of global consistency of a multimodel [6]. However, using this definition algorithmically as a specification of a workflow for global consistency checking would be impractical because of (a) costly (meta)model matching needed to specify the overlaps, and (b) necessity to build big and unfeasible merges of metamodels and models. A more efficient approach proposed in [2,6] prescribes to do matching, merging and checking not for entire component models but for their projections to the respective metamodel overlaps, hence, the name *local* consistency checking. It was a conjecture (not proven formally) that the local approach is sound and complete w.r.t. (i.e., equivalent to) the above mentioned definition of global consistency.

The present paper makes two essential contributions to the local approach. The first is pushing the local checking idea even further up to its extreme: we propose to check each global constraint C individually, and correspondingly do matching and merging as minimally as required for checking C, i.e., only using those (meta)model elements that affect the validity of C. Based on this technique, we can control the granularity of consistency checking by combining constraints into groups checked separately. (The two extremes are a multitude of groups having one global constraint each, and one big group embracing all global constraints.) Thus, while the original local approach of [6] reduces one huge global consistency check to a set of several lesser but still significant checks (with the correspondingly significant matches and merges), in this paper we propose an approach with a set of small checks (based on respectively easy matches and merges) in a size-controllable way. Correspondingly, we call the former local approach to consistency *collective*, while the latter one *individual*. Besides reduced matching and merging workload, additional advantages of the local-individual approach are (a) better tailored and stepwise model repairing (in the *per constraint* fashion), and (b) possibilities to realize the *living with inconsistency* paradigm [9], when non-urgent consistency repairs (together with the respective matching and merging) can be postponed.

Our second contribution to local checking is an accurately defined mathematical framework that allows us to prove that individual consistency checking is sound and complete w.r.t. the definition of global consistency, and is equivalent to collective checking of [6]. Having specification (definition) and implementation (algorithms) separated is always useful as the former defines an optimization space for the latter. In addition, although conditions for our equivalence results are not too restrictive, they are not absolutely universal and (as we will show) can be violated if the global constraint to be checked badly interacts with inter-model correspondence specification involving queries against component models.

The paper is structured as follows: Constraint checking in general is contained in Sects. 2.1 and 2.2. Multimodels are introduced in Sect. 2.3. Section 3 combines these two topics: it explains how global constraint declarations are managed and states the main theorem, which precisely formulates the above mentioned equivalence. Section 4 is devoted to related work, Sect. 5 concludes.

2   Background

Metamodels are usually specified by UML class diagrams. The compact syntax of the latter hides many details that need to be explicated and formalized to allow our machinery to work. In this section, we show how it can be done in the formal framework of typed graphs (e.g., [8]) and diagrammatic constraints. The formalism of diagrammatic constraints, first developed under the cryptic name of *generalized sketches* [3,5], and then promoted as the *Diagram Predicate Framework, DPF* [18,19], is less known, and we present in Sect. 2.2 its basics in the amount needed for our work in the paper to make it self-contained. Finally, Sect. 2.3 introduces multimodels.

2.1   From Class Diagrams to Graphs, I: Typing

The left lower quadrant of Fig. 1 presents a fragment of a simplified metamodel for UML class diagrams with several constraints declared. Three multiplicity constraints are depicted in the usual UML style. They prescribe each operation to have a name and belong to at most one class, and prohibit multiple inheritance. A more complex OCL-constraint is specified in the top right corner of the metamodel box and says that if there is no superclass, there should be at least one interface implementation and vice versa (which shall guide the developers to code their programs in a polymorphic style). The left upper quadrant shows a class diagram (model) instantiating the metamodel. To use our machinery, we

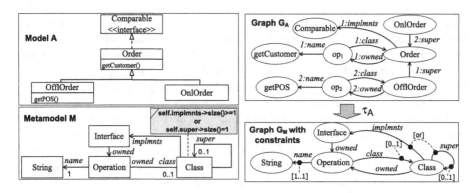

Fig. 1. UML model and metamodel represented as typed graph

need to translate the metamodel, the model, and the conformance relation into formal objects.

The right half of the figure shows the first step of the translation. The metamodel is presented by a pair $M = (G_M, C_M)$ with G_M a *type* graph and C_M a set of four constraint declarations. Each of them consists of a constraint name given in square brackets, and the constraint *scope* shown by dashed lines, i.e., set of elements over which the constraint is declared. The model is a pair $A = (G_A, \tau_A)$ with G_A a *data* graph, and $\tau_A : G_A \to G_M$ a *typing* mapping between graphs, which assigns types to every data element, e.g. $\tau_A(Order) = Class$, $\tau_A(op_1) = Operation$, $\tau_A(getCustomer) = String$, as well as $\tau_A(1:implmnts) = implmnts$, $\tau_A(1:super) = super$ and so on. Model A is a *typed graph* and we will also say that A is *typed over M*, and often write $a : T$ (read "element a is of type T") if $\tau(a) = T$. A standard formalization of the notion of graphs and mappings between them is briefly described below. Constraints and conformance of a model to constraints is specified in Sect. 2.2.

A *(directed multi-)graph* $G = (V_G, E_G, \mathsf{s}, \mathsf{t})$ consists of a set V of *vertices* (or *nodes*), a set E of *edges*, and two functions $\mathsf{s} : E \to V, \mathsf{t} : E \to V$ that assign to each edge its source and target. Writing $x \in G$ means that x is a node or an edge of G. We depict graph vertices by ellipses (or circles) and edges by arrows from their source to their target vertex, cf. Fig. 1, graphs G_A and G_M. A graph *mapping* or *morphism* $f : G \to G'$ is a pair of functions $f_V : V \to V'$ and $f_E : E \to E'$ preserving the incidence between vertices and edges. Since the definition of f on an edge e determines its values for e's source and target, we will often omit the latter from the mapping definition.

2.2 From Class Diagrams to Graphs, II: Diagrammatic Constraints

A key feature of constraints used in metamodeling is their *diagrammatic* nature: the set of elements over which a constraint is declared is actually a diagram of some shape specific for the constraint. For example, the shape of any multiplicity constraint is a single arrow, while the shape of the *or*-constraint is two arrows with a common source, see Table 1.

To declare a constraint over a metamodel graph G_M, we recognize the constraint shape in the graph and visualize it as was shown in Fig. 1. Formally, this recognition is a graph mapping $\delta : S^c \to G_M$ (called *(shape) binding*) from the shape S^c of a constraint with name c to graph G_M. E.g. in Fig. 1, we have constraint [*or*] declared by binding $\delta : S^{[or]} \to G_M$ ($S^{[or]}$ is

Table 1. Sample constraints

Name	Shape
[0..1]	$\textcircled{1} \xrightarrow{12} \textcircled{2}$
[or]	$\textcircled{1} \xleftarrow{01} \textcircled{0} \xrightarrow{02} \textcircled{2}$

shown in Table 1) with $\delta(01) = implmnts$, $\delta(02) = super$, i.e. $\delta(1) = Interface$, $\delta(0) = Class = \delta(2)$. The set of elements in G_M the shape is mapped to, is called the *image* of the binding. In the example, the image of δ consists of vertices *Interface* and *Class*, and edges *implmnts* and *super*.

The pair (c, δ) is a *constraint declaration*. The bindings of all relevant constraints of graph G_M are shown in detail in Fig. 2. Note the practicality of the DPF framework: for the [0..1]-declarations in G_M we can *reuse* shape $S^{[0..1]}$ in two different bindings: one of them maps edge 12 to edge *super*, the other maps 12 to edge *class*. Thus, validation logic is encapsulated and can be reused for all constraint declarations of type [0..1]. In the sequel, we write a pair (c, δ) as

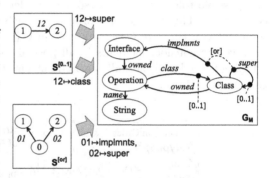

Fig. 2. Three constraint declarations

$c@\delta$, meaning *constraint c is imposed on metamodel G_M at the image of binding δ.*

In order to check consistency of model A, i.e. typed graph $A = (G_A, \tau_A)$, against a fixed constraint declaration $c@\delta$, we need to define c's *semantics* irrespective of A. This is done by programming a function VALIDATE$_c(B: Model)$: BOOLEAN which has input typed graph $B = (G_B, \tau_B)$ where $\tau_B : G_B \to S^c$, i.e. B is a model typed over c's shape only. For example, function VALIDATE$_{[or]}$ acts on models typed over $S^{[or]}$ (cf. Table 1): it returns *true* for a model $X = (G_X, \tau_X : G_X \to S^{[or]})$, iff each element of type 0 in G_X has an outgoing edge to some element of type 1 or to some element of type 2.

So defined semantics is used in the check function:

CHECK$(A: Model, c@\delta: Constraint)$: BOOLEAN

which, basically, performs three steps:

1. *Restrict* A to elements, whose types are in the image of δ in G_M.
2. *Retype* elements of this new structure to formal typing over S^c. This yields typed graph $B = (G_B, \tau_B)$.
3. Return the result of $validate_c(B)$.

We say that A *satisfies* $c@\delta$ and write $A \models c@\delta$, if CHECK$(A, c@\delta)$=*true*. Model A is a *legal* model over metamodel M, if it satisfies all constraints declared in M. For example, checking constraint declaration $[or]@\delta$ is shown in Fig. 3. The image of δ is shown in the lower right part (elements not in the image are greyed out), the restriction G_A is in the top right quadrant, and $B = (G_B, \tau_B : G_B \to S^{[or]})$ is the corresponding retyping. As $validate_{[or]}(B) = true$, we conclude $A \models [or]@\delta$. Note the copy procedure during retyping: for each *class*-instance in the restriction of G_A, we have to create *two* vertices in G_B, because we must incorporate their two possible roles as subclass (source of edge *super*) and superclass (target of edge *super*). This is a general procedure: each vertex or edge in G_A has to be represented n times in G_B, if its type in G_M has n preimages under δ. In this way, we can consider elements in all possible occupied roles. This "role-based" retyping procedure is actually carried out via the general mathematical *pullback* construction [1,13].

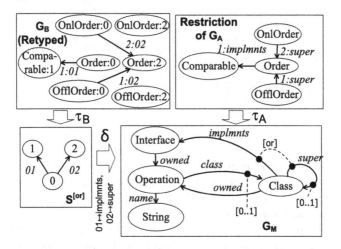

Fig. 3. How function CHECK works

2.3   Multimodeling

Modeling a complex system normally results in a *multimodel*, i.e., a set of heterogenous models each one conforming to its own metamodel. Besides class diagrams, other types of UML diagrams are produced, for instance sequence diagrams, statecharts, activity diagrams, etc. Even class diagrams may conform to different metamodels: Business analysts may use behavioural specifications only [10] with no attributes or associations, M_1 in Fig. 4, whereas for another modeling team, class models are more technically oriented and associations and attributes are used (M_2). In all cases, the models collectively represent a single system to be build, and any formal treatment has to consider *overlaps*, i.e. the definitions of common terminology in different models. E.g., the (meta) concept *class* occurs in both of the above-mentioned metamodels. Names of common concepts, however, may differ: one team may use the term *String*, while the other may use *Text*, yet speaking of the same concept.

In the binary case (two metamodels M_1 and M_2), *overlaps* can be specified by two graph mappings $M_1 \xleftarrow{r_1} M_{12} \xrightarrow{r_2} M_2$ in which M_{12} contains all common concepts. Any pair $x_1 \in M_1$ and $x_2 \in M_2$ is declared to be the same, if there is $x \in M_{12}$ such that $r_1(x) = x_1$ and $r_2(x) = x_2$. We call this configuration of metamodels and mappings a *multimetamodel* $\mathcal{M}$ and write $\mathcal{M} = (M_1, M_2, M_{12}, r_1, r_2)$ or shorter $\mathcal{M} = (r_1, r_2)$, if domain and codomain of r_1 and r_2 are clear from the context.

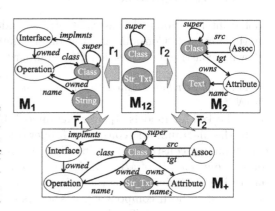

Fig. 4. Multimodel and merge

In the sequel, all (meta)models will be (typed) graphs, such that we simplify notation by using letters M (metamodels) and A (models) with subscripts to distinguish different graphs. A multimetamodel $\mathcal{M}$ is shown in Fig. 4: M_1 was already used in Sect. 2.1, Fig. 1. M_2 is the above mentioned technical metamodel. The overlap specification M_{12} declares *Class* together with its super-relation to be the same and, since $r_1(Str\_Txt) = String$ and $r_2(Str\_Txt) = Text$, it declares sameness of *String* and *Text* (see the shaded vertices). The *merge* (union) M_+ of the two components of $\mathcal{M}$ is shown in the lower half of Fig. 4. We introduce merges in Sect. 3.

3   Managing Global Constraints

In the present section we analyse *global* constraints, i.e., constraints that reside in neither of the component metamodels alone, and thus involve elements from several metamodels. Correspondingly, we use the name *inter-metamodel constraints* that accurately describes the case. In Sect. 3.1, we will state a *definition* of *global satisfaction* against an inter-metamodel constraint. The definition treats the binary case only, but the generalization for the N-ary case is straightforward. Models typed over different metamodels are said to be *globally* consistent if they satisfy all imposed inter-metamodel constraints. We will argue that it is impractical to use this definition as an algorithm for global consistency checking. Hence, in Sect. 3.2, we introduce another algorithm, in which global satisfiability against an inter-metamodel constraint is checked *locally*, and illustrate its advantages with a running example. Section 3.3 compares the global satisfaction definition of Sect. 3.1 with the local algorithm of Sect. 3.2 and, additionally, with the collective method of [6]. Finally, equivalence of all three methods is stated (main theorem).

3.1   Global Consistency

Global inter-metamodel constraints are spread over different components of a multimetamodel. Consider e.g. the binary multimetamodel in Fig. 4 with the following constraint declaration C (a standard requirement for Java Beans):

> *For each attribute named "n" there must be an accessor operation with name "getN"!*

to be checked for models A_1 over metamodel M_1 and A_2 over metamodel M_2.

In the diagrammatic constraint framework, to declare C, we need to find a corresponding constraint c and binding mapping $\delta: S^c \rightarrow M$. For this, we take for M the *merge* M_+ of M_1 and M_2 w.r.t. overlap M_{12}. This is shown in the lower half of Fig. 4. Basically, it is the union of M_1 and M_2 modulo M_{12}: Since *Class* is common to both components, it appears only once in the merge. The same is true for *String* and *Text* being represented by *Str_Txt* in M_+. However, the two edges labelled *name* in M_1 and M_2 are not unified: They are not declared the same in the overlap (one is an operation's name, the other the name of an attribute). $\bar{r}_1: M_1 \rightarrow M_+$ and $\bar{r}_2: M_2 \rightarrow M_+$ map all elements of M_1 and M_2 to the corresponding elements in the merge. Now we can impose c to M_+ via binding map δ. This is shown in Fig. 5.

c's intended semantics is controlled by function VALIDATE$_c$ (cf. Sect. 2.2), which has input graph $B = (G_B, \tau_B)$ typed over S^c. If S^c is bound as shown in Fig. 5, it will return true if and only if for each own class attribute with name n, there is an owned operation with name $getN$ in the same class. Note that the *super* relation is not included in the image of δ, because getters shall exist for *own* attributes only (inherited attributes already yield respective *get*-methods).

In Sect. 2.3, we described two modeling teams. Assume the first team creates legal model (one or more class diagrams) A_1 typed over metamodel M_1, and the other team creates legal model A_2 typed over metamodel M_2. Global consistency requires validity of the name alignment constraint $c@\delta$ introduced above. Conjoint treatment of models requires their *matching*, i.e., specifying their common concepts. But *model overlap* might not be possible to be inferred automatically: e.g., entity *Onl(ine)Order* in model A_1 may be called *Onl(ine)Purchase Order* in A_2, cf. Fig. 6. In general, cross-(meta)model terminology may be very heterogeneous, and the structure of models may vary significantly while still reflecting identical concepts. Given a significant size of practical models, model matching can be a costly procedure that needs special tools and user input.

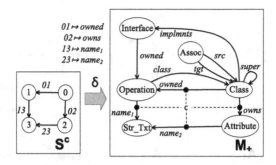

Fig. 5. Imposing global constraint on merged multimodel

Formally – and similarly to metamodels – one must determine two graph mappings $A_1 \xleftarrow{\ r'_1\ } A_{12} \xrightarrow{\ r'_2\ } A_2$ that are compatible with typing[1]. We call this configuration of models and mappings a *multimodel* A over multimetamodel $\mathcal{M}$ and write $A = (r'_1, r'_2)$[2]. Only now is it possible to merge multimodel A, which, basically, is performed in the same way as for metamodels: One constructs the union G_{A_+} of the data graphs of A_1 and A_2 wrt. to A_{12}. This yields a unique typing mapping $\tau_{A_+} : G_{A_+} \to M_+$ (this can formally be proved, because merging is a special case of the universal construction of pushouts [1]) and hence model merge $A_+ = (G_+, \tau_{A_+})$.

Definition 1 (Global Consistency [6,20]). Let $c@\delta$ be an inter-metamodel constraint over multimetamodel $\mathcal{M} = (r_1, r_2)$. We say that multimodel $A = (r'_1, r'_2)$ over $\mathcal{M}$ satisfies $c@\delta$, if the above constructed model merge A_+ satisfies $c@\delta$ over M_+. If A satisfies all inter-metamodel constraints imposed on $\mathcal{M}$, we call A *globally consistent*.

We remark that the binary case can be generalized to the N-ary case by constructing M_+ as *colimit*, a categorical construction encompassing binary merging [6,20].

Unfortunately, practical consistency checking along the lines of this definition, i.e., constructing *globally* typed data before checking, has major disadvantages:

1. One has to deal with the entire union of data (usually a huge structure) - independent of whether there is only a small portion being affected by the constraint.
2. To specify overlaps of typed data structures, this enormous collection of data has to be traversed manually or at least semi-automatically. Overlaps have to be complete, i.e. they are not specific to the given constraint declaration.

---

[1] Formally, r'_i ($i \in \{1,2\}$) map the data graph of A_{12} and respect behavior of r_i, i.e. $r'_i; \tau_i = \tau_{12}; r_i$.

[2] Again assuming domain and codomain of r'_1 and r'_2 to be clear from the context.

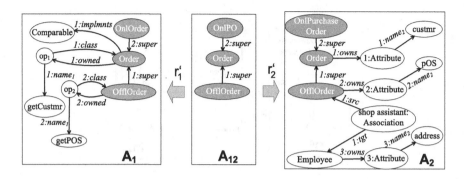

Fig. 6. Multimodel: models with overlap

Consider e.g. Fig. 6: A_1 contains owned operations and implemented interfaces of the order classes. A_2 represents the same order classes. Shaded nodes and their *:super*-links are in the overlap A_{12}, i.e. *OnlOrder* and *OnlPurchaseOrder* are declared to be the same classes despite their different names. Besides own attributes, A_2 contains the *shop assistant* who processed the offline order (via a directed association). A_+ is the union of all these elements w.r.t. the overlap. It is not reprinted due to lack of space.

If we want to check whether $\mathcal{A} = (r_1', r_2')$ satisfies constraint $c@\delta$, the above mentioned disadvantages manifest as follows:

1. Although $c@\delta$ only "talks" about classes and names of their attributes and operations, we have to deal with interface implementations and operation's reference to its class (from A_1), as well as (usually many) associations (from A_2) but also with superclass relations (in the overlap).
2. The user must search the set of all classes and all their superclass relations for identical concepts. In the example he must specify sameness of *OnlOrder* and *OnlPurchaseOrder*, the other two identities *Order* and *OfflOrder* may automatically be proposed based on identical naming, yet have to be confirmed by the user. The user also has to declare several superclass relations to be the same although the constraint declaration does not talk about inheritance relation.

Both aspects become more severe, if there is a big number of diagrams, probably stored with different techniques. Moreover, our examples are small compared with real diagrams, where the proportion of matching (i.e. overlap specification) of non-relevant data (being outside the fragment that matters for checking) will be significantly bigger.

3.2 Local-Individual Checking

Is there a technique for checking inter-metamodel constraints that would be more efficient than a direct execution of the definition (Definition 1 in Sect. 3.1) as proposed in [20]? A better approach would be to consider only those pieces of data and models and their overlaps that matter for checking, i.e., make checking constraints *as local as possible*:

Definition 2. The following algorithm for global consistency checking is called *local-individual* checking. Let $\mathcal{A} = (A_1, A_2, A_{12}, r'_1, r'_2)$ be a multimodel over multimetamodel $\mathcal{M} = (M_1, M_2, M_{12}, r_1, r_2)$. Let $\bar{r}_1$ and $\bar{r}_2$ be inclusion maps of M_1 and M_2 into the metamodel merge M_+ as is Fig. 4. An inter-metamodel constraint $c@\delta$ is verified as follows (the following four steps will be illustrated afterwards by way of example):

1. Let M_1^c, M_2^c, and M_{12}^c consist of all elements of M_1, M_2, and M_{12}, resp., which are mapped to the image of δ by $\bar{r}_1$, $\bar{r}_2$, and $r_1; \bar{r}_1$ ($= r_2; \bar{r}_2$), resp.[3]
2. Restrict models A_1 and A_2 to those elements being typed over M_1^c and M_2^c resp. Call this data A_1^c and A_2^c.
3. Determine overlap A_{12}^c of A_1^c and A_2^c.
4. Apply $check(A_+^c, c@\delta)$, where A_+^c is the local merge of A_1^c and A_2^c.

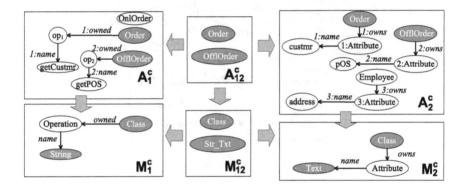

Fig. 7. Individually local consistency checking: steps 1 to 3

We illustrate application of the algorithm for our running example, where multimodel (r'_1, r'_2) from Fig. 6 will be checked against constraint declaration $c@\delta$ from Fig. 5. Steps 1 to 3 are illustrated in Fig. 7:

Step 1 : M_1^c, M_2^c, and M_{12}^c are depicted in the lower half. Once the complete overlap M_{12} is known, they are automatically derived from the scope of the constraint. Shaded vertices again depict overlap. The important improvement is that *Interfaces* together with their operations and interface implementations now vanish. In the same way, class membership of operations can be omitted. Since the constraint declaration does not involve superclass relations, they can be omitted, too. Moreover, we need not care about associations and their source and targets.

---

[3] We still consider $c@\delta$ to be imposed on the merge M_+ of M_1 and M_2, i.e. $\delta : S^c \to M_+$. Recall that the *image* of δ is the set of those elements in M_+, the shape of c is mapped to.

Step 2 : The upper half shows appropriately narrowed A_1^c and A_2^c. Again, this step can be carried out automatically (similar to the retype step of function CHECK as described in Sect. 2.2). Note that *OnlPurchaseOrder* is omitted since it does not possess own attributes and hence automatically satisfies constraint declaration $c@\delta$.

Step 3 : The only manual activity is overlap specification. It is now reduced to the selection of classes *Order* and *OfflOrder*. We do not have to deal with superclass relations and classes without attributes in the overlap. Additionally, no text matching is necessary, since model structures simplify accordingly. Moreover, declaration of *OnlOrder-OnlPurchaseOrder*-identity is no longer necessary.

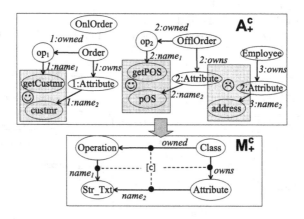

Fig. 8. Local consistency checking: step 4

Step 4 : Calculation of local merge A_+^c is again an automatic procedure. In Fig. 8, it is depicted together with the part M_+^c of the integrated metamodel that matters for checking. The resulting data space (A_+^c) now contains no superfluous elements. It is reduced to four involved classes only: *OnlOrder* still appears (but now only as automatic leftover from A_1). The other three classes can easily be traversed. Function CHECK has input a narrowed model (only those model elements typed over elements in the image of the binding). In the example it detects satisfaction for classes *Order* and *OfflOrder* but violation for class *Employee* (grey rectangles).

The reader may compare the unstructured contents of Fig. 6 with the reduced data in the upper half of Fig. 7. The presented technique obviously reduces model merging and matching workload, if constraints shall be checked in the *per constraint* fashion. It can also be applied, if it is temporarily possible to live with inconsistency, i.e. with delayed non-urgent consistency repairs [9].

It remains to ensure *global-local-equivalence*, i.e. the algorithm must always yield the same result as the global definition (cf. Definition 1). This equivalence may seem obvious, but it can be invalid for model structures richer than simple typed graphs. For instance, assume that (meta)models can be augmented with *derived associations*: if class C_1 has an association a to C_2 and C_2 has association b to C_3, then there is a derived association $/ab$ from C_1 to C_3 (note dashed arrow in M_+ in Fig. 9). In Fig. 9, model M_+ is the merge of M_1 and M_2, in which class C_2 is assumed to be common in both metamodels.

Now consider a constraint declaration. *"Each object instantiating C_1 must reference at least one C_3-object via an $/ab$-link."* Its binding map δ has image consisting of the derived association and classes C_1 and C_3. Then the global check procedure of Definition 1 for multimodel $\mathcal{A}$ with models (A_1, A_2) that share the object $:C_2$ (in Fig. 9, object identifiers are omitted) will construct the whole model merge with a derived $/ab$-link from the C_1-object to the C_3-object. Hence, $\mathcal{A}$ is consistent w.r.t. Definition 1.

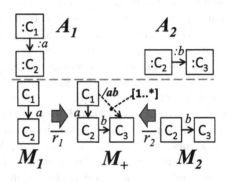

Fig. 9. Derived association

However, the local algorithm (Definition 2) hides class C_2 in step 1, because C_2 is not in the image of the constraint declaration. Hence, the restricted model A_1^c only contains object $:C_1$, and A_2^c only contains $:C_3$ (step 2), and we then necessarily have an empty overlap (step 3). The local merge (step 4) does not contain any association, and hence no derived one. Thus, in contrast to the global check, the local check returns *false*!

This mismatch shows that investigation of global-local equivalence must be carried out carefully, specifically, when dealing with correspondences involving derived elements [6]. However, in the next section we show that the equivalence always holds in the framework of typed graphs without derived elements.

3.3 Global-Local-Equivalence

In order to ensure that all proposed algorithms are correct in the context of typed graphs, we have to prove (a) that the new local-individual approach is correct w.r.t. the original definition of global consistency in Sect. 3.1, and (b) that local-individual checking is equivalent to the local-collective grouping technique proposed in [6], where special portions of the metamodel are determined such that constraint groups imposed on this portion can be checked simultaneously.

We include a short proof sketch of the global-local-equivalence theorem, which is stated in the end of this section (a detailed proof is given in [13]): both, the above definition and the invented algorithm contain a merging step: one for the entire metamodel (which yields M_+) and one for only those parts that matter for the constraint (which yields M_+^c). In the proof of our theorem we compare both approaches by - virtually - carrying them out in parallel: We use the fact that these *simultaneous merges* can be controlled with the so-called *Van*

Kampen Property [8], whenever one of the two graph mappings r_1 and r_2 is injective[4]. It is an exactness property for typed graphs, which guarantees that both operations, merge and restriction, behave and interact well. It fails in categories where augmentation effects as described above occur. Basically, one can show that the well-behavedness of the simultaneous metamodel merge (M_+ and M_+^c) carries over to the model level (A_+ and A_+^c). Then it is not difficult to deduce that $check(A_+, c@\delta) = validate_c(retype(A_+^c))$, where *retype* performs Step 2 of function CHECK in Sect. 2.2. Global-local-equivalence then follows, since, by construction, A_+^c is the restriction of A_+ (Step 1 of function CHECK).

It is also important to compare the approach with the local-collective method of [6], in which checking the global consistency of multimodel $\mathcal{A}$ against a *group* of constraints $C = \{c_1@\delta_1, \ldots, c_n@\delta_n\}$, which is locally satisfied by component models, is reduced to checking consistency against C at the model overlap. It is not difficult to show that this setting can be seen as a special case of our framework, in which a global constraint declaration $c@\delta$ encodes the entire group C: constraint c is a logical conjunction of constraints c_i in some precisely defined sense, and the image of δ is the union of images of $\delta_1, \ldots, \delta_n$. Then collective checking of group C is equivalent to individual checking of constraint $c@\delta$.

From all these considerations we deduce our *main theorem*:

Main Theorem. Let metamodels be graphs, models be typed graphs, and model mappings are typed graph morphisms. Let $\mathcal{M} = (\ M_1 \xleftarrow{\ r_1\ } M_{12} \xrightarrow{\ r_2\ } M_2\ )$ be a multimetamodel with r_1 or r_2 injective, $\mathcal{A} = (\ A_1 \xleftarrow{\ r_1'\ } A_{12} \xrightarrow{\ r_2'\ } A_2\ )$ be a multimodel over $\mathcal{M}$, and $c@\delta$ be an inter-metamodel constraint declaration over the merged metamodel M_+. Then the following statements are equivalent:

- $\mathcal{A}$ satisfies $c@\delta$ according to Definition 1.
- The local-individual algorithm of Definition 2 returns true for $c@\delta$.
- If $c@\delta$ encodes a group C of constraint declarations, then $\mathcal{A}$ satisfies C according to the local-collective approach of [6]. □

4 Related Work

Approaches to heterogeneous multimodeling can be roughly divided into *global* and *local*. For the former, heterogeneity is managed by relating all local models to one global model, and checking consistency wrt. this global model. In contrast, there is no global model in local approaches.

The most direct (and most well-known) global approach to consistency checking is via monitoring satisfiability of consistency rules. All local models are considered as instances of some all-embracing global model given a priori, and inter-model consistency is given by *rules* specified in a special language "understanding" all local models. A representative of this approach is described in [15]:

---

[4] All examples in the present paper are such that *both* r_1 and r_2 are injective.

inter-metamodel constraints are called inter- or multi-feature rules, and are investigated in the context of feature-oriented software development. Inconsistency detection, for instance, is performed by mapping feature models to propositional logic. Different to our approach, matching is only allowed when elements have same types *and* same names. Hence, matching can well be automated. A mini-survey of similar approaches can be found in [6].

Another global approach is *consistency checking via merging (CCVM)* proposed in [20] for homogeneous structural modeling, and earlier discussed in [7] for behavioral modeling; in [6], it was generalized for the heterogeneous case. The global model is not given a priori but is computed by merging all local models modulo their correspondences; the latter must be explicitly specified. An essential advantage of CCVM approaches over monitoring consistency rules is that complex types of model matching are allowed. Contributions of the present paper into CCVM were discussed in the introduction in detail.

For *local approaches*, explicit specification of inter-model correspondences is a central issue, and different types of notation and techniques were developed [17]. Besides the usual distinction between manual and (semi-)automatic procedures, e.g. [23], more sophisticated approaches have been elaborated [12]. A distinctive feature of our approach is that the set of correspondences is reified as a special model endowed with correspondence mappings – a span. This is a standard categorical idea, which was repeatedly employed in homogeneous multimodeling frameworks based on category theory, the most prominent being [21], where spans are themselves subject of evolution. The most difficult issue is *indirect correspondences*, when sets of elements in different models are related but their relationships cannot be specified by equating the elements. Such correspondences are usually specified by *correspondence rules* [17], but their formal treatment needs the machinery of Kleisli mappings [4]; incorporating the latter into the framework developed in this paper is our important future work.

Finally, the Van Kampen property (originally invented in algebraic topology) reveals a remarkable correspondence between software engineering and a mathematical method for inferring properties of a global structure from its known local characteristics, cf. [8,22]. Since our work is also about interconnection of the local and the global, it is not surprising that the Van Kampen property is fundamental for our framework as well.

5   Conclusion

We presented a new approach for local checking of constraints imposed on heterogeneous multimodels, which significantly reduces model matching and merging workload. Our second contribution is a formal underpinning of global consistency, which essentially employs the diagrammatic nature of constraint. In this framework, we were able to prove the equivalence of two local approaches to the global consistency definition, so that the latter provides an optimization space for the former.

The most important direction for future research is to generalize the proposed binary overlapping algorithm together with a necessary equivalence theorem for the general N-ary overlapping case considered in [6]. Moreover, view definitions (on metamodels) and view execution (on models) [6] should also be taken into consideration. The challenge will be to find appropriate generalization and extensions of our mathematical machinery for model correspondences involving derived elements. Another direction of future research is to extend the scope of underlying graphical structures beyond simple directed (typed) graphs and include, e.g., attributed graphs [8]. Obviously, this also requires a generalization of the underlying diagrammatic framework.

We also plan to evaluate the algorithm in the tooling framework developed at Bergen University College [14,16]. Our idea is to enhance DPF editors to make them inter-metamodel aware. Alternatively, we can try to integrate our approach with another constraint checking tools, e.g. USE, a tool to specify and check OCL constraints [11].

Acknowledgement. We are sincerely grateful to anonymous reviewers for useful comments and suggestions. Financial support was provided by Automotive Partnership Canada via the Network on Engineering Complex Software Intensive Systems (NECSIS).

References

1. Barr, M., Wells, C.: Category Theory for Computing Sciences. Prentice Hall, New York (1990)
2. Diskin, Z.: Towards generic formal semantics for consistency of heterogeneous multimodels. Tech. Rep. GSDLAB 2011–02-01, University of Waterloo (2011)
3. Diskin, Z., Kadish, B., Piessens, F., Johnson, M.: Universal arrow foundations for visual modeling. In: Anderson, M., Cheng, P., Haarslev, V. (eds.) Diagrams 2000. LNCS (LNAI), vol. 1889, pp. 345–360. Springer, Heidelberg (2000)
4. Diskin, Z., Maibaum, T., Czarnecki, K.: Intermodeling, queries, and kleisli categories. In: de Lara, J., Zisman, A. (eds.) Fundamental Approaches to Software Engineering. LNCS, vol. 7212, pp. 163–177. Springer, Heidelberg (2012)
5. Diskin, Z., Wolter, U.: A diagrammatic logic for object-oriented visual modeling. In: Proceedings of the Second Workshop on Applied and Computational Category Theory (ACCAT 2007), pp. 19–41. ENTCS (2007)
6. Diskin, Z., Xiong, Y., Czarnecki, K.: Specifying overlaps of heterogeneous models for global consistency checking. In: Dingel, J., Solberg, A. (eds.) MODELS 2010. LNCS, vol. 6627, pp. 165–179. Springer, Heidelberg (2011)
7. Easterbrook, S.M., Chechik, M.: A framework for multi-valued reasoning over inconsistent viewpoints. In: ICSE, pp. 411–420 (2001)
8. Ehrig, H., Ehrig, K., Prange, U., Taentzer, G.: Fundamentals of Algebraic Graph Transformations. Monographs in Theoretical Computer Science. An EATCS Series. Springer, Heidelberg (2006)
9. Fickas, S., Feather, M., Kramer, J.: Proceedings of ICSE 1997 Workshop on Living with Inconsistency, Boston, USA (1997)
10. Fowler, M.: Analysis Patterns: Reusable Object Models. Addison-Wesley, Reading (1997)

11. Gogolla, M., Büttner, F., Richters, M.: USE: a UML-based specification environment for validating UML and OCL. Sci. Comput. Program. **69**(1–3), 27–34 (2007). http://dx.doi.org/10.1016/j.scico.2007.01.013
12. Kessentini, M., Ouni, A., Langer, P., Wimmer, M., Bechikh, S.: Search-based metamodel matching with structural and syntactic measures. J. Syst. Softw. **97**, 1–14 (2014). http://dx.doi.org/10.1016/j.jss.2014.06.040
13. König, H., Diskin, Z.: Individually local checking of global consistency in heterogeneous multimodeling: the categorical story behind the scenery. Tech.rep., University of Applied Sciences, FHDW Hannover (2016). http://fhdwdev.ha.bib.de/public/papers/02016-01.pdf
14. Lamo, Y., Wang, X., Mantz, F., Bech, Ø., Sandven, A., Rutle, A.: DPF workbench: a multi-level language workbench for MDE. Proc. Est. Acad. Sci. **62**, 3–15 (2013)
15. Lopez-Herrejon, R.E., Egyed, A.: Detecting inconsistencies in multi-view models with variability. In: Kühne, T., Selic, B., Gervais, M.-P., Terrier, F. (eds.) ECMFA 2010. LNCS, vol. 6138, pp. 217–232. Springer, Heidelberg (2010)
16. Rabbi, F., Lamo, Y., Yu, I., Kristensen, L.: A diagrammatic approach to model completion. In: 4th Workshop on Analysis of Model Transformations Co-Located with MODELS 2015, pp. 56–65 (2015)
17. Romero, J., Jaen, J., Vallecillo, A.: Realizing correspondences in multi-viewpoint specifications. In: EDOC, pp. 163–172. IEEE Computer Society (2009)
18. Rutle, A., Rossini, A., Lamo, Y., Wolter, U.: A diagrammatic formalisation of MOF-based modelling languages. In: Oriol, M., Meyer, B. (eds.) Objects, Components, Models and Patterns. LNBIP, vol. 33, pp. 37–56. Springer, Heidelberg (2009). http://dx.doi.org/10.1007/978-3-642-02571-6_4
19. Rutle, A., Wolter, U., Lamo, Y.: A diagrammatic approach to model transformations. In: Proceedings of the 2008 Euro American Conference on Telematics and Information Systems (EATIS 2008), pp. 1–8. ACM (2008)
20. Sabetzadeh, M., Nejati, S., Liaskos, S., Easterbrook, S.M., Chechik, M.: Consistency checking of conceptual models via model merging. In: RE, pp. 221–230. IEEE (2007)
21. Schürr, A.: Specification of graph translators with triple graph grammars. In: Mayr, E.W., Schmidt, G., Tinhofer, G. (eds.) WG 1994. LNCS, vol. 903. Springer, Heidelberg (1995)
22. Sobociński, P.: Deriving process congruences from reaction rules. Tech. Rep. DS-04-6, BRICS Dissertation Series (2004)
23. de Sousa Jr., J., Lopes, D., Claro, D.B., Abdelouahab, Z.: A step forward in semi-automatic metamodel matching: algorithms and tool. In: Filipe, J., Cordeiro, J. (eds.) Enterprise Information Systems. LNBIP, vol. 24, pp. 137–148. Springer, Heidelberg (2009). http://dx.doi.org/10.1007/978-3-642-01347-8_12

Supporting the Linked Data Approach to Maintain Coherence Across Rich EMF Models

Jad El-Khoury[1](✉), Cecilia Ekelin[2], and Christian Ekholm[2]

[1] Department of Machine Design, KTH Royal Institute of Technology,
Stockholm, Sweden
jad@kth.se

[2] Advanced Technology and Research, Volvo Group Trucks Technology,
Gothenburg, Sweden
{cecilia.ekelin, christian.ekholm}@volvo.com

Abstract. In many development environments, Model-Driven Engineering (MDE) may well be limited to parts of the complete product development process due to the lack of interoperability mechanisms that connect the product data across the model-based engineering tools being used. This is especially the case if the tools are not designed to work tightly together, and/or if they do not share a common technological basis. In this paper, we investigate the use of the OASIS OSLC interoperability standard to facilitate the integration of models from different languages into a single coherent view. We evaluate a fully-automated code generator that provides OSLC interfaces for EMF-based modelling tools, allowing the exposure of modelling elements from any rich modelling language. We argue that such a generator is a critical component for reducing the cost of providing rich and specialized tool interfaces, generally needed when integrating modelling tools. The study is based on a case study that addresses the development process – and the corresponding integrated software engineering environment - at Volvo Trucks used when developing a new electronic architecture including heavy vehicle functions.

Keywords: Linked data · OSLC · Tool integration · Tool interoperability · EMF · Code generation · Model-driven engineering

1 Introduction

Model-driven engineering (MDE) is leading the effort of migrating engineering focus from text-based documentation to a digital representation of product data. Besides a model's ability to facilitate communication between individuals and teams, information conveyed in a model – when made electronically accessible – serves as a basis for analysis and synthesis activities throughout the product development life-cycle.

This MDE promise is currently best achieved with development activities constrained within a certain modelling tool, or a package of tools designed to work together. A first challenge arises with the need to maintain the MDE approach between activities relying on disparate tools. For example, the modelling tool MATLAB/Simulink [1] works well

© Springer International Publishing Switzerland 2016
A. Wąsowski and H. Lönn (Eds.): ECMFA 2016, LNCS 9764, pp. 36–47, 2016.
DOI: 10.1007/978-3-319-42061-5_3

with its own toolboxes, as well as with tightly integrated external products such as TargetLink from dSPACE [2]; while its integration with a UML tool is not so clearly defined. In the best case, this challenge can be handled if the tools happen to share common technologies (such as a modelling framework, storage technologies, etc.), making their integration readily possible. However, considering the variety of modelling technologies encountered during the life-cycle of a typical product development process, it is most likely that the effort needed to maintain the MDE approach across such activities becomes no longer sustainable. As a result, MDE and its benefits are typically constrained to a subset of the development life-cycle.

One approach to expand this subset is to impose the same technological space on tools throughout the development process, leading to the adoption of a more centralized platform (such as PTC Integrity [3] or MSR-Backbone [4]). While this may be feasible at a smaller scale, such centralized platforms cannot scale to handle the complete heterogeneous set of data sources normally found in a large organization. Such platforms may also be less flexible for changes over time, when additional tools need to be introduced.

A second approach is to integrate models across technologies, as advocated by solutions such as ModelBus [5]. In a sense, such solutions also assume a common technological space (that of the integration platform), which all models need to be mapped to, before they can be integrated. Typically, this relies on model transformations, leading to the risk of data duplication, and the challenge of maintaining the data synchronized and consistent across the tool chain.

In this paper, we investigate a third alternative, where one attempts to work in a technology-agnostic way, focusing instead on the model data that need to be integrated, while disregarding how the data is managed within each modelling tool. We apply the Linked Data principles [6], and in particular its manifestation in the OASIS OSLC [7] tool interoperability standard, to enable the cohesion of MDE across modelling tools.

In the next subsection, we give an overview of Linked Data and the OASIS OSLC standard, followed by an argument for our approach in adopting the standard for MDE. In Sect. 2, we present a case study performed at Volvo Trucks to investigate and validate our approach. Section 3 then presents the developed underlying infrastructure that was necessary to carry out the use case. A discussion of related work is presented in Sect. 4, before concluding the paper in Sect. 5.

1.1 Linked Data and the OASIS OSLC Standard

Linked Data is an approach for publishing structured data on the web, such that data from different sources can be connected, resulting in more meaningful and useful information. Linked Data builds upon standard web technologies such as HTTP, URI and the RDF family of standards.

OASIS OSLC is a standard that targets the integration of software tools. It builds upon the Linked Data principles, and its accompanying standards, by defining common rules and patterns to access, manipulate and query resources managed by the different tools in the tool chain.

This Linked Data approach to tool interoperability promotes a distributed architecture, in which each tool autonomously manages its own product data, while providing RESTful services through which other tools can interconnect. This leads to low coupling between tools, by reducing the need for one tool to understand the deep data of another. Moreover – like the web – the approach is technology-agnostic, where tools can differ in the technologies they use to handle their data. That is, both the data as well as the technology is decentralized.

Figure 1 illustrates a typical architecture of an OSLC tool interface, and its relation to the tool it is interfacing. With data exposed as RESTful services, such an interface is necessarily an "OSLC Server", with the connecting tool defined as an "OSLC Client". A tool interface can be provided natively by the tool vendor, or through a third-party as an additional adaptor. In either case, a mapping between the internal data and the exposed RDF resources needs to be done. Such mapping needs to deal with the differences in the technologies used. In addition, a mapping between the internal and external vocabulary is needed, since the vocabulary of the resources being exposed is not necessarily the same as the internal schema used to manage the data.

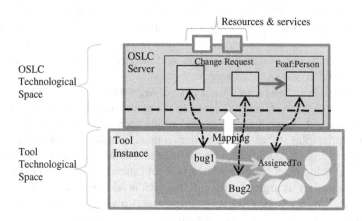

Fig. 1. Typical tool architecture, with an OSLC Server.

OSLC defines domain specifications, which include domain vocabularies (or information models) for specific lifecycle domains. The standardized domain specifications are minimalistic, focusing on the most common concepts within a particular domain, while allowing different implementations to extend this common basis. For an example of relevance to modelling tools, the Architecture Management Specification [8] only defines two resources Architecture Management and Link Type, where the former is used to represent any type of modelling elements such as a UML Class, Use Case, or Business Process Diagram.

1.2   Approach

While we agree with the minimalistic principle of the OSLC standard, it becomes apparent from our case study that a more detailed and specialized vocabulary is necessary to deal with the rich semantics generally available in many modelling tools. Modelling languages, such as UML, contain tens and hundreds of modelling artefacts that - depending on the tool usage scenarios - may need to be exposed. Moreover, these artefacts are hierarchically structured and contain relationships among themselves, creating a web structure that may also need to be exposed. As will be explained in the case study in Sect. 2, a typical integration scenario that require the exposure of many fine-grained resources is the linking of information across models at a fine level of details (for example, tracing a requirement to a specific class instead of a complete model or class diagram).

This needs not necessarily conflict with the minimalism of OSLC. As illustrated in Fig. 2, the rich and specialized vocabularies of MDE modelling languages (For a legible representation of EAST-ADL models the reader is referred to [12]), can build on the small but common foundation provided by OSLC domain specifications (such as Architecture Management [8] and Requirements Management [9]), which themselves build on the even more common OSLC Core vocabularies [10]. For ease of adoption and management, a common vocabulary needs to stay minimal; while a more specialized language can afford to be more detailed.

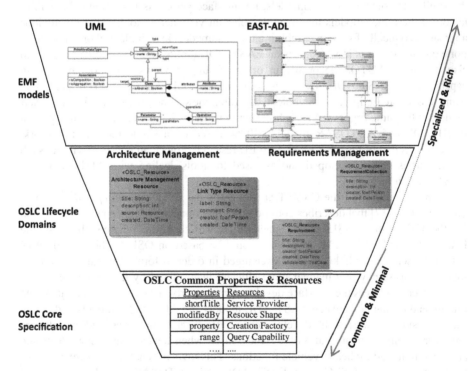

Fig. 2. The minimal and common basis of OSLC forms a foundation for the increasingly specialized and rich MDE modelling languages.

However, the development of an OSLC interface for a rich and specialized MDE tool may be potentially costly. First, a richer vocabulary - with the many fine-grained artefacts to be exposed at the interface - requires a larger development effort. Second, a specialized tool has normally few end-users upon which development costs can be shared. On the other hand, in the case when the metamodel of the artefacts is available in a digital format, it ought to be possible to automate the process of creating this OSLC interface. Such an approach is very advantageous since the same automation process can be reapplied to similar tools with similar technological basis, further lowering the threshold needed to adopt OSLC across the tool chain.

In this paper, we propose a fully-automated code generator that provides an OSLC interface for EMF-based modelling tools, allowing the exposure of modelling elements from any rich modelling language. Such a generator forms part of the tool support critical for reducing the cost of providing rich and specialized tool interfaces, generally needed when integrating modelling tools.

2   Case Study

AUTOSAR [11] and EAST-ADL [12] define two complementary and compatible metamodels for capturing design information for automotive embedded systems. They moreover define XML-based data exchange formats based on the metamodels. Despite the similarities of the two metamodels, no interface yet exists that allows the combination of these metamodels into a single coherent view across tools. That is, previous approaches typically focus on combining the metamodels in a single tool or framework. For example, Papyrus [13] supports an EAST-ADL profile and it would be possible to also define an AUTOSAR profile in order to support views based on the linking capabilities of EAST-ADL. Moreover, tools like EATOP [14] and ARTOP [15], both being based on Eclipse, could potentially offer view functionality by hosting their models in the same framework. It is however unnecessarily restrictive to assume that all EAST-ADL and AUTOSAR models will be based on a single tool or framework. Therefore, as part of the CRYSTAL [16] EU research project, an interface without such restrictions is being developed and assessed for tools dealing with AUTOSAR and EAST-ADL information.

A major delivery of the CRYSTAL project is the so called *interoperability specification (IOS)* [17] that describes common tool interoperability concepts. A foundation for the IOS is the OASIS OSLC standard. It was therefore inherent that also the EAST-ADL and AUTOSAR interfaces would be based on OSLC. This would allow data to be seamlessly linked and/or exchanged in order to form a global view and to maintain consistency in a manner more efficient than offered by file exchange.

In order to address the interface development properly, a case study containing data linking and exchange between EAST-ADL models and AUTOSAR models is defined. The case study addresses the development process – and the corresponding software engineering environment - at Volvo Trucks used when developing a new electronic architecture including heavy vehicle functions. This involves enabling data exchange – with the support of OSLC - for EAST-ADL and AUTOSAR models. A use case diagram for exchanging and linking EAST-ADL and AUTOSAR models is shown in

Fig. 3a. Color coding is used to improve readability of the diagram, where red represents AUTOSAR, blue represents EAST-ADL and green represents analysis combining both EAST-ADL and AUTOSAR. A typical usage scenario is illustrated in Fig. 3b, in which a Modeller and Implementer create EAST-ADL and AUTOSAR models respectively. The Modeller then uses the AUTOSAR OSLC adaptors to query and select a particular AUTOSAR model element (in particular a Software Component) and link it to a particular EAST-ADL element (DesignFunctionPrototype).

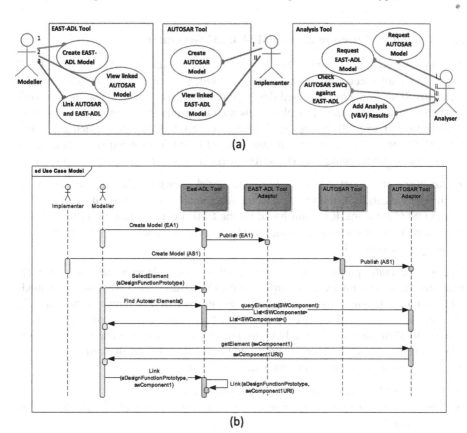

Fig. 3. (a) Use case diagram (b) A typical scenario for exchanging and linking EAST-ADL and AUTOSAR models (Color figure online)

3   Auto Generation of OSLC Interfaces for EMF-Based Models

A major cornerstone in realizing the above scenario is the ability to expose elements of the EAST-ADL and AUTOSAR models, as Linked Data resources and according to the OSLC standard. This requires the development of OSLC adaptors for the EAST-ADL and AUTOSAR tools managing their respective models.

The EAST-ADL and AUTOSAR metamodels contain hundreds of unique classes, with a complex hierarchy of multiple inheritances, and many associations between them. Early in the course of the project, it was concluded that a manual development of OSLC interfaces to expose these classes is prohibitive. Instead, the ability to automate the interface development is necessary. Several methods of automatic generation of OSLC adaptors were investigated, finally selecting the Eclipse Lyo Code Generator [18], which generates an OSLC adapter based on a specification model.

3.1   Overall Architecture of the EMF4OSLC Generator

The current Lyo code generator builds upon the Lyo OSLC4J SDK. While OSLC4J targets the implementation phase of adaptor implementation, the generator complements the SDK with a model-based development approach, which allows one to work at a higher level of abstraction, with models used to specify the adaptor design, without needing to deal with all the technical details of the OSLC standard (such as Linked Data, RDF, etc.). The generator can then be used to synthesis the specification model into a running implementation. The software consists of the following components:

- Adaptor meta-model – The adaptor meta-model allows for the graphical and intuitive specification of the OSLC adaptor functionality. It is designed to be loyal to the OSLC standard. It is built based on the EMF Ecore framework [19].
- Lyo code generator – generating the OSLC adaptor based on an instance of the adaptor meta-model.

The code generator produces most – but not all – of the code necessary for a complete ready-to-run adaptor interface, according to the OSLC standard. Only a set of methods that communicate with the source tool to access its internal data remain to be manually implemented (the dotted arrows "mapping" in Fig. 1 above). This communication is reduced to a simple set of methods to (a) get (b) create (c) search and (d) query each serviced resource. So, for a complete generation of the adaptor, the current generator needs to be complemented with two additional features:

- The automatic creation of the adaptor specification.
- The automatic generation of the necessary code to access and manipulate the data in the backend tool.

An additional component – EMF4OSLC - is hence developed that builds on top of this existing generator, in order to provide these two features. Given that the targeted modelling tools are EMF-based, EMF technologies can be readily used to (1) transform EAST-ADL/AUTOSAR metamodels into an adaptor specification model; and (2) provide the necessary Java code to access EMF model data at runtime. Figure 4 illustrates how this component fits with the current generator – as a separate component. Instead of tightly integrating the new component into the code generator, we envisage a pattern where additional components (the top-level dotted components in Fig. 4) can similarly build upon the current general-purpose generator. For example, another model generator can produce instances of the adaptor meta-model for SQL-based tools, and hence allowing for complete adaptor generation for such technologies. This naturally leads to

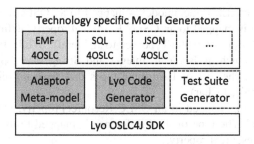

Fig. 4. The layered approach of the Lyo generator, building upon the Lyo OSLC4J SDK, and allowing for the proposed EMF4OSLC model generator.

the better interoperability between EMF-based tools and SQL-based tools, based on the technology-agnostic web services of Linked Data. Relating to the layers of Fig. 2, while the existing generator supports the OSLC core and domain specifications, the EMF4OSLC extends this support to cover the richer layers needed by EMF-based tools.

3.2 Adaptor Implementation

This section presents the implementation details of the EMF4OSLC component. While the process is identical for both EAST-ADL and the AUTOSAR metamodels, we will exemplify using the former. Figure 5 illustrates the resulting EAST-ADL data exchange infrastructure, where the model elements are handled in the tool EATOP. To implement a working OSLC adaptor from an EMF metamodel, as argued in Sect. 3, five steps are carried out, and will be described in the following subsections.

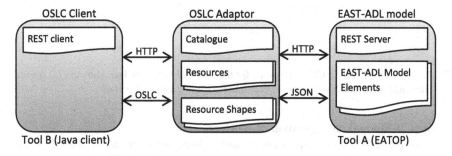

Fig. 5. EAST-ADL data exchange infrastructure

Step 1: Generating OSLC resource definitions.

As a first step, the EMF4OSLC generator imports an ECORE representation of the EAST-ADL metamodel (Version 2.1.12) [12] and traverses its elements (EClasses, EAttributes, etc.) in order to produce the corresponding OSLC Resource definitions according to the following mapping logic:

- Every EClass in the EMF metamodel is mapped to an OSLC Resource.
- Every EAttribute is mapped to an OSLC ResourceProperty, defined to be a Literal (i.e. a Property with oslc:valueType set to a literal). While the most common EAttribute types (such as Boolean, Integer and String) are supported by OSLC, EMF contains a richer set of EAttribute types that have no direct equivalent in OSLC (for example, EChar).
- Every EReference is mapped to an OSLC ResourceProperty, with oslc:valueType set to "Resource". The type of the EReference is mapped to the oslc:range of the corresponding ResourceProperty.
- For both EAttribute and EReference elements, the cardinality defined using the "lower bound" and "upper bound" properties are simply mapped to an equivalent OSLC cardinality description using the oslc:occurs of a ResourceProperty.
- Every EEnum enumeration type is mapped to an OSLC Property with an oslc: allowedValue set to the corresponding enumeration values.

As an example, the EClass VehicleFeature, found in the EAST-ADL metamodel, is translated to the OSLC resource definition VehicleFeature as illustrated in Fig. 6. In this example, the VehicleFeature Eclass inherits from another resource Feature. The resource definition also maps to four ResourceProperties. Each such ResourceProperty is in turn defined through constraints such as its range and cardinality.

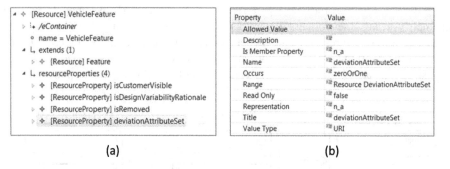

(a)   (b)

Fig. 6. The corresponding OSLC resource for the VehicleFeature EClass, showing (a) resource properties and inheritance structure (b) constraints defining each property.

Step 2: Manual configuration of services.

Once the resource definitions are created, it is necessary to define the OSLC Services (such as query capabilities, creation factories, and the RESTful operations) that are needed for the relevant resources. Not all resources would require such services, and the identification of the necessary services would depend on the usage scenario of the interfaces. For this reason, it remains a manual step to define the required services, through the graphical modelling support already provided by the base Lyo code generator.

Step 3: Definition of backend connection code.

When dealing with a big meta-model that contains hundreds of resources, writing the code connecting the OSLC adaptor with the backend tool (in this case EATOP) would be a laborious task. In this step, the EMF4OSLC component produces code templates for each of the Get/Create/Query methods of each serviced resource. The Lyo Generator in turn uses these templates to produce the appropriate final java methods. Figure 7 shows an example template for the Get-method of a resource.

```
backendCodeTemplate_getResource =
  "String url =
"http://ea_server.volvo.com/element/[ResourceClassName/]?get=app
lication/json&id=[Parameter2/]";
  aResource = new Gson().fromJson( sendGet(url), [
  ResourceClassName].class);"
```

Fig. 7. Resource get-method template code, where template parameters are marked in bold

Step 4: Automatic generation of the OSLC adaptor.
Once the resources are defined, and their corresponding services are configured, the OSLC adaptor is generated through the standard existing Lyo code generator functionality.
Step 5: Building and running the OSLC adaptor.
Steps 1-4 result in a fully functioning Eclipse project that is ready to run as an embedded OSLC web server. Such server can then be reached by an OSLC client using any of the OSLC defined discovery capabilities.

4 Related Work

The prototype proposed in [21] maps between EMF objects and RDF Resources, based on a mapping language between the EMF domain model and the corresponding RDF ontology. More generally, [20, 22] are representatives of a flora of solutions that attempt to translate between the RDF data model and the more traditionally encountered technologies. In particular, [20] provides a library for accessing RDF data from the dynamic object-oriented Ruby programs, while [22] provides a solution to publish relational databases as RDF graphs. While such approaches are crucial in defining the basic mapping between RDF and EMF, our work is dedicated towards the more specific OSLC standard, which is of most relevance to tool interoperability and MDE.

The work presented here is similar to the solution in [23], where an OSLC-based integration of EMF models is proposed in the Rational Software Architect Design Manager (DM) tool. DM allows its EMF-based models to be exposed as OSLC resources. This however assumes that the EMF models are defined and used within the DM tool itself. Instead, our approach provides a generic infrastructure that supports models from different EMF-based tools, and without necessarily knowing the internal mechanisms of the tools. This facilitates the integration of models across tools (EMF-based and/or otherwise). To ensure sustainability, we also desire an approach that builds on an established code generator for OSLC technologies, and which can be further extended to support other technologies as discussed in Sect. 3.1.

5 Conclusion

In this paper, we identified the need for efficient support in the development of tool interfaces in order to expose the rich and specialized semantics normally found in modern MDE tools. It is argued that such support can best be made possible by adopting the technology-agnostic Linked Data approach (and OSLC standard) to tool interoperability. In addition, one can take advantage of the digital access in model-based tools to automate the process of producing the needed interfaces.

A core component of such tool support is the proposed fully-automated code generator that provides an OSLC interface for EMF-based modelling tools, allowing the exposure of fine-grained elements from any rich modelling language. This approach was validated in an automotive case study at Volvo Trucks, using the EAST-ADL and AUTOSAR metamodels. Such metamodels contain hundreds of unique classes - with a complex hierarchy of multiple inheritances – that can now be exposed as OSLC resources for other tools to integrate with. Naturally, such mapping between the different paradigms (the classical object-oriented model of EMF and the RDF data model of Linked Data) is necessarily accompanied with complexities and compromises that one needs to deal with. The work presented here does not attempt to provide such a formal mapping, taking instead an initial hands-on approach. A discussion of the substantial differences in the underlying data models can be found in [20]. A practical issue from our own case study highlighted that while EAttributes and EReferences are defined within the context of their EClass, properties in Linked Data are stand-alone first-class entities that can be reused across many resources. In the case of rich modelling languages, this leads to an explosion in the number of properties that have no natural structuring entity. In addition, while the proposed generator allows for the exposure of the complete complex structure of an EMF model, the capability to configure and limit the hierarchy of artefacts being exposed would be desired.

While we have demonstrated our solution for the EMF technology, automation support is necessary for other technologies in order to ensure interoperability between a wider range of modelling tools. On-going work is under way to support SQL-based tools. By building upon the Lyo code generator and the architecture of Fig. 4, this further reduces the threshold of integrating modelling tools in a tool chain.

Acknowledgement. The research leading to these results has received partial funding from the European Union's Seventh Framework Program (FP7/2007-2013) for CRYSTAL – Critical System Engineering Acceleration Joint Undertaking under grant agreement No. 332830 and from Vinnova under DIARIENR 2012-04304.

References

1. MathWorks MATLAB/Simulink, April 2016. http://se.mathworks.com/products/simulink/
2. dSPACE TargetLink, April 2016. https://www.dspace.com/en/inc/home/products/sw/pcgs/targetli.cfm
3. PTC Integrity, April 2016. http://www.ptc.com/application-lifecycle-management/integrity

4. Weichel, B., Herrmann, M.: A backbone in automotive software development based on XML and ASAM/MSR. In: SAE Technical Papers (2004). doi:10.4271/2004-01-0295
5. Hein, C., Ritter, T., Wagner, M.: Model-driven tool integration with modelbus. In: Workshop Future Trends of Model-Driven Development (2009)
6. Berners-Lee, T.: Linked data design issues, April 2016. http://www.w3.org/DesignIssues/LinkedData.html
7. OASIS OSLC, April 2016. http://www.oasis-oslc.org/
8. OSLC architecture management specification version 2.0, 2011, April 2016. http://open-services.net/wiki/architecture-management/OSLC-Architecture-Management-Specification-Version-2.0/
9. OSLC requirements management specification version 2.0, 2012, April 2016. http://open-services.net/bin/view/Main/RmSpecificationV2
10. OSLC core specification version v2.0, 2013, April 2016. http://open-services.net/bin/view/Main/OslcCoreSpecification
11. AUTOSAR: automotive open system architecture, April 2016. http://www.autosar.org
12. EAST-ADL: electronic automotive systems architecture description language, April 2016. http://www.east-adl.info/
13. Papyrus - modeling environment, April 2016. https://eclipse.org/papyrus
14. EATOP EAST-ADL tool platform, April 2016. http://www.eclipse.org/eatop/
15. AUTOSAR tool platform (Artop), April 2016. https://www.artop.org/
16. CRYSTAL - critical system engineering acceleration - an artemis project, April 2016. http://www.crystal-artemis.eu/
17. Loiret, F., et al.: Draft proposal on EAST-ADL/AUTOSAR for IOS, in Interoperability Specification (IOS) - V2, CRYSTAL deliverable D601.022, 2015, pp. 183–188. http://www.crystal-artemis.eu/fileadmin/user_upload/Deliverables/CRYSTAL_D_601_022_v1.0.pdf
18. Eclipse Lyo code generator, April 2016. https://wiki.eclipse.org/Lyo/AdaptorCodeGenerator Workshop
19. Eclipse modeling framework project (EMF), April 2016. https://eclipse.org/modeling/emf/
20. Oren, E., Heitmann, B., Decker, S.: ActiveRDF: embedding semantic web data into object oriented languages. In: Web Semantics: Science, Services and Agents on the World Wide Web (2008)
21. Hillairet, G., Bertrand, F., Lafaye, J.Y.: Bridging EMF applications and RDF data sources. In: 4th International Workshop on Semantic Web Enabled Software Engineering (2008)
22. Bizer, C., Cyganiak, R.: D2R server: publishing relational databases on the SemanticWeb. In: Proceedings of the International SemanticWeb Conference (2003)
23. Elaasar, M., Neal, A.: Integrating modeling tools in the development lifecycle with OSLC: a case study. In: Proceedings of the 16th International Conference on Model Driven Engineering Languages and Systems, MODELS, pp. 154–169 (2013)

Stress-Testing Centralised Model Stores

Antonio Garcia-Dominguez$^{(\boxtimes)}$, Konstantinos Barmpis,
Dimitrios S. Kolovos, Ran Wei, and Richard F. Paige

Department of Computer Science, University of York, York, UK
{antonio.garcia-dominguez,konstantinos.barmpis,
dimitrios.kolovos,ran.wei,richard.paige}@york.ac.uk

Abstract. One of the current challenges in model-driven engineering is
enabling effective collaborative modelling. Two common approaches are
either storing the models in a central repository, or keeping them under
a traditional file-based version control system and build a centralized
index for model-wide queries. Either way, special attention must be paid
to the nature of these repositories and indexes as networked services: they
should remain responsive even with an increasing number of concurrent
clients. This paper presents an empirical study on the impact of certain
key decisions on the scalability of concurrent model queries, using an
Eclipse Connected Data Objects model repository and a Hawk model
index. The study evaluates the impact of the network protocol, the API
design and the internal caching mechanisms and analyzes the reasons for
their varying performance.

1 Introduction

Model-driven engineering (MDE) has received considerable attention due to its
demonstrated benefits of improving productivity, quality and maintainability.
However, industrial adoption has ran into various challenges regarding the current maturity and scalability of MDE.

In their 2012 study [1], Mohagheghi et al. interviewed four companies and
noted that they considered that the tools at the time did not scale to the large
projects that would merit the use of MDE. Several ways in which MDE practice
could learn from widely-used programming environments to handle large models
better were pointed out in [2], with a strong focus on the need for modularity
in modelling languages to improve scalability and simplify collaboration. Three
categories of scalability issues in MDE were identified in [3]: model persistence
issues, model querying and transformation issues, and collaborative modelling
issues.

Focusing on collaborative modelling, one common approach is storing the
models in a *model repository* that keeps track of revisions and resolves conflicts
between users. Another approach is using a file-based version control system for
storage and version control and creating a *model index* that can efficiently answer
model-wide queries and provide integrated views of all the model fragments.
These tools are typically deployed as a service within a network, in order to
make the models available from any device within the organisation.

© Springer International Publishing Switzerland 2016
A. Wąsowski and H. Lönn (Eds.): ECMFA 2016, LNCS 9764, pp. 48–63, 2016.
DOI: 10.1007/978-3-319-42061-5_4

There are strong implementations of both approaches, but little attention has been paid to their inherent nature as networked services: most studies have either focused on local scenarios where the client and the server reside in the same machine, or considered only the simple case with a single remote user. It can be argued that even with the right features, a collaborative system that is not responsive under load would not be widely adopted.

In this empirical study we evaluate the impact of several design decisions in one functionality common to both model repositories (e.g. CDO) and model indices (e.g. Hawk): querying remote models. The study aims to inform developers and end users of remote model stores on the real tradeoffs between several common choices: which network protocol to use, how to design the API and which types of caches are most effective.

The rest of this work is structured as follows: Sect. 2 provides a discussion on existing work on model repositories and model indices, Sect. 3 introduces the research questions and the design of the experiment, Sect. 4 discusses the obtained results and Sect. 5 presents the conclusions and future lines of work.

2   Background and Related Work

Persisting and managing large models has been extensively investigated over the past decade. This section presents the main state-of-the-art tools and technologies and briefly describes the two tools used in this empirical study.

2.1   File-Based Model Persistence

One of the most common approaches to storing models is serializing them to a textual file-based form. Tools like the Eclipse Modeling Framework (EMF) [4], ModelCVS [5], Modelio[1] and MagicDraw[2] all use XML-based model serialization. While this approach offers a structured platform-independent way for storing models, it has been shown by various works such as [3,6] to lack scalability as it requires loading the entire text file in order to retrieve any information needed from the model.

2.2   Database-Backed Model Persistence

In light of the scalability limitations resulting from storing models as text files, various database-backed model persistence formats have been proposed. Teneo/ Hibernate[3] allows EMF models to be stored in relational databases. NeoEMF [6] and MongoEMF[4] all use NoSQL databases to store EMF models. Database persistence allows for partial loading of models as only accessed elements have to be loaded in each case. Furthermore, such technologies can leverage the use of database indices and caches for improving element lookup performance as well as query execution time.

---

[1] https://www.modelio.org/.
[2] http://www.nomagic.com/products/magicdraw.html#Collaboration.
[3] http://wiki.eclipse.org/Teneo/Hibernate.
[4] https://github.com/BryanHunt/mongo-emf/wiki.

2.3 Model Repositories

When collaborative modeling is involved, simply storing models in a scalable form such as inside a database stops being sufficient; in this case issues such as collaborative access and versioning need to also be considered. Examples of model repository tools are Morsa [7], ModelCVS[5], Connected Data Objects (CDO)[6], EMFStore [8], Modelio, MagicDraw and MetaEdit+[7]. Model repositories offer capabilities for allowing multiple developers to manage models stored in a centralized repository by ensuring the models remain in a consistent state, while persisting the models in a scalable form, such as in a database.

CDO in particular is one of the most mature solutions, having been developed for over 7 years as an Eclipse project and being currently maintained by Obeo[8]. It implements a pluggable storage architecture, being able to use various solutions such as relational databases (H2, MySQL) or document-oriented databases (MongoDB), among others. CDO includes Net4j, a messaging library that provides bidirectional communications over TCP, HTTP and in-memory connections, and uses it to provide a remote API that exposes remote models as EMF resources. In addition to storing models, CDO includes a CDOQuery API that makes it possible to run queries remotely on the server and retrieve directly the results, reducing the necessary bandwidth.

2.4 Heterogeneous Model Indexing

An alternative to using model repositories for storing models used in a collaborative environment is to store them as file-based models in a classical version control system. As discussed in [9] this leverages the benefits of widely-used file-based version control systems such as SVN and Git, but retains the issues file-based models face. To address this issue a model indexer can be introduced that monitors the models and indices them in a scalable model index. The model index is synchronized with the latest version of the models in the repository and can be used to perform efficient queries on them, without having to check them out or load them into memory.

Hawk is an example of such a technology: it can maintain a graph database with the contents of one or more version control systems and perform very efficient queries on them. More recently, Hawk has been embedded into a server that provides a service-oriented API based on the Apache Thrift[9] library.

3 Experiment Design

As mentioned in the introduction, effective collaborative modelling requires not only having the right features, but also making sure that the system stays responsive as the number of clients increases. This section presents the design of an

---

[5] http://www.modelcvs.org/versioning/index.html.

[6] http://wiki.eclipse.org/CDO.

[7] http://www.metacase.com/.

[8] As stated in http://projects.eclipse.org/projects/modeling.emf.cdo.

[9] http://thrift.apache.org/.

empirical study that evaluates the impact of several factors in the performance of remote queries on a model repository (CDO) and a model index (Hawk).

3.1   Research Questions

RQ1. *What is the impact of the network protocol on remote query times and throughputs?*

In order to connect to a remote server, two of the most popular options are using raw TCP connections (for the sake of performance and flexibility) or sending HTTP messages (for compatibility with web browsers and interoperability with proxies and firewalls). Both Hawk and CDO support TCP and HTTP.

Properly configured HTTP servers and clients can reuse the underlying TCP connections with HTTP 1.1 pipelining and avoid repeated handshakes, but the additional overhead imposed by the HTTP fields may still impact the raw performance of the tool.

RQ2. *What is the impact of the design of the remote query API on remote query times and throughputs?*

Application protocols for network-based services can be stateful or stateless. Stateful protocols require that the server keeps track of part of the state of the client, while stateless protocols do not have this requirement. In addition, the protocol may be used mostly for transporting opaque blocks of bytes between server and client, or it might have a well-defined set of operations and messages.

While a stateful protocol may be able to take advantage of the shared state between the client and server, a stateless protocol is generally simpler to implement and use. Service-oriented protocols need to also take into account the granularity of each operation: "fine" operations that do only one thing may be easier to recombine, but they will require more invocations than "coarse" operations that perform a task from start to finish.

CDO implements a stateful protocol on top of the Net4j library, which essentially consists of sending and receiving buffers of bytes across the network. On the other hand, Hawk implements a stateless service-oriented API on top of the Apache Thrift library, exposing a set of specific operations (e.g. "query", "send object" or "register metamodel"). The Hawk API is generally coarse: most queries only require one pair of HTTP request/response messages.

While the stateful CDO clients and servers may cooperate better with each other, the simpler and less granular API in Hawk may reduce the total network roundtrip for a query by exchanging less messages.

RQ3. *What is the impact of the internal caching and indexing mechanisms on remote query times and throughputs?*

Database-backed systems generally implement various caching strategies to keep the most frequently accessed data in memory, away from slow disk I/O. At the very least, the DBMS itself will generally keep its own cache, but the system might use additional memory to cache especially important subsets or to keep them in a form closer to how it is consumed.

Another common strategy is to prepare indices in advance, speeding up queries. DBMSs already provide indices for common concepts such as primary keys and unique values, but these systems may add their own application-specific indices that precompute parts of the queries to be run.

3.2 Experiment Setup

In order to provide answers for the above research questions, a networked environment was set up to emulate increasing numbers of clients interacting with a model repository (CDO 4.4.1.v20150914-0747) or a model index (Hawk 1.0.0. 201602231713) and collect query response times. The environment is outlined in Fig. 1, and consists of the following:

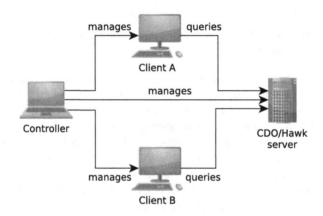

Fig. 1. Network diagram for the experimental setup

– **One "Controller" machine** that supervises the other machines through SSH connections managed with the Fabric Python library[10]. It is responsible for starting and stopping the client and server processes, monitoring their execution, and collecting the measured values. It does not run any queries itself, so it has no impact on the obtained results.
– **Two "Client" machines** that invoke the queries on the server, fetch the results and measure query response times. The two client machines were running Ubuntu Linux 14.04.3, Linux 3.19.0-47-generic and Oracle Java 8u60 on an Intel Core i5 650 CPU, 8 GiB of RAM and a 500 GB SATA3 hard disk. The client machines had two client programs installed: one for CDO and one for Hawk. Only one of these programs ran at a time. Each of these programs received the address of the server to connect to, the size of the Java fixed

---
[10] http://www.fabfile.org/.

thread pool to be used, the number of queries to be distributed across these threads and a template for the query to be run.

- **One "Server" machine** that hosts the CDO model repository and the Hawk model index, and provides TCP and HTTP ports exposing the standard CDO and Hawk APIs for remote querying. The server machine had the same configuration as the client machines.

  The server machine had two server programs installed: one for CDO and one for Hawk. Again, only one of these programs ran at a time. Both server programs were Eclipse products based on Eclipse Mars and used the same embedded HTTP server (Eclipse Jetty 9.2.13). Both systems were configured to use up to 4096 MB of memory (`-Xmx4096m -Xms2048m`)[11].

  In particular, the CDO server was based on the standard CDO server product, with the addition of the experimental HTTP Net4j connector. No other changes were made to the CDO configuration. The database backend was H2, the most mature and feature-complete option at the time of writing.

- **One 100 Mbps network switch** that connected all machines together in an isolated local area network.

As the study was intended to measure query performance results with increasing numbers of concurrent users, the client programs were designed to first warm up the servers into a *steady state*. Query time was measured as the time required to connect to the server, run the query on the server and retrieve the model element identifiers of the results over the network. Queries would be run 1000 times in all configurations, to reduce the impact of variations due to external factors (CPU and I/O scheduling, Java just-in-time recompilation, disk caches, virtual memory and so on).

Several workloads were defined. The lightest workload used only 1 client machine with 1 thread running 1000 queries in sequence. The other workloads used 2 client machines, each running 500 queries, with increasingly large pools of 2, 4, 8, 16, and 32 threads. These workloads would simulate between 1 and 64 clients running queries concurrently.

3.3 Queries Under Study

After defining the research questions and preparing the environment, the next step was to populate CDO and Hawk with the contents to be queried, and to write equivalent queries in their back-end independent languages: OCL for CDO and the Epsilon Object Language [10] (EOL) for Hawk.

CDO and Hawk were populated through the MoDisco use case titled *SharenGo Java Legacy Reverse-Engineering*[12] that was presented at the GraBaTs 2009 contest [11]. This use case involved reverse-engineering increasingly large Java codebases in order to extract knowledge models. The largest codebase

---

[11] The Neo4j performance guide suggests this amount for a system with up to 100M nodes and 8GiB RAM, to allow the OS to keep the graph database in its disk cache.

[12] http://www.eclipse.org/gmt/modisco/useCases/JavaLegacyRE/.

Listing 1. GraBaTs query written in OCL (OQ) for evaluating CDO.

```
1    DOM::TypeDeclaration.allInstances()→select(td |
2        td.bodyDeclarations→selectByKind(DOM::MethodDeclaration)
3            →exists(md : DOM::MethodDeclaration |
4            md.modifiers
5                →selectByKind(DOM::Modifier)
6                →exists(mod : DOM::Modifier | mod.public)
7            and md.modifiers
8                →selectByKind(DOM::Modifier)
9                →exists(mod : DOM::Modifier | mod._static)
10           and md.returnType.oclIsTypeOf(DOM::SimpleType)
11           and md.returnType.oclAsType(DOM::SimpleType).name.fullyQualifiedName
12           = td.name.fullyQualifiedName))
```

Listing 2. GraBaTs query written in EOL (HQ1) for evaluating Hawk.

```
1    return TypeDeclaration.all.select(td|
2        td.bodyDeclarations.exists(md:MethodDeclaration|
3        md.returnType.isTypeOf(SimpleType)
4        and md.returnType.name.fullyQualifiedName == td.name.fullyQualifiedName
5        and md.modifiers.exists(mod:Modifier|mod.public==true)
6        and md.modifiers.exists(mod:Modifier|mod.static==true)));
```

in the case study was selected, covering all the `org.eclipse.jdt` projects and producing over 4.9 million model elements. The H2 and Neo4j databases in CDO and Hawk grew to 1.4 GB and 1.9 GB, respectively.

These model elements conformed to the Java Development Tools AST (JDTAST) metamodel, which is described in works such as [3] or [7]. Some of the types within the JDTAST metamodel include the TYPEDECLARATIONs that represent Java classes and interfaces, the METHODDECLARATIONs that represent Java methods, and the MODIFIERs that represent Java modifiers on the methods (such as `static` or `public`).

Based on these types, task 1 in the GraBaTs 2009 contest required defining a query (from now on referred to as the GraBaTs query) that would locate all possible applications of the Singleton design pattern in Java [12]. In other words, it would have to find all the TYPEDECLARATIONs that had at least one METHODDECLARATION with `public` and `static` modifiers that returned an instance of the same TYPEDECLARATION.

To evaluate CDO, the GraBaTs query was written in OCL as shown in Listing 1. The query (named OQ after "OCL query") filters the TYPEDECLA-

Listing 3. GraBaTs query written in EOL (HQ2) using derived attributes on the METHODDECLARATIONs for evaluating Hawk.

```
1    return MethodDeclaration.all.select(md |
2        md.isPublic and md.isStatic and md.isSameReturnType
3    ).collect( td | td.eContainer ).asSet;
```

Listing 4. GraBaTs query written in EOL (HQ3) using derived attributes on the TypeDeclarations for evaluating Hawk.

```
1   return TypeDeclaration.all.select(td|td.isSingleton);
```

RATIONS by iterating through their MethodDeclarations and their respective Modifiers.

To evaluate Hawk, we used the three EOL implementations of the GraBaTs query of our previous work [13]. The first version of the query ("Hawk query 1" or HQ1, shown in Listing 2) is a translation of OQ to EOL, and follows the same approach.

The second version (HQ2), shown in Listing 3, assumed that the user instructed Hawk to extend MethodDeclarations with three derived attributes: *isStatic* (the method has a `static` modifier), *isPublic* (the method has a `public` modifier), and *isSameReturnType* (the method returns an instance of its TypeDeclaration). The query starts off from the MethodDeclarations so Hawk can take advantage of the fact that derived attributes are also indexed, so Hawk can use lookups instead of iterations to find the methods of interest. A detailed discussion about how derived attributes are declared in Hawk and how they are incrementally re-computed upon model changes is available in our previous works [9,14].

The third version (HQ3), shown in Listing 4, assumed instead that Hawk extended TypeDeclarations with the *isSingleton* derived attribute, setting it to true when the TypeDeclaration has a `static` and `public` MethodDeclaration returning an instance of itself. This derived attribute eliminates one more level of iteration, so the query only goes through the TypeDeclarations.

The GraBaTs query has been translated to 1 OCL query (OQ) and 3 possible EOL queries (HQ1 to HQ3). It must be noted that since CDO does not support derived attributes like Hawk, it was not possible to rewrite OQ in the same way as HQ1. Since the same query would be repeatedly run in the experiments, the authors inspected the code of CDO and Hawk to ensure that neither tool cached the results of the queries themselves: this was verified by re-running the queries while adding unique trivially true conditions, and comparing execution times.

4   Results and Discussion

The previous section described the research questions to be answered, the environment that was set up for the experiment and the queries to be run. This section will present the obtained results, answer the research questions (with the help of additional data in some cases) and discuss potential threats to the validity of the work.

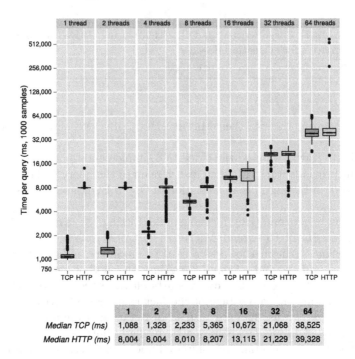

	1	**2**	**4**	**8**	**16**	**32**	**64**
Median TCP (ms)	1,088	1,328	2,233	5,365	10,672	21,068	38,525
Median HTTP (ms)	8,004	8,004	8,010	8,207	13,115	21,229	39,328

Fig. 2. OQ execution times (CDO, OCL)

4.1 Measurements Obtained

The obtained results for OQ, HQ1, HQ2 and HQ3 are shown in Figs. 2, 3, 4 and
5. These are notched box plots that show the distribution of query execution
times over $n = 1000$ samples, using a logarithmic scale on the y axes. Results are
faceted over the total number of client threads (from 1 to 64) and then separated
by protocol (TCP or HTTP). Each figure also includes a data table with the
median query execution times in milliseconds by thread count and protocol,
for direct numerical comparison between the alternatives. Shapiro-Wilk tests
rejected the null hypothesis ("the sample comes from a normal distribution")
with p-values < 0.01 for almost all combinations of query, protocol and thread
count. This was confirmed with Q-Q plots as well. For the purposes of this study,
we will assume that the query execution times are not normally distributed and
use non-parametric tests.

The box plots include dots with the outliers detected among the 1000 samples: these are the values above and below 1.5 times the interquartile distance
(IQR) from the third and first quartile, respectively. These outliers are assumed
to originate from thread ramp-up and ramp-down and from variations in the
I/O and CPU schedulers of the operating system and the underlying caches.

While they are not formal statistical tests, the notches serve as approximate
confidence intervals for the real median, based on $median \pm IQR/\sqrt{n}$ [15].

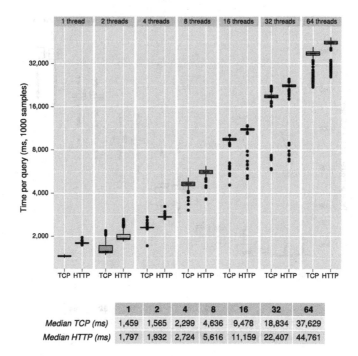

	1	**2**	**4**	**8**	**16**	**32**	**64**
Median TCP (ms)	1,459	1,565	2,299	4,636	9,478	18,834	37,629
Median HTTP (ms)	1,797	1,932	2,724	5,616	11,159	22,407	44,761

Fig. 3. HQ1 execution times (Hawk, EOL, no derived attributes)

Most configurations (CDO with TCP, all versions of Hawk) ran all queries correctly, producing the expected 164 results. However, CDO with HTTP resulted in several queries failing to respond or returning incorrect results with 4 threads (3 out of 1000), 8 (8), 16 (22), 32 (18) and 64 (2). CDO with HTTP also produced four especially notable outliers: 2 took 268.5 s, one took 535.5 s and the last one took 590.5 s.

4.2 RQ1: Impact of Protocol

Regarding the impact of the protocol on the performance and throughput of the remote queries, both CDO and Hawk confirm that there is a certain overhead involved in using HTTP rather than TCP. However, the actual overhead is very different depending on the tool and the query:

- OQ (Fig. 2) shows that CDO over HTTP has a striking overhead with low thread counts, taking nearly 8 times as much time per query as CDO over TCP for only 1 client thread. Kruskall-Wallis tests confirm significant differences for all thread counts (all p-values are < 0.01).
- HQ1 (Fig. 3) over HTTP has a consistent overhead over using TCP, but not as striking as CDO's case for OQ. Comparing the medians between TCP and HTTP, using HTTP increased query times between 17.74 % and

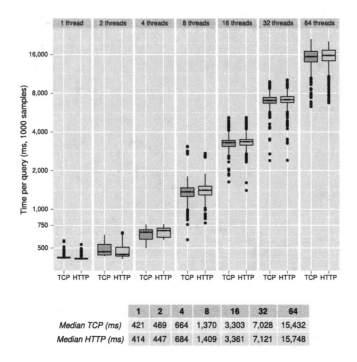

Fig. 4. HQ2 execution times (Hawk, EOL, extended METHODDECLARATIONS)

23.45 %. Kruskall-Wallis tests confirmed significant differences for all numbers of threads, with p-values < 0.01.

– The lower query times for HQ2 (Fig. 4) and HQ3 (Fig. 5) reduce CPU contention and make HTTP and TCP more alike. However, there are still significant differences, with Kruskall-Wallis p-values slightly higher but consistently below 0.02 for all numbers of threads.

4.3   RQ2: Impact of API Design

One striking observation from RQ1 was that CDO over HTTP had much higher overhead than Hawk over HTTP. Comparing the medians of OQ and HQ1 with 1 client thread, CDO+HTTP took 635.66 % longer than CDO+TCP, while Hawk+HTTP only took 23.17 % longer than Hawk+TCP. This contrast showed that CDO and Hawk used HTTP to implement their APIs very differently.

To clarify this issue, the Wireshark packet sniffer was used to capture the communications between the server and the client for one invocation of OQ and HQ1. These captures showed quite different approaches for an HTTP-based API:

– **CDO** involved exchanging 58 packets (10203 bytes), performing 11 different HTTP requests. Many of these requests were very small and consisted of exchanges of byte buffers between the server and the client, opaque to the HTTP servlet itself.

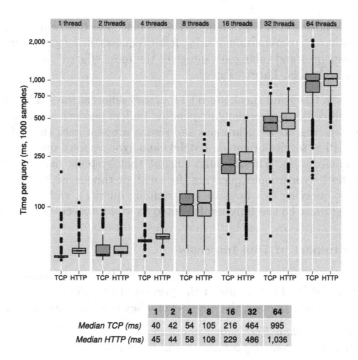

	1	2	4	8	16	32	64
Median TCP (ms)	40	42	54	105	216	464	995
Median HTTP (ms)	45	44	58	108	229	486	1,036

Fig. 5. HQ3 execution times (Hawk, EOL, extended TYPEDECLARATIONS)

Most of these requests were either within the first second of the query execution time or within the last second. There was a gap of approximately 6 seconds between the first group of requests and the last group. Interestingly, the last request before the gap contained the OCL query and the response was an acknowledgment from CDO. On the first request after the gap, the client sent its session ID and received back the results from the query.

The capture indicates that these CDO queries are asynchronous in nature: the client sends the query and eventually gets back the results. While the default Net4j TCP connector allows the CDO server to talk back to the client directly through the connection, the experimental HTTP connector relies on polling for this task. This has introduced unwanted delays in the execution of the queries. The result suggests that an alternative solution for this bidirectional communication would be advisable, such as WebSockets.

– **Hawk** involved exchanging 14 packets (2804 bytes), performing 1 HTTP request and receiving the results of the query in the same response. Since its API is stateless, there was no need to establish a session or keep a bidirectional server–client channel: the results were available as soon as possible.

While this synchronous and stateless approach is much simpler to implement and use, it does have the disadvantage of making the client block until all the results have been produced. Future versions of Hawk could also implement asynchronous querying in a similar way to what was suggested for CDO.

One side note is that Hawk required using much less bandwidth than CDO: this was due to a combination of using fewer requests, using `gzip` compression on the responses and taking advantage of the most efficient binary encoding available in Apache Thrift (*Tuple*).

In summary, CDO and Hawk use HTTP in very different ways. The CDO API is stateful and consists of exchanging pending buffers between server and client periodically: queries are asynchronous and results are sent back through polling. The Hawk API is service-oriented, stateless and synchronous: query results are sent back immediately. These results suggest that systems may benefit from supporting both synchronous querying (for small or time-sensitive queries) and asynchronous querying (for large or long-running queries), and that asynchronous querying must be carefully implemented to avoid unnecessary delays.

4.4   RQ3: Impact of Tool Internals

This section will focus on the results from the TCP variants, since they outperformed all the HTTP variants in the previous tests. Comparing the results produced by the four queries, there are several key observations to make:

O1. *OQ ran faster than HQ1 with 1 and 2 threads.*
O2. *HQ1 ran faster than OQ between 8 and 64 threads.*

O1 was somewhat unexpected: it was assumed that the join-free adjacency of the Neo4j graph database used in Hawk would give it an edge over the default H2 relational backend in CDO. Enabling the SQL trace log in CDO showed that after the first execution of OQ, later executions only performed one SQL query to verify if there were any new instances of TYPEDECLARATION.

Previous tests had already rejected the possibility that CDO was caching the query results. Instead, an inspection of the CDO code revealed a collection of generic caches. Among others, CDO keeps a CDOEXTENTMAP from ECLASSes to all their EOBJECT instances, and also keeps a CDOREVISIONCACHE with the various versions of each EOBJECT. In comparison, Hawk only uses the DBMS cache and an internal type cache, so it needs to retrieve the objects from the DBMS every time they are needed.

On the other hand, O2 shows that the lighter caching and Neo4j backend of Hawk allow it to scale better with demand: with 8 threads, the median time with Hawk is 4.64 s instead of the 5.37 s of CDO.

O3. *HQ2 ran faster than HQ1 and OQ for all thread counts.*
O4. *HQ3 ran faster than HQ2 for all thread counts.*

O3 and O4 confirm the findings of our previous work in scalable querying [9, 14]: adding derived attributes to reduce the levels of iteration required in a query speeds up running times by orders of magnitude, while adding minimal overhead due to the use of incremental updating. These derived attributes can be seen as application-specific caches that precompute parts of a query, unlike the application-agnostic caches present in CDO.

In particular, HQ3 takes two orders of magnitude less time than OQ and HQ1 for 1 thread, and is still faster than the best results of OQ and HQ1 even when handling 64 threads. While the *isSingleton* derived attribute in HQ3 might be considered too specialized for most cases, the *isStatic*, *isPublic* and *isSameReturnType* attributes in HQ2 are more generally useful and still produce significant time savings over OQ and HQ1.

4.5   Limitations and Threats to Validity

The presented study has several limitations that may threaten the internal and external validity of the results. Regarding the internal validity of the results:

- There is a possibility that CDO or Hawk could have been configured or used in a more optimal way. Since the authors developed Hawk, this may have allowed them to fine-tune Hawk better than CDO. However, the servers did not show any undesirable virtual memory usage, excessive garbage collection or disk I/O. The H2 backend was chosen for CDO due to its maturity in comparison to the other backends, and the Neo4j backend has consistently produced the best results for Hawk according to previous work. Finally, the authors contacted the CDO developers regarding how to compress responses and limit results by resource, to make it more comparable with Hawk, and were informed that these were not supported yet[13].
- The queries for CDO and Hawk were written in different languages, so part of the differences in their performance may be due to the languages and not the systems themselves. The aim in this study was to use the most optimized language for each system, since Hawk does not support OCL and CDO does not support EOL. Analytically, we do not anticipate that this is likely to have a strong impact on the obtained results as both languages are very similar in nature and are executed via mature Java-based interpreters. A future study could extend CDO or Hawk to fully address this issue.

As for the external validity of the results, this first study has not considered running several different queries concurrently, and has only considered one particular configuration for Hawk and CDO. While this configuration would be quite typical in most organisations, further studies are needed that mix different queries running in different models concurrently, and configure Hawk and CDO with different backends, memory limits, and model sizes.

5   Conclusions and Further Work

The results from the study suggest that the network protocol can have very different impacts on the performance of the model repository or model index, depending on how it is used: while CDO over HTTP had a dramatic overhead

---

[13] https://www.eclipse.org/forums/index.php?t=rview\&goto=1722258 and https://www.eclipse.org/forums/index.php?t=rview\&goto=1722096.

of 640%, Hawk over HTTP had a more reasonable 20%. The 20% overhead is a reasonable price to pay for the simpler operation across firewalls and its availability from Web browsers. A packet capture revealed that the problem with CDO over HTTP was the naïve way in which server-to-client communications had been implemented, which used simple polling instead of state-of-the-art approaches such as WebSockets. The study also showed that while CDO's extensive application-agnostic caching was somewhat faster than Hawk with no derived attributes, Hawk with derived attributes (a form of application-specific caching) could outperform CDO by two orders of magnitude and still be faster for large numbers of concurrent clients. As a general conclusion, this study confirms that the apparent performance of a highly efficient model access API can be severely degraded by minor details in the communications layer, and that having a few and well-placed application-specific caches can be much more effective than a comprehensive set of application-agnostic caches.

We plan to extend the present study to cover more situations, with more configurations of Hawk and CDO, a wider assortment of queries and a larger number of clients. Another direction of future work is analyzing the queries to split the work in a query efficiently between the client and the server, using the server for model retrieval and using the client to transform the retrieved values.

Acknowledgments. This research was part supported by the EPSRC, through the Large-Scale Complex IT Systems project (EP/F001096/1) and by the EU, through the MONDO FP7 STREP project (#611125).

References

1. Mohagheghi, P., Gilani, W., Stefanescu, A., Fernandez, M.A.: An empirical study of the state of the practice and acceptance of model-driven engineering in four industrial cases. Empirical Softw. Eng. **18**(1), 89–116 (2012)
2. Kolovos, D.S., Paige, R.F., Polack, F.A.C.: Scalability: the holy grail of model driven engineering. In: Proceedings of the Workshop on Challenges in MDE, Collocated with MoDELS 2008, Toulouse, France (2008)
3. Barmpis, K., Kolovos, D.S.: Evaluation of contemporary graph databases for efficient persistence of large-scale models. J. Object Technol., 13–3: 3: 1–26, July 2014. doi:10.5381/jot.2014.13.3.a3
4. Paternostro, M., Steinberg, D., Budinsky, F., Merks, E.: EMF: Eclipse Modeling Framework, 2nd edn. Addison-Wesley Professional, Reading (2008)
5. Kramler, G., Kappel, G., Reiter, T., Kapsammer, E., Retschitzegger, W., Schwinger, W.: Towards a semantic infrastructure supporting model-based tool integration. In: Proceedings of the 2006 International Workshop on Global Integrated Model Management, GaMMa 2006, pp. 43–46. ACM, New York (2006)
6. Gómez, A., Tisi, M., Sunyé, G., Cabot, J.: Map-based transparent persistence for very large models. In: Egyed, A., Schaefer, I. (eds.) FASE 2015. LNCS, vol. 9033, pp. 19–34. Springer, Heidelberg (2015)
7. Pagán, J.E., Cuadrado, J.S., Molina, J.G.: A repository for scalable model management. Softw. Syst. Model., 1–21 (2013). doi:10.1007/s10270-013-0326-8

8. Koegel, M., Helming, J.: EMFStore: a model repository for EMF models. In: Proceedings of the 32nd ACM/IEEE International Conference on Software Engineering, vol. 2, pp. 307–308. ACM (2010)

9. Barmpis, K., Shah, S., Kolovos, D.S.: Towards incremental updates in large-scale model indexes. In: Taentzer, G., Bordeleau, F. (eds.) ECMFA 2015. LNCS, vol. 9153, pp. 137–153. Springer, Heidelberg (2015)

10. Kolovos, D.S., Paige, R.F., Polack, F.A.C.: The Epsilon Object Language (EOL). In: Rensink, A., Warmer, J. (eds.) ECMDA-FA 2006. LNCS, vol. 4066, pp. 128–142. Springer, Heidelberg (2006)

11. GraBaTs. 5th Int. Workshop on Graph-Based Tools (2009). http://is.tm.tue.nl/staff/pvgorp/events/grabats2009/. Accessed 29 Feb 2016

12. Sottet, J.-S., Jouault, F.: Program comprehension. In: Proceedings of the 5th International Workshop on Graph-Based Tools (2009). http://is.tm.tue.nl/staff/pvgorp/events/grabats2009/cases/grabats2009reverseengineering.pdf. Accessed 29 Feb 2016

13. Barmpis, K., Kolovos, D.S.: Towards scalable querying of large-scale models. In: Cabot, J., Rubin, J. (eds.) ECMFA 2014. LNCS, vol. 8569, pp. 35–50. Springer, Heidelberg (2014)

14. Barmpis, K., Kolovos, D.S.: Towards scalable querying of large-scale models. In: Cabot, J., Rubin, J. (eds.) ECMFA 2014. LNCS, vol. 8569, pp. 35–50. Springer, Heidelberg (2014)

15. Chambers, J.M., Cleveland, W.S., Tukey, P.A., Kleiner, B.: Graphical Methods for Data Analysis, 1st edn. Duxbury Press, Boston (1983). ISBN 978-0-534-98052-8

Language Engineering

Compositional Language Engineering Using Generated, Extensible, Static Type-Safe Visitors

Robert Heim[1]([✉]), Pedram Mir Seyed Nazari[1], Bernhard Rumpe[1,2], and Andreas Wortmann[1]

[1] Software Engineering, RWTH Aachen University, Aachen, Germany
heim@se-rwth.de
[2] Fraunhofer FIT, Aachen, Germany
http://www.se-rwth.de
http://www.fit.fraunhofer.de

Abstract. Language workbenches usually produce infrastructure to represent models as abstract syntax trees (AST) and employ processing infrastructure largely based on visitors. The visitor pattern suffers from the expression problem regarding extensibility and reuse. Current approaches either forsake static type safety, require features unavailable in popular object-oriented languages (e.g., open classes), or rely on procedural abstraction and thereby give up the object-oriented data encapsulation (the AST) itself. Our approach to visitors exploits knowledge about the AST and generation of statically type-safe external visitor interfaces that support extensibility in two dimensions: (1) defining new operations by implementing the interface and (2) extending the underlying data structure, usually without requiring adaptation of existing implemented visitors. We present a concept of visitor development for language engineering that enables an adaptable traversal and provides hook points for implementing concrete visitors. This approach is applicable to single DSLs and to language composition. It thus enables a transparent, easy to use, and static type-safe solution for the typical use cases of language processing.

Keywords: Visitor pattern · Compositional language engineering · Language workbenches

1 Introduction

Many language workbenches (LWBs) employ context-free grammars (CFGs) to describe modeling languages [4]. From these grammars, LWBs derive the abstract syntax of languages in form of abstract syntax trees (ASTs). Parsers process models into instances of the ASTs. Processing ASTs requires to define traversal algorithms on the underlying tree data structure. Separating these algorithms from operations that perform on the AST liberates from reimplementing traversal strategies for different operations. The visitor design pattern [6] enables such separation by providing a traversal definition and **visit** methods that act as

© Springer International Publishing Switzerland 2016
A. Wąsowski and H. Lönn (Eds.): ECMFA 2016, LNCS 9764, pp. 67–82, 2016.
DOI: 10.1007/978-3-319-42061-5_5

hook points for AST node instances during traversal of the AST. For each visited AST node the traversal algorithm calls the appropriate `visit` method which then performs the specified operations. Thereby, the visitor pattern facilitates to *add new operations* on data structures, while *adding new types* (for instance when new productions are added to the related languages' AST) to data structures is effortful. In the original visitor pattern, visitor implementations must be extended with an additional `visit` method for each added data type. The problem of supporting extensibility in both dimensions is also known as the *expression problem* [20]. Approaches to it either require features unavailable in popular object-oriented languages (e.g., mixins [5] or open classes [3]), demand advanced type systems [15], forsake static type safety [2,16], or rely on procedural abstraction – and thereby abandon the object-oriented data encapsulation of the AST [14].

We contribute a concept to generate visitor infrastructures from CFGs that support language engineers with *statically type-safe* interfaces to work on the AST for model analysis and transformation. The visitor infrastructure facilitates development of reusable model processing infrastructures for single languages and supports integration of visitor implementations for combined languages. It is based on the single-dispatch language Java as the most popular object-oriented language[1] and we demonstrate a realization within the language workbench MontiCore [10][2].

Section 2 introduces MontiCore and its language processing mechanisms. Afterwards, Sect. 3 presents the visitor infrastructure generation approach for single languages and Sect. 4 for combined languages. Section 5 discusses our approach, before Sect. 6 debates related work and Sect. 7 concludes.

2   Preliminaries

MontiCore [10] is a language workbench for the engineering of compositional modeling languages. It provides an extended CFG format for integrated specification of concrete and abstract syntax. From these grammars, MontiCore derives the Java AST classes of a language and its parsers instantiate these classes to represent processed models.

We present quintessential concepts of MontiCore's grammar by the example of the grammar for class diagrams depicted in Fig. 1: it begins with the keyword `grammar` (l. 1), followed by its name and a body in curly brackets. The body contains productions to describe the structure of the CD language. The grammar's main production is `CDDef`, the definition of a class diagram consisting of the model keyword `classdiagram` (everything in quotation marks is part of the concrete syntax only), a name, classes, and associations (l. 2). The production `Name` is part of

---

[1] http://www.tiobe.com/index.php/tiobe_index.

[2] MontiCore is open source (https://github.com/MontiCore/monticore) and running visitor examples as described in this paper are available online (http://www.se-rwth.de/materials/mcvisitors/).

```
                                                    ┌──────────────┐
                                                    │        MCG   │
  ┌─────────────────────────────────────────────────────────────────┐
1 │ grammar CD {                                                      │
2 │   CDDef = "classdiagram" Name "{" ( Class | Association )* "}";    │
3 │   Class = "class" Name ( "extends" super:Name)? "{" Method* "}";   │
4 │   interface Method;                                                │
5 │   MethodSignature implements Method = type:Name Name ParameterList ";"; │
6 │   ParameterList = "(" (Parameter || ",")* ")";                     │
7 │   Parameter = type:Name Name;                                      │
8 │   // associations ...                                              │
9 │ }                                                                  │
  └─────────────────────────────────────────────────────────────────┘
```

Fig. 1. An exemplary MontiCore grammar for definition of simplified class diagrams.

MontiCore primitives. The body of a class diagram is delimited by curly brackets and contains arbitrary many (denoted by the star operator *) associations and classes in arbitrary order (via disjunction operator |). The production for classes begins with the model keyword `class`, followed by a name, optionally followed by the keyword `extends` with another name, and a body delimited by curly brackets (l. 3). The body contains arbitrary many instances of `Method`, which is an interface production (l. 4) that is implemented by the production `MethodSignature` (l. 5). Thus, `MethodSignature` can be used whenever a `Method` is required – for instance in the `Class` production (l. 3). This enables to add new implementing productions to the grammar a-posteriori without modifying the interface production itself, which is essential for language inheritance (see Sect. 4). The production `MethodSignature` consists of a type, a name, and a list of parameters. The `ParameterList` (l. 6) consists of comma-separated `Parameter` instances in brackets[3], where each `Parameter` (l. 7) has a type and a name. From the grammar depicted in Fig. 1, MontiCore generates an AST node class for each production. Figure 2 depicts these classes. The names of AST classes begin with "AST" and are followed by the name of the production they are derived from (such as `ASTCDDef`). The non-terminal `Name` results to a field `name` of Java type `String` in the AST class. MontiCore enables to define the names of AST fields, as for example via `type:Name` in the production `Parameter`. This results in the field `String type` of `ASTParameter`. References to other non-terminals in a production become associations between the corresponding AST classes. They have the same cardinalities as specified in the grammar. For instance, `CDDef` uses the non-terminal `Class`, thus `ASTCDDef` is associated to `ASTClass`. For the interface production `Method`, MontiCore generates the interface `ASTMethod`. As the production `MethodSignature` implements the interface production `Method`, its AST class `ASTMethodSignature` implements `ASTMethod` as well.

3   Generating the Visitor Pattern as DSL Infrastructure

We exploit knowledge on the automated generation of AST node classes to produce visitor interfaces for CFGs. These interfaces prescribe separate methods

---

[3] For a production P and a separator s the expression (P || "s")* denotes an arbitrary count of P separated by s. There is no s at the end.

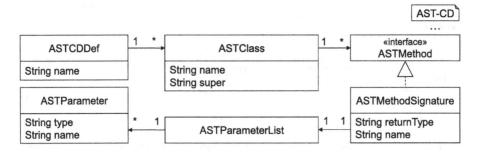

Fig. 2. The AST node classes MontiCore derives from the CD grammar of Fig. 1.

for traversal and visiting that are connected by methods to handle their interaction. For each production of the CFG, the generated visitor interface yields the methods visit, endVisit, and handle to handle operations on these nodes. For concrete class nodes, we also generate a traverse method for subtree traversal. All methods have default implementations[4] and hence do not require an implementation. Instead, they are best understood as hook points.

Derived from the CD language presented in Fig. 1, the generated visitor interface CDVisitor is as depicted in Fig. 3. The methods visit and endVisit for an AST node type enable to process instances of that node before and after its traversal, respectively. By default they do nothing and hence the default implementation is an empty method body (omitted in Fig. 3).

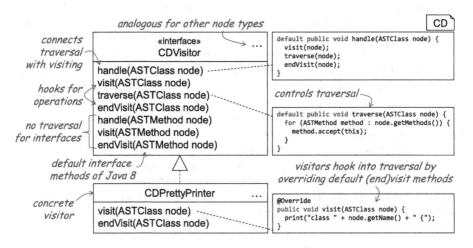

Fig. 3. The CDVisitor interface generated for the CD language and a concrete visitor.

Reusing a traversal algorithm can be achieved by implementing it in a super type that is meant to be inherited by concrete visitor implementations.

---

[4] Default implementations are available since Java 8.

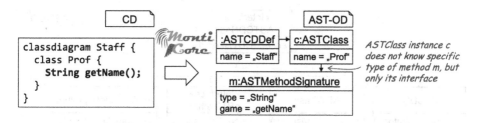

Fig. 4. A CD model and the resulting AST instance with an ASTClass not knowing that m is of type ASTMethodSignature.

By providing such an implementation in a class it requires software components that are based on the visitor infrastructure to extend it. This, however, contradicts flexibility in software design during language engineering as the component then is defined as a specialization of the visitor infrastructure and multi-inheritance is not supported in Java. Also, with respect to semantics, it is better to leave the specialization characteristics open to the language engineer. For example, a pretty printer could specialize an abstract pretty printer that defines constants regarding whitespaces. To this effect, MontiCore's visitor infrastructure is not based on classes but on interfaces which enable easier integration with other software components. This becomes even more relevant in language composition (cf. Sect. 4), when concrete visitors require extension and composition.

The top-right side of Fig. 3 illustrates the default implementations of the CDVisitor interface: The handle method takes care of visiting and traversal. The traverse method implements a climb-down strategy (e.g., order) to traverse the children. This separation enables to easily change the traversal order in subclasses while shielding the developer from involuntary changing the overall traversal strategy or missing to call the visit methods. The CDVisitor interface does not provide traversal methods for AST nodes of interface types derived from interface productions of the CFG, because interfaces do not have children. AST nodes of interface types (e.g., ASTMethod) are never instantiated. Instead, MontiCore enforces that each CFG contains at least one implementation for each interface production. Consequently, there always exists a concrete AST node class that implements the interface. Figure 4 elucidates this with a CD model (left) and the resulting AST instance (right). The CD model contains the class Prof, which has a method getName(). Although the ASTClass instance c has an instance of ASTMethodSignature, the class ASTClass knows this instance only via its interface ASTMethod.

For traversing the children of the ASTClass associated ASTMethod instances have to be considered. To call the most specific handle method for each of the children, a mechanism to calculate the most specific type of each child is required. This mechanism should not make use of type-introspection, but instead dispatch dynamically by itself. To simulate double dispatch in the single dispatch language Java, MontiCore generates an interface with a single accept method responsible

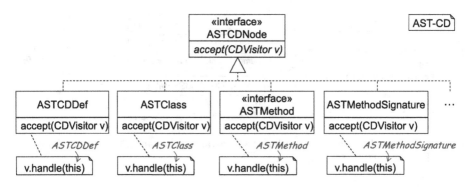

Fig. 5. All AST node types implement the `accept` method for the language's visitor.

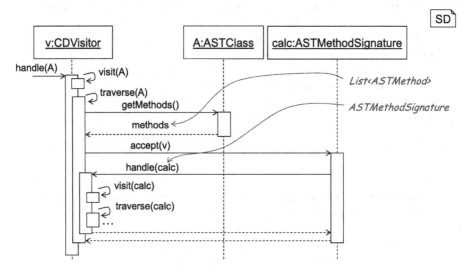

Fig. 6. Traversing a class requires identifying the runtime type of the methods in order to call the most specific `handle` methods. To this effect, a double dispatch is simulated.

for calling the visitors' `handle` methods with the most specific type. Figure 5 shows this interface and its implementations. The purpose of the `accept` methods is to dispatch to the most specific `handle` method of the given `CDVisitor` for each AST node type. Consequently, MontiCore generates AST nodes in such a way that they dispatch on the language's visitor to the `handle` method with themselves as argument (i.e. `this`). Although the implementation looks similar among the AST types, it differs in the specific type of `this`. Thereby, the most specific `handle` method is called. The sequence diagram in Fig. 6 illustrates the double dispatching of `ASTMethods` when handling the `ASTClass` shown in Fig. 4.

Until now, it was assumed that defining operations on a language's AST always relates to the most specific node types. This, however, is not true: For example, defining an operation to count all methods should be based on the

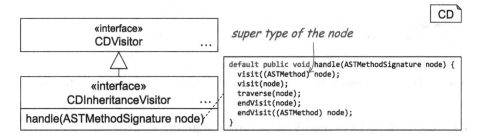

Fig. 7. The inheritance visitor visits nodes also in all their super types.

visit method for `ASTMethod`, but the double dispatching always calls the most specific `visit` hooks during traversal. Hence, such a method counter must hook into all `visit` methods for nodes that refine `Method`. While in the example only one production (`MethodSignature`) is effected, MontiCore enables implementing interface productions multiple times. All specific `visit` hooks would require to implement the same code. To prevent such code repetitions, MontiCore provides an extended visitor interface called *inheritance visitor* (see Fig. 7). While the formerly described visitor interface only calls `visit` hooks for the specific types, the inheritance visitor exploits knowledge about the grammars and the relation between their rules to call all `visit` methods that a node type is applicable for. This requires casting the nodes (cf. Fig. 7) in the `handle` methods, but is statically type-safe and more importantly generated. By extending this inheritance visitor instead of the common one, operations can be defined on all node types.

Implementing visitors using the presented infrastructure is straightforward and statically type-safe. It does not require knowledge about the double dispatch mechanism when depth-first traversal suffices. Adapting traversal requires calling `accept` methods and, hence, some knowledge about the visitor pattern.

For example, pretty printers, which transform an AST instance to a string representation, often are implemented as visitors. Figure 3 (bottom) depicts an excerpt of a pretty printer for the CD language. The `CDPrettyPrinter` implements the visitor interface `CDVisitor` and thus inherits the default implementations for traversing and handling a CD AST. By overriding `visit` and `endVisit` methods it hooks into the default traversal to execute operations on specific nodes.

4   The Visitor Pattern for Compositional Languages

In software language engineering, non-invasive reuse of languages and related infrastructures can greatly improve development. In this context, extending and composing visitors is of particular interest. The following section describes an extension of the CD language and demonstrates how its visitors can be easily reused in the sub language. Afterwards, we describe how visitors of multiple super languages can be composed.

74   R. Heim et al.

| | MCG |

```
1 grammar CDWithConstructor extends CD {
2   ConstructorSignature implements Method = Name ParameterList ";"
3 }
```

Fig. 8. The `CDWithConstructor` language extends the `CD` language by constructors.

4.1 Extending Concrete Visitors for Language Extension

MontiCore supports language extension [8], where sub languages inherit the productions of their parents. For instance, Fig. 8 depicts the `CDWithConstructor` language, which extends `CD` (l. 1) and introduces constructors (l. 2). Constructors implement the interface production `Method`, enabling to use these whenever an instance `Method` is required.

The resulting AST is illustrated in Fig. 9. The AST nodes `ASTMethod` and `ASTParameterList` (not shown in the figure) of `CD` are reused by the new `ASTConstructorSignature` AST node type of `CDWithConstructor`. MontiCore also produces the interface `CDWithConstructorVisitor` for the sub language. Generated visitor interfaces extend the visitor interfaces of all their super languages to inherit their default implementations. Here, the visitor interface `CDWithConstructorVisitor` extends `CDVisitor` and adds default implementations for the new node type `ASTConstructorSignature`. Using this inheritance relation all default implementations of the super language's visitor interface are reused. Hence, when implementing a visitor for the new language the aggregated default implementations are available. Consequently, the pretty printer for the sub language (`CDWithConstructorPrettyPrinter`) can be implemented by extending the `CDPrettyPrinter` of the super language (l. 1 of Fig. 10). It thereby reuses the pretty printing for all nodes of the super language and only adds pretty printing for constructors. For example, the reused production `ParameterList` (l. 2 in Fig. 8) is printed using the inherited implementation of `CDPrettyPrinter`.

Visitors of a super language are unaware of new AST node classes introduced in sub languages. For example, the pretty printer of the `CD` language is able to handle `ASTClass` nodes. An AST instance of the sub language (i.e. a model) reuses the exact same class and hence it is possible to hand this model to the `handle(ASTClass)` method of the `CDPrettyPrinter`. However, double dispatching the children of type `ASTMethod` to their specific types is only possible for types defined in the super language itself. In case of a `ASTConstructorSignature` the most specific type known by the super language's visitor is `ASTMethod`. Hence `handle(ASTMethod)` would be executed. This is unintuitive, because the most specific type at runtime is `ASTConstructorSignature`. Consequently, MontiCore forbids directly applying a visitor implemented for a specific language on any of its sub languages. A compiler cannot statically check this which leads to Monti-Cores convention to only run visitors on their own language. This also means that a concrete visitor implementation must be adjusted to be reused on a sub language, even if nothing changes. This, however, is very easy and requires minimal

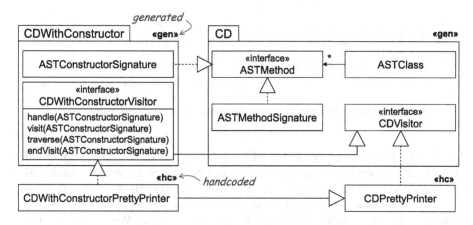

Fig. 9. A subset of CD's and CDWithConstructor's language infrastructure.

```Java
 1  class CDWithConstructorPrettyPrinter extends CDPrettyPrinter implements
        CDWithConstructorVisitor {
 2    @Override
 3    public void visit(ASTConstructorSignature node) {
 4      print(node.getName());
 5    }
 6    @Override
 7    public void endVisit(ASTConstructorSignature node) {
 8      print(";");
 9    }
10  }
```

Fig. 10. Extending a concrete visitor of a single super language is straightforward. Only the additional nodes must be considered. For nodes of the super language, the super language's pretty printer CDPrettyPrinter is reused.

glue code. For example, reusing the pretty printer without adding anything is as easy as defining a class similar to Fig. 10, but with an empty class body.

Another issue with this implementation is that extension of AST types in sub languages results in an unexpected accept call. For example, the node type ASTConstructorSignature implements the interface ASTMethod and thereby inherits CD's accept method with the visitor parameter being of static type CDVisitor. The CDWithConstructorVisitor calls this method when traversing the ASTClass instead of the intuitively expected accept method with parameter of static type CDWithConstructorVisitor This occurs because the inherited traversal is defined in the super language. This traversal calls accept on the ASTMethod children. While the type of the child is dispatched dynamically, choosing the accept method within it uses method overloading based on the static type of the visitor that defines traversal (i.e. CDVisitor). Consequently, the wrong accept method is executed. This cannot be solved by simulating another double dispatch, because the super language never statically is aware of types of a sub language. Hence, this is a limitation of our approach. Our solution to

```
                                                        ┌──────────────┐
                                                        │         MCG  │
  ┌─────────────────────────────────────────────────────┴──────────────┴───┐
1 │ grammar Automaton {                                                       │
2 │   Automaton =  "automaton" Name "{" (State | Transition)* "}";            │
3 │   State = "state" Name ";";                                               │
4 │   Transition = from:Name "-" input:Name ">" to:Name ";";                  │
5 │ }                                                                         │
  └──────────────────────────────────────────────────────────────────────────┘
```

Fig. 11. The MontiCore grammar for a language to model automata.

this is overriding the `accept` method for visitor interfaces of super languages in affected AST types (e.g., `accept(CDVisitor)` of `ASTConstructorSignature`). The generated implementation checks at runtime, whether the given visitor stems from the correct sub language. In this case, the call is delegated to the correct `accept` method by casting the visitor to the specific type. We argue, that this solution still is a good tradeoff between static type safety and flexibility in reuse, because (a) the AST types and this mechanism are generated and (b) the visitor interfaces remain statically type-safe. Implementing as well as reusing concrete visitors do neither require manual type-introspection nor casts. Also, the former problem does not occur when reusing non-terminals of super languages as done with `ParameterList`. Here, traversal (of `ASTConstructorSignature`) resides in the sub language and the generated traversal is aware of relations to the super language and consequently is statically type-safe.

4.2 Composing Concrete Visitors During Language Embedding

MontiCore enables language embedding by inheritance of grammars and provides adaptation mechanisms on a symbolic level [8,9]. These adaptation mechanisms depend on visitor composition for, e.g., building symbol tables. The same holds true for other software components such as validation or pretty printers. In this section we first show the embedding of automata into the CD language on the grammar level and then demonstrate the resulting visitor interfaces as well as composing existing pretty printers of both the CD language as well as the pretty printer of the `Automaton` language to a new pretty printer for the integrated language. Figure 11 depicts the `Automaton` language that describes automata (l. 2) using states (l. 3) and transitions (l. 4). We assume an implemented `AutomatonPrettyPrinter` (analogous to `CDPrettyPrinter`) that implements the `AutomatonVisitor` interface to pretty print an automaton.

Figure 12 depicts the MontiCore grammar that embeds automata into class diagrams. Automata are integrated as methods by implementing the interface production `Method` of the CD language. Figure 13 shows the resulting structure. The `ASTAutomatonEmbedding` implements the `ASTMethod` interface of the CD language and has a `ASTAutomaton` of `Automaton` language as child. The visitor interface of the new language extends both super language's visitor interfaces to inherit their default implementations.

Implementing a pretty printer for this language cannot make use of the approach shown in Sect. 4.1, because Java does not allow multi-inheritance of classes

```
                                                                    ┌─────────┐
                                                                    │   MCG   │
  ┌─────────────────────────────────────────────────────────────┴─────────┴──┐
 1│ grammar CDWithAutomaton extends CD, Automaton {                            │
 2│   AutomatonEmbedding implements Method = Automaton;                        │
 3│ }                                                                          │
  └────────────────────────────────────────────────────────────────────────────┘
```

Fig. 12. The CDWithAutomaton language's grammar extends the grammars of the languages CD and Automaton and provides a production that embeds automata as methods.

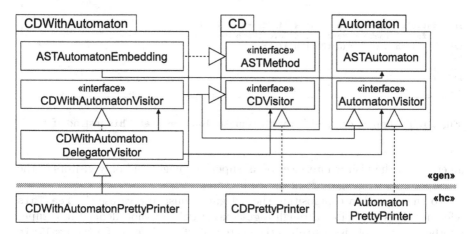

Fig. 13. A subset of the resulting infrastructure when embedding the Automaton language into the CD language.

and hence, it is not possible to extend both languages' pretty printers. Instead, MontiCore generates a visitor implementation for the new language, that is capable of composing visitors of all super languages using a delegator pattern (cf. CDWithAutomatonDelegatorVisitor in Fig. 13). It provides setters for visitors of all (potentially transitive) super languages. MontiCore exploits knowledge of the AST model by generating this delegator visitor in such a way that it delegates all handle, traverse, and visit calls to the concrete super visitor of the language that the current node stems from. This behavior is adjustable by extending this delegator visitor and overriding the corresponding methods.

As this approach to composition is based on delegation, it requires *inversion of control*. For example, when handling a node the delegator delegates the handling to the visitor that is registered for that specific node. Executing the visit hooks and traversal, however, should not directly take place in the delegate, but the delegator should control these operations as well. In MontiCore this inversion of control is called the *realThis pattern*. It describes that in composable objects (such as concrete visitors) the this reference should not be used, but instead a realThis reference. A composer then can set this realThis reference to itself and thereby gain control over all methods within the delegates. Consequently, a composer must implement a super set of the aggregated interfaces of all composed objects, which holds true for the visitor infrastructure as visitor interfaces

```Java
 1  public interface CDVisitor {
 2    public CDVisitor getRealThis();
 3    public void setRealThis(CDVisitor realThis);
 4
 5    default public void handle(ASTClass node) {
 6      getRealThis().visit(node);
 7      getRealThis().traverse(node);
 8      getRealThis().endVisit(node);
 9    }
10
11    default public void traverse(ASTClass node) {
12      for (ASTMethod method : node.getMethods()) {
13        method.accept(getRealThis());
14      }
15    }
16    // ...
17  }
```

Fig. 14. To support composition visitors must always use `realThis` instead of `this`.

inherit from the visitor interfaces of all super languages and only visitors of the corresponding languages are meant to be composed.

To enable such a composition the delegates must always use the `realThis` reference. It is accessible through a `getRealThis()` method defined in a super interface. In case of visitors this is the visitor interface. A setter for the `realThis` reference then enables changing it. The composed delegates must implement both methods to manage the `realThis` reference, which initially equals `this`. Figure 14 depicts the actual default implementations of the visitor interface that enable visitor composition by using `getRealThis()` (ll. 6–8, 13).

For transitive delegation (e.g., composing already composed visitors) a delegator must transitively ensure the correct `realThis` reference when itself gets composed. This is achieved by transitively setting `realThis` for all delegates in case that the own `realThis` changes.

Figure 15 depicts an example by composing the concrete pretty printer visitors of `CD` and `Automaton` to a pretty printer for the new language. The composition extends the delegator visitor `CDWithAutomatonDelegatorVisitor` (l. 2) that provides statically typed methods for the composition (used in ll. 4–5).

```Java
1  class CDWithAutomatonPrettyPrinter
2                  extends CDWithAutomatonDelegatorVisitor {
3    public CDWithAutomatonPrettyPrinter() {
4      setCDVisitor(new CDPrettyPrinter());
5      setAutomatonVisitor(new AutomatonPrettyPrinter());
6      setCDWithAutomatonVisitor(new EmptyCDWithAutomatonVisitor());
7    }
8  }
```

Fig. 15. Implementing a pretty printer for the combined language reuses existing pretty printers of the super languages. For the new AST node `ASTAutomatonEmbedding` nothing is printed, which is why only an empty implementation is chosen (l. 6).

A setter for a visitor of the own language (l. 6) ensures that the new AST node `ASTAutomatonEmbedding` can be traversed. In this example the pretty printer is solely based on the pretty printers of the super languages and does not require any additional output for the embedding production. Hence, an empty visitor is used that only inherits the default implementation from the visitor interface, but does not hook into any of its methods.

5   Discussion

The visitor pattern and its derivatives suffer from the expression problem [20] and so does our approach. Nevertheless, the presented infrastructure makes minimal use of type-introspection that is (a) hidden when implementing and composing visitors and (b) automatically generated and, thus, less error prone. To this effect, our main contribution is enabling language engineers to implement visitors in a statically type-safe fashion. Also, the generated visitor interfaces are semantically bound to the languages to support comprehensibility. Experience with language engineering has shown that depth-first traversal (with the same order of child traversal as they occur in the grammar) is sufficient for most model processing tasks. Hence, handcrafted visitor implementations, which inherit traversal and hooks from the generated interface, usually do not require adjustments. When necessary, traversal can be adapted in specific visitors by overriding the inherited default traversal. Being interface-driven, our approach furthermore does not enforce implementing operations on the AST by extending visitors, which enables developers to use the inheritance relation to flexibly integrate visitors with other software components.

The main limitation of the presented visitor infrastructure resides in overridden traversals. While our approach enables adaptation of traversal by overriding the default implementation, it might require manual adjustments when the CFG of the language changes.

When a non-terminal is added on the right-hand side of a production, the corresponding AST node gets a new child that must be traversed. In this case, manual adaptation of overridden traversals in concrete visitors is required, which a compiler does not identify statically.

However, removing complete productions or changing their names can be statically identified and evolution efforts can be minimized by employing refactoring mechanisms. Nonetheless, our approach is affected by the expression problem as changing the AST of a language might require adaptation of all its visitors. When depth-first traversal is sufficient this rarely occurs, because default implementations are generated.

MontiCore supports overriding non-terminals in sub languages. The full-qualified names of the generated AST nodes include the languages' names and hence are unique. Consequently, the generated visitor interfaces support overridden non-terminals since they are based on the full-qualified names of the corresponding AST nodes as well.

6   Related Work

In contrast to established visitor combinators [18] our solution is statically type-safe in liberating language developers from manually casting generic types (such as `AnyVisitable` [18]) to specific types. Instead, our solution provides a statically type-safe visitor interface that supports visitor composition. It enables implementing a concrete visitor by hooking into a predefined traversal for specific AST nodes, but also enables to adapt the traversal for specific visitors.

The original visitor pattern [6] describes the traversal algorithms as part of the data structure (within the `accept` methods). This prohibits adjusting traversal in specific AST visitors as they all share the same AST implementation. Oliveira [13] distinguishes between *internal visitors* that define traversal within the data structure and *external visitors* that define it in the visitors. Also, the original visitor pattern stores the result of a visitor run as state in the visitor. This *imperative* calculation is distinguished by Oliveira [13] from a *functional* style, where all corresponding methods aggregate and return results. Based on this categorization MontiCore's visitor infrastructure is external and imperative.

Various approaches that solve the underlying expression problem rely on mechanisms not available to popular object-oriented languages: Advanced type systems can solve the expression problem [15] and enable to implement visitors as type-safe reusable components. Other approaches employ mixins [5] or open classes [3] to overcome the expression problem. However, utilizing such features requires to forsake existing language workbench infrastructure and enforces engineers to learn less supported languages.

To circumvent the cyclic dependency between the visitor interface and the data structure the Acyclic Visitor pattern [11] splits all visit methods into their own data-specific visitor interface. Thereby, the different visitor interfaces are semantically bound to a specific data type, but they require type-introspection to cast the generic visitor interface to the specific one. Consequently, this approach is similar to the one in MontiCore, with the difference that MontiCore semantically binds visitor interfaces to a language instead of their concrete nodes.

Another recent solution to the underlying expression problem, that is applicable in common object oriented languages, is given by Object Algebra (OA) [14]. It, however, gives up representation of a language's AST as types. Instead, using constructor overloading the AST for a given model is only implicitly constructed during a concrete calculation on it. It thereby introduces a different approach to language engineering which requires language engineers to change their understanding of DSL implementation in general. Currently, there is limited experience [7,17,21] about OA's main advantages and limitations and hence it is not yet clear whether such investment pays off for language engineers.

Other LWBs, such as Xtext [1], build on the Eclipse Metamodeling Framework (EMF) using Ecore models to describe the AST [12,19]. EMF trees are traversed using tree iterators[5] that require clients to implement the method

---

[5] http://download.eclipse.org/modeling/tmf/xtext/javadoc/2.9/org/eclipse/xtext/nodemodel/BidiTreeIterator.html.

`getChildren(Object)`, which defines an iterator over all children of the object. The parameter is of the most generic type `Object` and returning one iterator for all children requires to cast them to a common super type as well. Thus, using this infrastructure depends on type-introspection in client-code to differentiate between specific AST node types. Commonly, Xtext-based DSLs use Xtend [1] for implementing code generators. Xtend is a Java dialect that compiles into Java code and claims to enable multi-dispatching. However, the multi-dispatching is implemented using type-introspection in switch statements[6].

7 Conclusion

We demonstrated a concept to derive visitor infrastructures from context-free grammars to support language engineers to work with ASTs for model analysis, transformations, and code generation. It separates AST traversal from operations that hook into the traversal. In order to define new operations on ASTs, it provides language engineers with generated statically type-safe visitor interfaces that foster reuse during language composition and allow for traversal adaptation if required. With the infrastructure being interface-driven, developers may flexibly integrate other software components with concrete visitor implementations. To this effect, we described how a sophisticated combination and extension of software patterns support compositional language engineering and presented a realization in the language workbench MontiCore.

References

1. Bettini, L.: Implementing Domain-Specific Languages with Xtext and Xtend. Packt Publishing, Birmingham (2013)
2. Carlisle, M.C., Sward, R.E.: An Automatic "Visitor" Generator for Ada. Ada Letters (2002)
3. Clifton, C., Leavens, G.T., Chambers, C., Millstein, T.: MultiJava: modular open classes and symmetric multiple dispatch for Java. In: Proceedings of the 15th ACM SIGPLAN Conference on Object-oriented Programming, Systems, Languages, and Applications (2000)
4. Erdweg, S., et al.: The state of the art in language workbenches. In: Erwig, M., Paige, R.F., Van Wyk, E. (eds.) SLE 2013. LNCS, vol. 8225, pp. 197–217. Springer, Heidelberg (2013)
5. Flatt, M., Krishnamurthi, S., Felleisen, M.: Classes and Mixins. In: Proceedings of the 25th ACM SIGPLAN-SIGACT Symposium on Principles of Programming Languages (1998)
6. Gamma, E., Helm, R., Johnson, R., Vlissides, J.: Design patterns: Elements of Reusable Object-oriented Software. Addison-Wesley Professional, Boston (1995)
7. Gouseti, M., Peters, C., van der Storm, T.: Extensible Language Implementation with Object Algebras (Short Paper). SIGPLAN Not. (2014)

---

[6] https://eclipse.org/xtend/documentation/202_xtend_classes_members.html.

8. Haber, A., Look, M., Mir Seyed Nazari, P., Navarro Perez, A., Rumpe, B., Völkel, S., Wortmann, A.: Composition of heterogeneous modeling languages. In: Desfray, P., Filipe, J., Hammoudi, S., Pires, L.F. (eds.) MODELSWARD 2015. CCIS, vol. 580, pp. 45–66. Springer, Heidelberg (2015)
9. Hölldobler, K., Nazari, P.M.S., Rumpe, B.: Adaptable symbol table management by meta modeling and generation of symbol table infrastructures. In: Proceedings of the Workshop on Domain-Specific Modeling (2015)
10. Krahn, H., Rumpe, B., Völkel, S.: MontiCore: a framework for compositional development of domain specific languages. Int. J. Softw. Tools Technol. Transf. (STTT) **12**(5), 353–372 (2010)
11. Martin, R.C., Riehle, D., Buschmann, F. (eds.): Pattern Languages of Program Design 3. Addison-Wesley Longman Publishing Co., Inc., Boston (1997)
12. Merkle, B.: Textual modeling tools: overview and comparison of language workbenches. In: Proceedings of the ACM International Conference Companion on Object Oriented Programming Systems Languages and Applications Companion (2010)
13. Oliveira, B.C.S.: Genericity, Extensibility and Type-Safety in the Visitor Pattern. Oxford University, Oxford (2007)
14. Oliveira, B.C.D.S., Cook, W.R.: Extensibility for the masses: practical extensibility with object algebras. In: Proceedings of the 26th European Conference on Object-Oriented Programming (2012)
15. Oliveira, B.C.D.S., Wang, M., Gibbons, J.: The visitor pattern as a reusable, generic, type-safe component. In: SIGPLAN Notices (2008)
16. Palsberg, J., Jay, C.B.: The essence of the visitor pattern. In: Proceedings of the 22Nd International Computer Software and Applications Conference (1998)
17. Rendel, T., Brachthäuser, J.I., Ostermann, K.: From object algebras to attribute grammars. In: SIGPLAN Notices (2014)
18. Visser, J.: Visitor combination and traversal control. In: SIGPLAN Notices (2001)
19. Vlter, M., Benz, S., Dietrich, C., Engelmann, B., Helander, M., Kats, L.C.L., Visser, E., Wachsmuth, G.: DSL Engineering - Designing, Implementing and Using Domain-Specific Languages (2013). dslbook.org
20. Torgersen, M.: The expression problem revisited. In: Odersky, M. (ed.) ECOOP 2004. LNCS, vol. 3086, pp. 123–146. Springer, Heidelberg (2004)
21. Zhang, H., Chu, Z., Oliveira, B.C.D.S., Storm, T.V.D.: Scrap Your boilerplate with object algebras. In: SIGPLAN Notices (2015)

Demystifying Ontological Classification
in Language Engineering

Colin Atkinson[1] and Thomas Kühne[2]([⊠])

[1] University of Mannheim, B6, C2.11, Mannheim, Germany
atkinson@informatik.uni-mannheim.de
[2] Victoria University of Wellington, P.O. Box 600, Wellington 6140, New Zealand
Thomas.Kuehne@ecs.victoria.ac.nz

Abstract. The introduction of ontological classification to support domain-metamodeling has been pivotal in the emergence of multi-level modeling as a dynamic research area. However, existing expositions of ontological classification have only used a limited context to distinguish it from the historically more commonly used linguistic classification. In important areas such as domain-specific languages and classic language engineering the distinction can appear to become blurred and the role of ontological classification is obscured, if not fundamentally challenged. In this paper we therefore examine critical points of confusion regarding the distinction and provide an expanded explanation of the differences. We maintain that optimally utilizing ontological classification, even for tasks that traditionally have only been viewed as language engineering, is critical for mastering the challenges in complex systems modeling including the validation of multi-language models.

Keywords: Ontological classification · Linguistic classification · Semantic classification · Language engineering · Metamodeling · Multi-paradigm modeling

1 Introduction

Ontological classification was originally suggested in conjunction with linguistic classification as part of a dual classification scheme to address inconsistencies in the original four-layer architecture associated with the UML [8]. Without an improved understanding of the precise nature of the four layers and the relationships between them, it was not possible to reconcile the intended linear organization of the layers [28] with the overall architecture's claims to strictness [3]. Recognizing two different classification principles and combining them in a dual classification architecture turned out to be the key to allow strictness to be enforceable in two orthogonal dimensions [7].

Being explicit about the ontological and linguistic classification dichotomy also proved to be useful for achieving a better understanding of tool infrastructure choices [9], and most importantly, provided a foundation for deep modeling, i.e., the idea of explicitly using multiple ontological classification levels for

© Springer International Publishing Switzerland 2016
A. Wąsowski and H. Lönn (Eds.): ECMFA 2016, LNCS 9764, pp. 83–100, 2016.
DOI: 10.1007/978-3-319-42061-5_6

domain modeling. This approach helped shift the focus from metamodeling as a tool building technique to a user-centered, ontological modeling paradigm [8]. Often found in combination with various forms of deep characterization [6], dual classification has therefore become the foundation for a number of research tools [4,14,21,22,32], and a growing research community [1].

In this regard, dual classification (i.e., the distinction between ontological and linguistic classification and their combined usage), has been a success. However, while the distinction between the two classification flavors is straightforward in certain architectures and application contexts [7], recognizing the two flavors and fully utilizing their strengths can be challenging in less clear-cut contexts. For instance, at first sight there does not appear to be a difference between a linguistically defined domain-specific language and an ontological multi-level model for the same domain. Some tools hence allow, if not promote, the use of ontological classification levels for doing what would widely be regarded as language engineering [5,23] even though such practice seems at odds with the ontological versus linguistic dichotomy. Such apparent interchangeability of linguistic and ontological classification makes it very difficult to judge which form of classification is, or should be, used for particular purposes, and ultimately challenges the foundations of the distinction.

In this paper we first briefly summarize the existing main expositions of ontological and linguistic classification (Sect. 2) and then elaborate the previously alluded to points of confusion (Sect. 3). Subsequently we present an expanded explanation of the distinction (Sect. 4) to then show how it can resolve all points of confusion (Sect. 5). We conclude by arguing that a proper use of both ontological and linguistic classification will be pivotal in addressing modern modeling challenges (Sect. 6).

2   Background

Figure 1 illustrates a classic, clear-cut application of dual classification in the OCA [7]. A linguistic type model comprising the linguistic types (in the right-hand side level labeled "Linguistic Types") plays the role of a traditional language definition which controls the form of entities and their relationships in user models (in the middle-column "Model ..." levels). In contrast, the ontological types in the user type model level (middle-top "Model Types" level) represent domain classifiers, such as the Platonic idea of "Track Piece" (light bulb in the "Universe of Discourse" (UoD)). Classification relationships (labeled "ontological") between elements in adjacent user model levels represent respective classification relationships in the UoD.

Existing descriptions of the dual classification approach referred to the linguistic types as controlling "form" and the ontological types as controlling "content" [9]. Furthermore, linguistic types (such as Object) directly classify elements of language usage (such as main47), whereas ontological types (such as Track-Piece) only classify elements of language usage (such as main47) via proxy with respect to the UoD, meaning that ontological classification relationships are

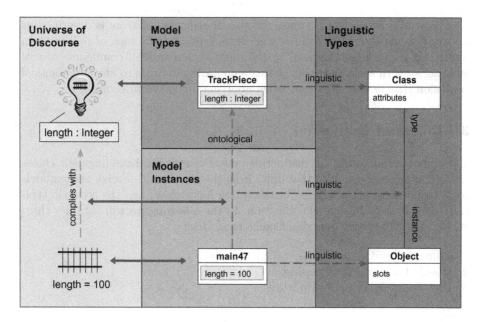

Fig. 1. Classic dual classification example

always motivated by respective classification in the UoD [20]. Linguistic types have therefore been characterized as giving rise to a notation/language whereas ontological types have been understood as reflecting classifiers in the domain (which may or may not exist and which may or may not have types themselves, depending on the domain).

We may observe that linguistic classification, as described above, has a long tradition in computer science. A classic language grammar can be regarded as linguistically classifying the allowed sentences of a language [19] and most so-called "metamodels" [28] are linguistic type models of the models they support the generation of [20]. Figure 1 is not an attempt to accurately reflect part of the UML "metamodel" but intentionally uses a simplified approach to illustrate that Track-Piece and main47 can be regarded as modeling elements created from linguistic types Class and Object respectively. Such language definitions may incorporate well-formedness constraints that go beyond simple syntactic construction rules (static semantics [16]), but typically defer the definition of the semantics of a language (dynamic semantics [16]) to a separate transformation (Kermeta being one of the notable exceptions [27]).

We may further observe that ontological classification is intended to accurately capture the relationship between the meanings of a user-created type (here a UML class TrackPiece) and a user-created instance (here a UML object main47). The user-created type does not linguistically classify the user-created instance – i.e., it does not give the latter the ability to have a name, slots, and links – but rather just constrains the compliance of the content of the main47 object to the content of the TrackPiece class.

When the distinction between the two classification flavors is described as above it seems that they form a true dichotomy and the task of telling them apart is a trivial one. However, in the next section we will enumerate several situations which seem to challenge this assumption in order to identify points of confusion that may easily occur when applying dual classification.

3   Points of Confusion

The apparent blurring of the distinction between ontological and linguistic classification appears in scenarios that differ from the use of multi-level domain models to describe naturally occurring classification hierarchies, i.e., the scenario typically used to explain dual classification. In the following we will consider three such scenarios of particular significance to modelers:

1. Domain-Specific Languages.
2. Classic Language Engineering.
3. Dichotomy-Ambivalent Modeling.

3.1   Domain-Specific Languages

In Fig. 2 we use the standard OCA coloring of levels to illustrate a case when TrackPiece is used as a linguistic type. Such a scenario occurs when a language engineer uses a metacase tool like AtoMPM [30] or just a classic textual grammar approach [19] to define a domain-specific language which aims at specifically representing elements of interest to the language user, in this example a language for train control. We are not excluding the possibility that the language engineer may also associate a domain concept "Track Piece" with the type TrackPiece they are including in their language definition, but the tool choice and the modeler's primary intent – to create signs/tokens such as main47 that are devoid of meaning unless a semantics is associated with them via a transformation – technically makes TrackPiece a linguistic type (cf. Sect. 2).

However, this interpretation of TrackPiece creates a tension with the prior understanding of TrackPiece as being an ontological type (cf. Fig. 1). The TrackPiece types in Figs. 1 and 2 are indistinguishable from each other, including the choice of attributes. Apparently the choice of a domain-specific language, rather than a general-purpose language that contains more generic types such as Object, made

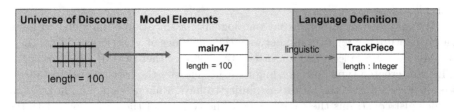

Fig. 2. A domain-specific modeling language fragment for train control

the previously distinct difference between ontological and linguistic classification dissolve.

This raises the question as to whether ontological classification is just a way of introducing domain-specificity into general purpose languages and, hence, whether it is then worth maintaining a dual classification scheme. At the very least the examples shown in Figs. 1 and 2 illustrate that a modeler may find it hard to ascertain whether TrackPiece should be regarded as an ontological or a linguistic type.

3.2   Classic Language Engineering

Figure 3 depicts the case of using ontological levels (i.e., "Model Types" and "Model Instances") to perform classic language engineering, i.e., to define a language (here, in level "Model Types") to be used for some purpose (here in level "Model Instances", to represent a track piece). Note that in this scenario the purpose of Object is not to represent a domain concept but merely to create tokens such as main47 so that the latter can subsequently be used for purposes like analysis, simulation, and code generation. Therefore we did not associate

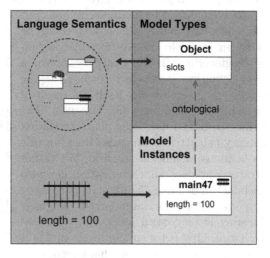

Fig. 3. Defining notation within ontological levels

the usual light bulb with Object but just an extension of all notational elements classified by Object. This, however, can be regarded as shortcut for a light bulb concept in the semantic domain of "language semantics" that has the set shown in Fig. 3 as its extension. This approach is consistent with the traditional association of a so-called "extensional semantics" for types like Object.

Tools like Melanee and MetaDepth have been shown to be usable for language engineering purposes [5,23], so it seems that Fig. 3 visualises the corresponding scenario of using ontological classification for what appears to be linguistic control.

Note that element main47 is presented using a user-friendly concrete syntax. Instead of showing the underlying representation – a slot list containing an entry that has a length name and a 100 value – main47 is presented in a manner that focuses on the content rather than the representation. Such presentation choices can go as far as rendering main47 as an icon that looks like a track piece [5]. The availability of presentation alternatives contributes to blurring the distinction between ontological classification and linguistic classification because it makes it appear that the former can now be perfectly used in place of the latter in order to perform language engineering.

However, if the use of ontological classification is not in conflict with such examples then how is it possible to determine whether a type like Object truly is a linguistic classifier or an ontological classifier?

3.3   Dichotomy-Ambivalent Modeling

The scenario shown in Fig. 4 is meant to show a multi-level model whose interpretation is ambiguous. On the one hand, the model could be read as a domain-model representing agent activities, concepts that govern those activities, and meta-concepts that govern the latter. In this case, the classification relationships between levels should be characterized as "ontological" (cf. Sect. 2).

On the other hand, the model could be read as an example of two-tier, classic language engineering. In the example shown, a process definition language is defined at the "Model Types" level and is itself the result of using a process metamodeling language. The fact that the model uses deep characterization (a potency-two attribute duration) does not rule out a language definition scenario, but rather illustrates how deep characterization can also be useful when defining (families of) languages. In any event, as the intention in language engineering is to control form, the classification relationships between the levels in Fig. 4 therefore appear to be best characterized as "linguistic".

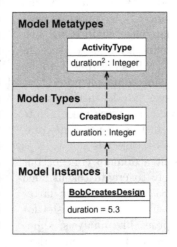

Fig. 4. Dichotomy-Ambivalence

Both of the aforementioned interpretations of Fig. 4 appear to be equally valid depending on perspective and purpose. This implies that even if one interpretation was intended at the time of creation of the model, re-purposing it for the opposing interpretation seems to be seamlessly supported. Hence, it could be argued that tools like Melanee or MetaDepth that are regularly used for defining languages as well as for domain modeling [5, 23] could be regarded as not only supporting a dual purpose but, beyond that, enabling modelers to be ambivalent about their actual purpose, thus freeing the modeler from difficult deliberations. Arguably,

- the same classification compliance rules can be used for both classification flavors,
- user interactions with classifiers are the same regardless of their flavor, and
- types like ActivityType apparently can be equally given an ontological as well as a linguistic reading.

Therefore, the questions arise as to

1. how one can claim that the classification flavors form a dichotomy, and
2. why one should burden users of multi-level tools with difficult deliberations about which classification principle they intend, if ambivalence even seems preferable?

That said, there is of course still a fundamental question of whether the use of ontological levels for defining languages is in accordance with the principles of dual classification (cf. Sect. 2) and, if not, whether that suggests that the principles of dual classification are a hindrance to optimal modeling pragmatics.

Summarizing, all three scenarios presented in this section strongly suggest that ontological and linguistic classification do not appear to form a long-implied "black and white" dichotomy. If types like TrackPiece and Object can interchangeably appear in both ontological and linguistic type levels and it seems best to not assign a flavor to types like "Process Type" then on what basis can anyone decide which classification flavor a type should have?

In order to answer this question in the next section, we describe the basis for the dual classification principle at a deeper level.

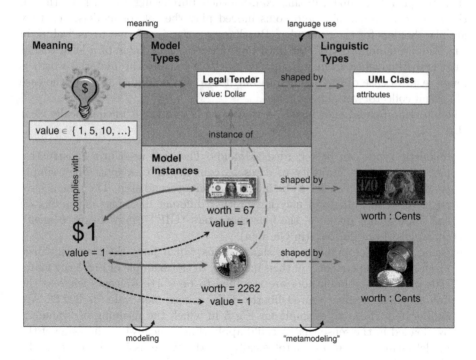

Fig. 5. Dual classification

4   Illuminating Dual Classification

Figure 5 attempts to shed more light on the distinction between linguistic and ontological classification by

- using an example that better highlights the fundamental differences, and
- illustrating a differentiating aspect that publications on the OCA have hitherto neglected.

We deliberately presented the model in Fig. 5 in a manner that allows two readings:

1. a real world scenario in which the four modeling elements dollar bill, coin, banknote mold, and coin mold can be regarded as real-world items.
2. a multi-language model that uses a domain-specific presentation for some of its modeling elements.

The idea behind the first "real world" reading of Fig. 5 is to view items of legal tender, such as a dollar bill or a dollar coin, as being formed by bill printing and coin minting molds respectively. The formed tokens (bills and coins) are then assigned "meaning", in this example their purchasing power. Note that in the real world dollar bills and coins indeed play the role of models, i.e., they are placeholders for their meaning. Purchasing power is referred to as "value" in Fig. 5 and amounts to "$1" for both bill and coin. This *value* of a legal tender item is distinguished from its *material worth*. Typically the material worth is lower (e.g., in case of the dollar bill) but it can also be higher (e.g., in the case of special collector variants of coins).

The intention behind allowing the first reading is to make it unequivocally clear that

- linguistic types can be regarded as molds. They are used in a constructive mode in the vast majority of cases to coin model elements. They simply produce tokens which are to be interpreted in a second step. The tokens have no intrinsic meaning and may have rather different meanings depending on the context. For instance, the four characters "GIFT" may mean "present" (in English) or "poison" (in German).
- generated model elements are signs/tokens which have their own intrinsic properties, independently of their meaning. In the example of Fig. 5 the materials used for the bank note are assumed to be worth 67 cents whereas the dollar coin is a silver seated liberty dollar whose melt value is $22.62. We deliberately chose an example for Fig. 5 in which the meaning of "value" is overloaded in the sense that it could apply (linguistically) to the value of the model element itself, or (ontologically) to the value assigned to the model element via an interpretation. This resolvable overloading illustrates that one must be careful to identify the subject, i.e., either the model element itself or its meaning, when attributing properties.

– generated model elements may have various meanings. In descriptive models they represent elements in the UoD but they can also have a prescriptive role, e.g., prescribing a system to be built, or simply be assigned some semantics, i.e., execution semantics. Sometimes such additional semantics are referred to as interpretations [29]. In the example in Fig. 5, the ontological interpretation of the items of legal tender is an abstract "$1" concept that only exists due to the notion of legal tender, i.e., nowadays "fiat money".

– the semantic domain of a model can reasonably be thought of containing (Platonic) ideas [7]. In the example we again use a light bulb to denote the logical idea which specifies the requirements on legal tender. Such ideas are represented by model elements at the "Model Types" level. Note that they do not specify properties of model elements, i.e., in the example LegalTender neither characterizes the dollar bill nor the dollar coin. In particular, LegalTender is not a generalization of all model element types that characterize legal tender tokens. Rather LegalTender characterizes the abstract money concept of "$1" and, of course, other amounts.

The above elaborations help to re-iterate the fact that ontological types do not directly characterize model instances. Ontological types rather represent ideas which in turn characterize instances, with the latter being represented by model instances. Linguistic types, on the other hand, directly describe properties of the tokens they produce. For example in "Love is a four-letter word" the predicate "four-letter word" applies to the word "love" itself, i.e., is a linguistic characterization. From an ontological viewpoint, the classification of "love" should be "Love is an emotion", i.e., refer to the meaning of the word "love".

With the above in mind, we may now observe that Fig. 5 illustrates an aspect of ontological classification that has so far not been mentioned in previous publications on the OCA:

– Ontological classification does not require literal conformance, i.e., in contrast to linguistic types, ontological types do not have to stipulate syntactic compliance.

In the example of Fig. 5, the seated liberty dollar absolutely must have certain physical properties, otherwise it could not be considered to be a linguistic instance of the minting mold that coined it. As the minting mold imprints all its features on all coins, they are all guaranteed to have the respective features. In the example we are assuming that the same materials will always be used in production hence every coin will feature the same material worth.

In contrast, the ontological type LegalTender specifies a requirement – i.e., for all instances to have a certain purchasing power – that is not directly expressed in its instances. None of the LegalTender instances directly carry a value feature. Whether or not they have a value is determined by looking up what they represent in the semantic domain. Only through referencing the meaning of model instances do we obtain the knowledge that both dollar bill and coin are instances of LegalTender with the value "$1" (hence the arrows from "$1" to the "value = 1"-properties in Fig. 5).

The fact that legal tender items have their intended value printed on them should not be mistaken with an expression of "meaning" as a physical property. For instance, if dollar bills were taken out of circulation then they would still claim a nominal face value of "$1" but their meaning would be "$0".

In the light of the above, we can therefore confirm that ontological instantiation can be regarded as semantically-founded and does not require literal compliance between model instances and their model types. We may thus alternatively refer to ontological classification as "semantic classification", whereas linguistic classification may be referred to as "syntactic classification". A linguistic type should be thought of syntactically classifying tokens (which may be given meaning in a subsequent step) whereas an ontological type should be thought of as semantically classifying tokens by representing a domain concept which in turn has domain instances which are represented by said tokens.

In practice, it makes sense for most ontological (semantic) classification relationships to rely on syntactic conformance as well, i.e., be no more flexible than linguistic classification. A syntactic conformance check is trivial to implement while a true semantic check would require an explicit representation of a semantic domain, the definition of a corresponding mapping, and the definition of a semantic check within the semantic domain. This significant difference in complexity explains why simple syntactic checking is almost universally accepted as a shortcut for semantic checking. Arguably, however, some languages like Eiffel [25] and JML [24], attempt to approximate a semantic check for objects by allowing the specification of pre- and post-conditions, albeit only in terms of a testing semantics. This latter limitation of ambition highlights another problem with a full semantic check: in general, its computation may be intractable or even undecidable.

5   Points of Confusion Clarified

Equipped with the above clarifications, we are now in a position to revisit the points of confusion around the dual classification principle identified in Sect. 3.

5.1   Ontological Types Used for Linguistic Classification

The first challenge we elaborated upon in Sect. 3 stemmed from the fact that any domain model involving types and instances can be regarded as a (domain-specific) language definition (model types) with its corresponding language use (model instances).

However, with the function of linguistic classifiers confirmed as merely producing tokens that do not carry any inherent meaning within themselves, it becomes clear that even though types in a domain-specific language definition could have the appearance of ontological types, they do not in any way fulfill the same function.

The linguistic TrackPiece type with its attribute "length : Integer" in Fig. 2 only creates a token (placeholder) that is able to capture a value for the key "length". The ontological type TrackPiece in Fig. 1, on the other hand, denotes the existence of the Platonic idea "Track Piece" as part of a railway system where the "length" of a piece has implications for the trains that run on it, giving rise to pieces that may or may not allow collisions of trains, etc. While the actual semantics associated with the ontological TrackPiece and its main47 instance may be rather simple or may even not have a representation at all, at least in terms of potential the ontological type TrackPiece signifies something entirely different to the linguistic type TrackPiece (cf. the "value" discussion in Sect. 4).

More specifically, while the two occurrences of TrackPiece in Figs. 1 and 2 look identical and interchangeable, this observation only holds with respect to their form outside a particular context. Just as a UML class diagram may be read as a type model (e.g., with its types classifying elements in the UoD) or as a token model (e.g., with its types being tokens which represent respective Java classes) [20], it is possible to read one and the same TrackPiece type as a linguistic type or as an ontological type.

This room for interpretation, however, must not be confused with arbitrariness or a fuzzy demarcation line. Just as with the type model versus token model analogy, it is not possible to ascertain the nature of a type's classification principle from the type alone. In the absence of any knowledge regarding the role the type is playing, it is not possible to make any statement about its function and/or nature. However, once the role is known, it is no longer possible to mistake one role with the other.

As a result, arguably the choice of name for the linguistic TrackPiece type is a poor one. After all, the type actually classifies model elements, i.e., tokens, as opposed to track pieces themselves. Strictly speaking, the appropriate name for the linguistic TrackPiece type should be "TrackPieceToken" (or similar).

Note that in contrast the name for the ontological type TrackPiece should not be "TrackPieceObject" (or similar). In the ontological dimension the intent is to actually classify the domain instances themselves. Model elements such as main47 (referred to as "instance specifications" in the UML) represent domain instances but whenever they are referenced, e.g., as instances of TrackPiece, one intends to refer to their meaning, i.e., the domain instances themselves. The importance of understanding the different functions of linguistic versus ontological types, and hence the significance of proper naming, can be illustrated by analyzing what the respective types fix and what they leave open. Figure 5 illustrates a scenario where two different tokens (coin and bill) have the same meaning, i.e., could be regarded as being synonyms. In this example, linguistic diversity is supported but semantic ambiguity is ruled out.

However, there are also homonyms, i.e., signs that are indistinguishable from each other but have different meanings. For example the sentence "*I seem to be having tremendous difficulty with my lifestyle*" has only one linguistic type (e.g., "Sentence") but depending on its ontological type (e.g., "Casually_Muttered_Phrase" versus "Dreadful_Insult_In_The_Vl'Hurg_Tongue"), it could either represent a personal self-reflection or an insult that leads to the decimation of an entire galaxy [2]. It therefore becomes obvious that knowing main47's linguistic type amounts to entirely different knowledge compared to knowing its ontological type, even though the two can seem indistinguishable on the surface.

Despite their arguably somewhat misleading naming choices (i.e. using "TrackPiece" rather than "TrackPieceToken"), classic language engineers are obviously aware that their types only define a notation, rather than capture semantic properties. After all, they use the term "metamodel" whenever they use a linguistic type model to define the syntax of a language. In contrast, a regular UML modeler would not refer to a UML class diagram which only contains simple types that represent domain concepts as a "metamodel", even though the class diagram could be regarded as a model of other models, i.e., object diagrams.

As mentioned before, we are not excluding the possibility that a language engineer may also associate a domain concept "Track Piece" with their linguistic type, thus giving more credence to their naming choice. However, as the above analysis shows, it is important to keep the two different purposes apart. Unconsciously confounding them is akin to failing to acknowledge the difference between the properties of real world elements and the properties of model elements that model them [17].

5.2   Linguistic Types Used in Ontological Levels

In Sect. 3 we observed an apparent conflict due to the fact that it seemed possible to view a linguistic type like Object as an ontological type (cf. Fig. 3). Closer scrutiny reveals that two ingredients are necessary for this apparent conflict to arise:

1. the ability to choose "language engineering" as the semantic domain, and
2. the possibility to reinterpret a classification relationship.

Ontological classification between model elements mirrors logical instantiation in the domain, so when one chooses a domain in which language elements playing the role of instances are classified by language elements playing the role of types then the respective classification relationships give rise to respective ontological classification. In short, a notation and its definition can be given a structural semantics which in turn gives rise to semantic classification between the notation and its definition. This first ingredient therefore stems from the fact that any language definition combined with its corresponding language use can be regarded as a domain model with types (the language definition) and instances (the language use). In other words, a "linguistic meaning" is one of the many meanings ontological classification can embody.

Yet, this does not constitute any conflicts regarding the nature of a classifier. The ontological classifier Object in Fig. 3 has a linguistic purpose, i.e., to control the form (not the meaning) of main47. However, it achieves this purpose through ontological classification, i.e., by representing the Platonic concept of a token type (here Object).

There are two options for making this token type control instances (e.g., main47): First, the semantic domain of the token type is defined to be the ontological level where the target instances (e.g., main47) reside. This would amount to hosting actual linguistic types in ontological levels as the characteristic "compliance" relationship (cf. Fig. 5) would be missing. The second option is to choose the semantic domain of the token type to be in the same "Language Semantics" domain as the token type and defining the meaning of the target instances to be that of their counterparts in the semantic domain. A semantic check within the semantic domain validates whether there is syntactic compliance and if the latter is established then it confirms the ontological "instance of" relationship between main47 and its ontological type Object. This would support a pure ontological understanding of the form control exerted by the token type. This approach could readily be supported by any tool featuring ontological levels and the ability to map their contents into a semantic domain with an associated semantic checking function.

The fact that semantic (ontological) classification can be "downgraded" to effectively fall back to a syntactic (linguistic) check as in option 2 above, makes it impossible to judge the ultimate purpose of a type by just looking at it, even when its ontological role is known. However, any ambiguity is resolved when the context is provided. With the intended universe of discourse or semantic domain known, the type's purpose will be revealed to either classify the domain instances or the model elements.

It is worth pointing out that not every ontological type can play the role of a linguistic classifier for its model instances. While the ontological type Track-Piece in Fig. 1 could indeed play the role of a linguistic classifier for main47, the ontological type LegalTender could not play the role of a linguistic classifier for a coin, as the latter does not have a physical "value" property (only a "worth" and a mapping to a semantic domain that assigns it a value). This suggests a partial litmus test for ontological types: If the conformance between model instance and its type is not literal, i.e., not a plain syntactic conformance, then the type cannot be a linguistic type.

Since ontological classification entails an inherent ambiguity regarding the ultimate purpose (in the absence of any knowledge about the intended semantic domain), it would seem advisable to use some notation to signify the purpose of ontological types (i.e. domain modeling versus notation definition), similar to a clef in musical notation which clarifies the absolute pitch of the notes that follow it.

5.3   Postponing Role Assignments

The conclusions from section Sect. 4 and the previous analyses established that a dual interpretation of types is possible but that the respective meanings associated with the different roles are fundamentally different. Of course, this has implications for the idea of a perspective-based interpretation of types and/or the flexible re-purposing of types in approaches/tools that aim to allow users to be ambivalent about the type roles.

The premise that both ontological and linguistic classification can be supported by a tool assuming a single classification principle is correct in the sense that the types as such do not imply a commitment. Even if such a tool essentially only supports structural control over instances then it will obviously support language engineering, as well as domain modeling. However, there are disadvantages to such an approach:

Lack of Semantic Typing. True semantic checking which involves transformations into the semantic domain and a subsequent check within the semantic domain is not supported. That leaves modelers with the limited expressiveness and flexibility of syntactic typing, denying them the additional abstraction that semantic typing affords.

Only Simple Language Support. Ontological classification hierarchies are linear by nature. If language engineering is restricted to a linear hierarchy, however, it is difficult to cleanly support languages with a built-in notion of classification. Enabling a nesting of levels to accommodate language engineering would also be at odds with the premise that no commitment to a classification role is ever required since nesting would not make sense for an ontological interpretation.

Ambiguity Considered Harmful. Arguably, it makes sense for a modeler to be conscious about what classification flavor they have in mind. The choice of features and their names, for example, can depend on whether one intends a semantic or a syntactic commitment (cf. Sect. 4, regarding the overloading of "value" for coins). Also, in the case of a semantic commitment description logics could be used to capture semantic knowledge in the domain whereas in the case of a syntactic classification only, simple attributes are sufficient as a specification. Finally, if a modeler is not clear about the intended role, they may mix linguistic and ontological roles in a single model without realizing the inconsistencies. In one type an attribute may be labeled "nameString" (indicating a linguistic intent) whereas an associated type could use "name" (indicating an ontological intent).

The first issue from above could be addressed by choosing an ontological interpretation as the default and viewing applications of language engineering as ontological modeling with respective structural checks performed in the semantic domain. The second issue, however, points out a real limitation of tools supporting linear classification levels with respect to defining languages that feature a notion of instantiation. While it is possible to model such instantiation relationships, the tool would not be able to recognize and support their significance. The last point suggests that future work should clarify which kinds of ambivalence are welcomed as supporting re-purposing and which may be considered harmful as they mask fundamental differences.

6   Conclusion

Linguistic classification has an undisputed role in computer science as the basis for formalization and classic language engineering. While the recognition of ontological classification has helped to spawn a research field, its previous expositions have also created misunderstandings [10] and made it difficult to distinguish it from linguistic classification in certain scenarios (cf. Sect. 3).

In order to clarify the role of ontological classification, in this paper we identified critical differences between linguistic and ontological classification that have not been highlighted before. We observed that

- *"semantic classification"* could be an alternative name for ontological classification as it emphasizes the inherent reference to a UoD or a semantic domain.
- ontological classification does not require literal conformance as it captures semantic properties of subject instances, as opposed to creating carriers for semantics.
- the use of the name "linguistic classification" should not be construed to imply that all language definition must exclusively occur through linguistic classification.

Earlier publications on the ontological versus linguistic dichotomy only dealt with straightforward scenarios and hence did not highlight the above aspects. In this paper we furthermore made the key observation that in order to avoid confusion one must reject the assumption that a type is intrinsically either an ontological or a linguistic type. We clarified that one and the same type may play an ontological role in one context and a linguistic role in another context (cf. Sect. 4). We thus emphasized that a type's purpose in a particular context is important to understand its role and that the dichotomy therefore does not apply to types themselves, but to the roles they play.

Yet, even if an ontological role is confirmed, e.g. by applying respective litmus tests (cf. Sect. 5.2), the intended use of the type may not be entirely clear. In Sect. 5.2 we noticed that this stems from the fact that a semantic test can boil down to a structural conformance check and that the respective ontological classification can hence be indistinguishable from linguistic classification, in terms of its effect and in the absence of knowledge about the semantic domain.

Section 3.3 made the case that such ambiguity could be the basis for an approach that promotes dichotomy ambivalence as a feature. However, we also pointed out a list of limitations associated with linear hierarchies built on this principle (cf. Sect. 5.3). We believe future work should provide a comprehensive analysis of the trade-offs involved in using the "ambivalent classification" approach. On the one hand it appears to liberate modelers from potentially difficult deliberations, but on the other hand modeler obliviousness may cause inconsistencies and even inappropriate modeling (cf. Sect. 5.1). There is no immediate resolution to this issue since – as we mentioned in Sect. 3.1 – the definition of a notation need not always be in conflict with simultaneously capturing domain semantics. Hence, the options of banning ontological classification from only exerting form control, explicitly distinguishing within ontological hierarchies between domain semantics versus form control, or promoting ambivalence or even agnosticism should be evaluated in future work.

Undoubtedly, however, we expect ontological classification to play an integral role in the future of modeling when used with the expanded interpretation we have offered in this paper. First, by exploiting the liberation from syntactic conformance it is possible to accommodate more flexible classification relationships based on meaning rather than syntax. For example, immaterial differences, such as different naming choices like "diameter" versus "width", do not prevent instances from being recognized as belonging to the same category (e.g., "Shape"). Such emphasis on the meaning rather than the structure of data is the underpinning for the "Semantic Web" and its associated "Web Ontology Language".

Second, ontological classification provides a new means of injecting semantics into modeling. In contrast to Barroca et al. [11] who use ontological types to support the reuse of property definitions (e.g. "liveliness", "safety", etc.) that are otherwise often captured with additional property specification languages [26], we suggest that ontological types should also incorporate domain semantics for natural types such as "SpecialistWorker", etc. In other words while we support the use of ontological (property) types to represent so-called "appredicators", we believe ontological types will also prove to be very useful for representing so-called "(eigen-)predicators".

We thus advocate ontological types as a bridge [18] between the semantically-oriented world of ontology engineering [12] and the syntactically-oriented word of classic language engineering [19]. Enhancing traditional language definitions with semantic properties that advanced tools will be able to validate through checks ranging from simple conformance checking involving name mapping, through simulations, to model-checking and automated proofs, will make modeling more meaningful than it has been in the context of software engineering. The systems modeling community has a longer tradition of associating semantics to languages [26] but even for this community the use of user-defined semantics represented with ontological types is a novel concept.

We support the view taken by Vangheluwe et al. that tackling the challenges involved in modeling complex systems, such as cyber-physical systems [15], requires the use of multiple languages/formalisms and the incorporation of semantics [13,31]. Introducing semantic properties, validating them, and demanding their preservation in modeling transformations will be a crucial tool to master the complexity of modeling and generating contemporary systems.

In this paper we have not attempted to identify the optimal architecture for supporting multiple languages along with a semantic perspective on the UoD. However, we hope that our clarification of the distinction between ontological classification and linguistic classification will contribute towards identifying useful roles for ontological classification in the context of classic language engineering. It is in this light that we emphasize there are no grounds for the assumption that claiming a difference between ontological and linguistic classification creates more problems than it solves. On the contrary, we believe ontological classification should be given more consideration in classic language engineering than it has been given to date.

References

1. MULTI-LEVEL MODELING WIKI (2014). http://homepages.ecs.vuw.ac.nz/ Groups/MultiLevelModeling/
2. Adams, D.: The Hitchhiker's Guide to the Galaxy. Del Rey, September 1995
3. Atkinson, C.: Meta-modeling for distributed object environments. In: Enterprise Distributed Object Computing, pp. 90–101. IEEE Computer Society, October 1997
4. Atkinson, C., Gerbig, R.: Melanie: multi-level modeling and ontology engineering environment. In: Proceedings of Modeling Wizards 2012. ACM (2012)
5. Atkinson, C., Gerbig, R., Kennel, B.: Symbiotic general-purpose and domain-specific languages. In: Proceedings of the 34th International Conference on Software Engineering, ICSE 2012, pp. 1269–1272. IEEE Press, Zurich, Switzerland (2012)
6. Atkinson, C., Kühne, T.: The essence of multilevel metamodeling. In: Gogolla, M., Kobryn, C. (eds.) UML 2001. LNCS, vol. 2185, pp. 19–33. Springer, Heidelberg (2001)
7. Atkinson, C., Kühne, T.: Model-driven development: a metamodeling foundation. IEEE Softw. 20(5), 36–41 (2003)
8. Atkinson, C., Kühne, T.: Rearchitecting the UML infrastructure. ACM Trans. Model. Comput. Simul. 12(4), 290–321 (2003)
9. Atkinson, C., Kühne, T.: Concepts for comparing modeling tool architectures. In: Briand, L.C., Williams, C. (eds.) MoDELS 2005. LNCS, vol. 3713, pp. 398–413. Springer, Heidelberg (2005)
10. Atkinson, C., Kühne, T.: In defence of deep modelling. Inf. Softw. Technol. 64, 36–51 (2015)
11. Barroca, B., Kühne, T., Vangheluwe, H.: Integrating language and ontology engineering. In: Proceedings of the 8th Workshop on Multi-Paradigm Modeling, vol. 1237, pp. 77–86. CEUR-Workshop Proceedings, September 2014
12. Carvalho, V.A., Almeida, J.P.A., Fonseca, C.M., Guizzardi, G.: Extending the foundations of ontology-based conceptual modeling with a multi-level theory. In: Johannesson, P., Lee, M.L., Liddle, S.W., Opdahl, A.L., López, O.P. (eds.) ER 2015. LNCS, vol. 9381, pp. 119–133. Springer, Heidelberg (2015)
13. Combemale, B., Deantoni, J., Baudry, B., France, R., Jézéquel, J.M., Gray, J.: Globalizing modeling languages. Computer 47, 68–71 (2014)
14. Demuth, A., Lopez-Herrejon, R.E., Egyed, A.: Cross-layer modeler: a tool for flexible multilevel modeling with consistency checking. In: 19th Symposium on the Foundations of Software Engineering (FSE), Szeged, Hungary, pp. 452–455 (2011)
15. Derler, P., Lee, E.A., Sangiovanni-Vincentelli, A.: Modeling cyber-physical systems. Proc. IEEE (special issue on CPS) 100(1), 13–28 (2012)
16. Harel, D., Rumpe, B.: Modeling languages: Syntax, semantics and all that stuff - part I: The basic stuff. Technical report MCS00-16, The Weizmann Institute of Science, Israel, September 2000
17. Jackson, M.: Some basic tenets of description. SoSyM 1(1), 5–9 (2002)
18. Kappel, G., Kapsammer, E., Kargl, H., Kramler, G., Reiter, T., Retschitzegger, W., Schwinger, W., Wimmer, M.: Lifting metamodels to ontologies: a step to the semantic integration of modeling languages. In: Wang, J., Whittle, J., Harel, D., Reggio, G. (eds.) MoDELS 2006. LNCS, vol. 4199, pp. 528–542. Springer, Heidelberg (2006)
19. Klint, P., Lämmel, R., Verhoef, C.: Toward an engineering discipline for grammarware. ACM Trans. Softw. Eng. Methodol. 14(3), 331–380 (2005)

20. Kühne, T.: Matters of (meta-) modeling. SoSyM **5**(4), 369–385 (2006)
21. Lamo, Y., Wang, X., Mantz, F., MacCaull, W., Rutle, A.: DPF workbench: a diagrammatic multi-layer domain specific (meta-)modelling environment. In: Lee, R. (ed.) Computer and Information Science 2012. SCI, vol. 429, pp. 37–52. Springer, Heidelberg (2012)
22. de Lara, J., Guerra, E.: Deep meta-modelling with METADEPTH. In: Vitek, J. (ed.) TOOLS 2010. LNCS, vol. 6141, pp. 1–20. Springer, Heidelberg (2010)
23. Lara, J., Guerra, E., Cuadrado, J.S.: Model-driven engineering with domain-specific meta-modelling languages. Softw. Syst. Model. **14**(1), 429–459 (2015)
24. Leavens, G.T., Baker, A.L.: Enhancing the pre- and postcondition technique for more expressive specifications. In: Wing, J.M., Woodcock, J., Davies, J. (eds.) FM 1999. LNCS, vol. 1709, pp. 1087–1106. Springer, Heidelberg (1999)
25. Meyer, B.: Object-Oriented Software Construction, 2nd edn. Prentice Hall, Upper Saddle River (1997)
26. Meyers, B., Wimmer, M., Vangheluwe, H., Denil, J.: Towards domain-specific property languages: the promobox approach. In: Proceedings of DSM 2013, pp. 39–44. ACM (2013)
27. Muller, P.-A., Fleurey, F., Jézéquel, J.-M.: Weaving executability into object-oriented meta-languages. In: Briand, L.C., Williams, C. (eds.) MoDELS 2005. LNCS, vol. 3713, pp. 264–278. Springer, Heidelberg (2005)
28. OMG: Unified Modeling Language Infrastructure Specification, Version 2.0 (2004)
29. Seidewitz, E.: What models mean. IEEE Softw. **20**(5), 26–32 (2003)
30. Syriani, E., Vangheluwe, H., Mannadiar, R., Hansen, C., Mierlo, S.V., Ergin, H.: AToMPM: a web-based modeling environment. In: Joint Proceedings of MODELS 2013 and ACM Student Research Competition, pp. 21–25 (2013)
31. Vangheluwe, H., de Lara, J., Mosterman, P.: An introduction to multi-paradigm modelling and simulation. In: Proceedings of the AIS 2002 Conference, Portugal, pp. 9–20 (2002)
32. Volz, B., Jablonski, S.: OMME - a flexible modeling environment. In: Proceedings of SPLASH Workshop on Flexible Modeling Tools (FlexiTools) (2010)

Example-Based Generation
of Graphical Modelling Environments

Jesús J. López-Fernández[(✉)], Antonio Garmendia,
Esther Guerra, and Juan de Lara

Universidad Autónoma de Madrid, Madrid, Spain
jesusj.lopez@uam.es

Abstract. Domain-Specific Languages (DSLs) present numerous benefits like powerful domain-specific primitives, an intuitive syntax for domain experts, and the possibility of advanced code generation for narrow domains. While a graphical syntax is sometimes desired for a DSL, constructing graphical modelling environments is a costly and highly technical task. This relegates domain experts to play a passive role in their development and hinders a wider adoption of graphical DSLs.

Targeting a simpler DSL construction process, we propose an example-based technique for the automatic generation of modelling environments for graphical DSLs. This way, starting from examples of the DSL likely provided by domain experts using drawing tools like yED, our system is able to synthesize a graphical modelling environment that mimics the syntax of the provided examples. This includes a meta-model for the abstract syntax of the DSL, and a graphical concrete syntax supporting spatial relationships like containment or attachment. The system is implemented as an Eclipse plugin, and we demonstrate its usage on a running example in the home networking domain.

Keywords: Domain-specific modelling languages · Graphical modelling environments · Example-based meta-modelling · Flexible modelling

1 Introduction

Model-Driven Engineering (MDE) is founded on the use of models to describe the systems to be built. Often, these models are defined using Domain-Specific Languages (DSLs) tailored to a particular field [7]. Hence, the need to create DSLs and their associated modelling environments is recurring in MDE projects.

The concrete syntax of a DSL may be graphical or textual, though in this paper we focus on graphical DSLs [10]. Many tools have emerged along the years to build environments for graphical DSLs [3,5,6,10,11,17]. However, building such environments still remains a technical, complex and time-consuming task. For example, building a graphical editor with Graphiti [5] requires manual programming based on a large Java API. In the case of GMF [6] and Sirius [17], it is necessary to describe the different aspects of the editor by building one or more models. These models may become very detailed, large and hard to build

© Springer International Publishing Switzerland 2016
A. Wąsowski and H. Lönn (Eds.): ECMFA 2016, LNCS 9764, pp. 101–117, 2016.
DOI: 10.1007/978-3-319-42061-5_7

and maintain for non-experts – especially for DSLs beyond toy examples – and frequently they must be constructed using unhandy tree-based editors.

Apart from the technical difficulties, a salient issue with most graphical language workbenches is the need to construct a meta-model upfront, and to describe the features of the concrete syntax and the modelling environment using a technical language or notation. This hinders the active participation of domain experts in the DSL construction process, who might find more familiar working with examples than with meta-models [1,12] and might lack the technical knowledge to define complex environment specifications. However, the active involvement of domain experts is crucial for the success of the DSL to be built [9].

To avoid these difficulties, we propose a novel technique for the automatic generation of graphical modelling environments starting from examples of the DSL. Hence, instead of building a meta-model first and describing its concrete syntax at the meta-model level, our proposal is to collect examples built by domain experts using drawing tools like Powerpoint, Dia or yED. Our framework processes the provided examples to induce a meta-model by using the techniques presented in [12], and it also extracts a description of the graphical concrete syntax that includes graphical forms for classes (*svg* files), edge styles, and spatial relations like containment or attachment. This information is used to synthesize a graphical modelling environment that mimics the graphical syntax used in the examples, but in addition, it enforces the well-formedness rules of the DSL and enables the creation of models (in contrast to drawings) that can be manipulated using MDE technology (e.g., transformations and code generators). As a result, a graphical DSL environment is generated with no need to code or create complex technical specifications. Our proposal is backed by a working prototype, available as an Eclipse plugin at http://miso.es/tools/metaBUP.html.

Paper Organization. Section 2 presents an overview of our approach and a running example. Section 3 introduces example-based meta-modelling. Section 4 shows our approach to extract concrete syntax information from graphical examples. Section 5 describes the synthesis of graphical modelling environments from the extracted information. Section 6 presents tool support. Finally, Sect. 7 discusses related research and Sect. 8 concludes the paper.

2   Overview and Running Example

Figure 1 outlines our process for the example-based generation of graphical modelling environments. It involves two roles: the *Domain Expert*, who provides graphical examples and ultimately validates the generated environment, and the *Modelling Expert*, who monitors the meta-model induction process from which the desired DSL environment is derived.

The core part of our process, gray-shaded in Fig. 1, is iterative. Here, the domain expert provides input examples made with tools like yED, portraying how models should look like (label 1). These examples may represent complete models, or they may focus on a particular aspect of interest and therefore be

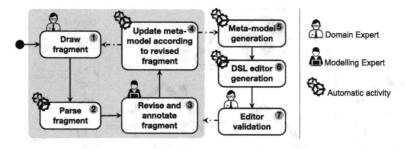

Fig. 1. Bottom-up graphical DSL development process.

partial, in which case we call them *fragments*. Then, the examples are automatically parsed into models, which are more amenable to manipulation (label 2). The parsed models are represented textually, making explicit the existing objects, attributes and relations in the examples, annotated with information regarding their graphical rendering (e.g., spatial relationships between objects or line styles). The modelling expert can edit this textual representation (label 3) to set more appropriate names to the derived relations, or to trigger refactorings in the meta-model induction process which takes place next (label 4). Thus, an iteration step finishes when the meta-model under construction is evolved to accept the revised fragment.

After processing all provided examples, the modelling expert can export the induced meta-model to a suitable format (Ecore in our current implementation, label 5), and invoke our editor generator to obtain a fully operating editor mimicking the concrete syntax of the examples (label 6). Moreover, the examples are migrated into models and can be edited and visualized in the generated editor. The domain expert can validate the editor (label 7), perhaps based on the converted examples, and if necessary, he can refine the DSL by providing further examples and re-generating the editor.

2.1 Running Example

As a running example, we develop a DSL in the home networking domain. In this DSL, we would like to represent the contracts that internet service providers (ISPs) hold with customers, the possible configurations of home networks, and their connection with the ISP infrastructure. Customer homes are connected via cable modems to the ISP network. Typically, each home has a (normally Wi-Fi-enabled) router to which the landline phone is connected, and with a number of Ethernet cable ports. Wi-Fi networks are password protected and work in a frequency range. Moreover, each home may have both cabled (e.g., PCs, printers or laptops) and wireless devices (e.g., smartphones, tablets or laptops).

Using our approach, domain experts provide example fragments that illustrate interesting network configurations and depict the desired graphical repre-

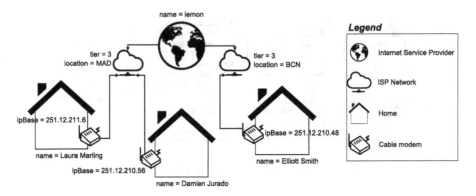

Fig. 2. Fragment showing a connection between customer homes and an ISP.

sentation for them. As an example, Fig. 2 shows one fragment built with yED[1], representing the connection between some customer homes and the ISP through cable modems. The elements in the drawing define some properties, like the ipBase of cable modems, the name of the home owner, the tier and location of the ISP network, and the name of the ISP. The legend to the right assigns a name to every picture used in the drawing.

3   Example-Based Meta-modelling

In [12], we introduced a bottom-up meta-modelling technique that enables the automatic induction of a meta-model starting from sketches[2], built using drawing tools. In order to facilitate the meta-model induction process, sketches are complemented by a legend that assigns a name to each different symbol in the drawing, as shown in Fig. 2. Such names are used as identifiers for the induced meta-model classes.

The meta-model induction process starts by parsing the provided fragment into a textual internal representation that is easier to manipulate by the modelling expert. The fragment, once revised by the modelling expert, is fed into our system. This may produce an update of the current version of the meta-model so that it "accepts" the provided fragment. For example, if a fragment contains objects of an unknown type, this type is incorporated into the meta-model. Similarly, if an object has new features not present in its type, then its meta-class is extended with these new features. Fragments have an *open-world* semantics: they only convey the relevant information for the scenario, and may omit additional information that will be given in further sketches. As explained in Sect. 2, examples are a special kind of fragments used to represent complete models, and they have a *closed-world* semantics.

---

[1] https://www.yworks.com/products/yed.

[2] We call these examples *sketches* to distinguish them from models conformant to a meta-model, though they are not hand-drawn but made with diagramming tools.

For instance, Listing 1 shows the textual model obtained from parsing the fragment in Fig. 2. Every object (e.g., h1 in line 2) receives a type as indicated in the legend (e.g., Home), and may contain slots (e.g., name in line 3) and links (e.g., modem in line 6) according to the original fragment.

```
1  fragment fragment1 {                          24    cm1 : CableModem {
2      h1 : Home {                                25        attr ipBase = "251.12.211.6"
3          attr name ="Elliott Smith"             26        ref isp = ispn1
4          @overlapping                           27    }
5          @composition                           28    cm2 : CableModem {
6          ref modem = cm3                         29       attr ipBase = "251.12.210.56"
7      }                                          30        ref isp = ispn1
8      isp1 : InternetServiceProvider {           31    }
9          attr name = "lemon"                    32    cm3 : CableModem {
10         ref infrastructure = ispn1, ispn2      33        attr ipBase = "251.12.210.48"
11     }                                          34        ref isp = ispn2
12     h2 : Home {                                35    }
13         attr name = "Damien Jurado"            36    ispn1 : ISPNetwork {
14         @overlapping                           37        attr tier = 3
15         @composition                           38        attr location = "MAD"
16         ref modem = cm2                         39   }
17     }                                          40    ispn2 : ISPNetwork {
18     h3 : Home {                                41        attr tier = 3
19         attr name = "Laura Marling"            42        attr location = "BCN"
20         @overlapping                           43    }
21         @composition                           44 }
22         ref modem = cm1
23     }
```

Listing 1. Textual representation of the fragment in Fig. 2

Figure 3 shows the meta-model induced from this fragment. As this is the first fragment, the meta-model was initially empty, and so four new classes are added, each containing the necessary attributes for the slots in the class' objects. We use simple heuristics to type primitive attributes, like setting the type to int when all slots within a fragment are compatible with that type (e.g., tier in the example). If a subsequent fragment invalidates such an assumption, then the type will

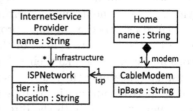

Fig. 3. Meta-model induced from the fragment in Listing 1.

be changed to String. References are assigned cardinality * as soon as an object points to two or more objects using edges with the same style (e.g., infrastructure). We also detect spatial relations between objects, like overlapping and containment, in which case compositions are created in the meta-model. In the example, the system detects overlapping between each CableModem object and a Home object.

Objects, slots and links in the textual fragment can be annotated manually by the modelling expert. Such annotations can provide design or domain information accounting for well-formedness constraints of the DSL (see [12]), or they can refer to concrete syntax details. In addition, some concrete syntax annotations are automatically produced by the fragment importer. In Listing 1, the importer added annotation @overlapping in lines 4, 14, and 20, to convey the fact that Home and CableModel objects overlap each other. We will detail the use of this kind of annotations in Sect. 4. In [12], we reported on another use of annotations, as a means to encode meta-model integrity constraints, like @composition in lines 5, 15, and 21. As we will see in Sect. 4, the @composition annotation was heuristically added due to the existence of overlapping.

The meta-model changes after each fragment is processed may trigger recommendations (refactorings). For example, if two classes have similarities (common attributes or references pointing to the same class) the system suggests applying the *extract superclass* refactoring, to factor out the common information [12].

Our technique is incremental, as new examples and fragments can be provided to make the meta-model evolve. Moreover, it fosters the active participation of domain experts in the meta-model construction process, as they can contribute with fragments (sketches) which are no longer passive documentation, but they are used to derive a meta-model. Up to now, our technique has been only able to derive the abstract syntax of the DSL [12]. In the following, we elaborate on the main contribution of this paper, which is the extension of our approach to derive a concrete syntax for the DSL (Sect. 4) and to synthesize a graphical modelling environment that emulates the syntax of the fragments (Sect. 5).

4   Example-Based Concrete Syntax Inference

We take advantage from the graphical information already encoded in sketches for both minimising the job of the modelling expert and deriving a concrete syntax close to the domain expert's conception.

Figure 4 shows the graphical properties that we extract from sketches and use to derive the concrete syntax of the DSL. Some are explicit features from the icons in the drawing, like their colour or size. Other properties are implicit relationships concerning the relative position of icons, like overlapping or adjacency, and are derived automatically by studying the size and location of each icon. For adjacency, we check both the direction (e.g., two objects adjacent left-to-right) and if in addition they are aligned and how (e.g., at the bottom).

Graphical properties are encoded as annotations of the corresponding objects and links in the textual fragment. Then, these annotations are transferred to the appropriate meta-model classes and references when the fragment is processed. Figure 4 shows the correspondence between the graphical properties and the elements they can annotate.

Next, we explain how we extract and manipulate this graphical information.

4.1   Detection of Icons and Line Styles

We retrieve each icon employed in the provided sketches, since this is the most relevant aspect of the appearance that the domain expert expects from the final DSL. Since the drawing tools we work with demand the definition and usage of palettes with all available icons, technically, we provide a directory where we store a copy of the files containing the icons as they are added to the palette.

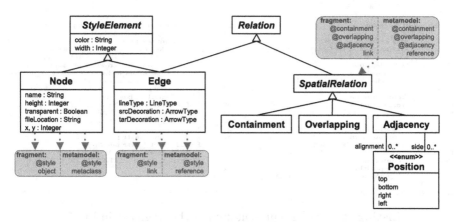

Fig. 4. Graphical properties inferable from sketches, and corresponding annotations.

These files are employed both in the serialization of fragments and in the generation of the concrete syntax, and are named according to the icon they contain. For instance, Fig. 5 shows to the right the *Legend* folder that contains the *svg* files used to represent each domain object in the fragment to its left.

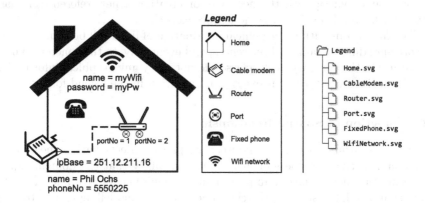

Fig. 5. Fragment with spatial features (left). Content of the *legend* folder (right).

Additionally, we detect and classify the style of edges in sketches. This feature can be deactivated if the edge style is irrelevant for the domain. If active, we identify and record the colour, line width, style (e.g., dotted) and source and target decorations of edges. As an example, Fig. 5 contains an edge linking a Router and a Cable modem. When the fragment is imported, the link is annotated with the identified style (lines 26–28 in Listing 2).

```
 1  fragment fragment2 {                        23        @adjacency(side = bottom)
 2      Home_1 : Home {                          24        ref ports = Port_1, Port_2
 3          attr phoneNo = 5550225               25        @composition
 4          attr name = "Phil Ochs"              26        @style ( color = "#000000", width = 3,
 5                                               27               line = dashed, source = none,
 6          @overlapping                         28               target = crows-foot-many )
 7          @composition                         29        ref '00000_3_dashed_none_crows_foot_many'
 8          ref modem = CableModem_1             30            modem = CableModem_1
 9                                               31        }
10          @containment                         32        FixedPhone_1 : FixedPhone { }
11          @composition                         33        WifiNetwork_1 : WifiNetwork {
12          ref electronicDevices = Router_1     34            attr name = "myWifi"
13                                               35            attr password = "myPw"
14          @containment                         36        }
15          @composition                         37        Port_1 : Port { attr portNo = 2 }
16          ref phones = FixedPhone_1            38        Port_2 : Port { attr portNo = 1 }
17                                               39        CableModem_1 : CableModem {
18          @containment                         40            attr ipBase = "251.12.211.16"
19          @composition                         41        }
20          ref wifiNetworks = WifiNetwork_1    42  }
21      }
22      Router_1 : Router {
```

Listing 2. Textual representation of the fragment in Fig. 5

Note that the name inferred for this link was not modem, but the one struck out (see lines 29–30 in Listing 2). Because we allow the modelling expert to edit the text fragments, he has replaced the inferred name with one closer to the domain. What is interesting about this operation is that, from this moment on, each time a link with the same style between a router and a cable modem is imported, it will be automatically named modem. If the modelling expert renames the feature in the future, he will be offered two options: either to replace the previous name modem with the new one, or creating a new reference in class Router which would coexist with the feature modem.

The annotations with the graphical information of links will be transferred to the corresponding meta-model references, and eventually, to the concrete syntax generator. On the contrary, meta-classes do not carry any graphical information with them, since we store their exact representation in the legend folder.

4.2 Detection of Spatial Relationships

Sometimes, spatial relationships between graphical objects have a meaning in the domain and need to be modelled. It is even likely that the domain expert is unaware of whether layout implies domain requirements. We automatically detect spatial relationships in sketches, and leave the modelling expert to keep or discard them by editing the textual fragments. We currently support three kinds of spatial relationships:

- *Containment*: a graphical object is within the bounds of another.
- *Adjacency*: two graphical objects are joined or very close. The maximum distance with which adjacency is to be considered is user-defined (*0* by default). Two optional properties are likewise detected: the side(s) from which objects are attached to each other, and alignment, a special type of adjacency.
- *Overlapping*: two graphical objects are superimposed (but not contained).

Detecting one of these relationships implies adding a reference to the meta-model. In the case of containment, the reference goes from the container to the containee. For adjacency and overlapping, we use this heuristic: if an object o overlaps (or is adjacent) to more than one object of the same kind, the reference stems from o's class; otherwise, the reference stems from the class of the bigger object. The rationale is that, frequently, the different parts of bigger objects are represented as smaller affixed elements (e.g., a component with affixed ports).

The fragment in Fig. 5 illustrates all supported spatial relationships, which are automatically detected when the fragment is imported (see Listing 2). On one hand, the Home contains a Router, a Fixed Phone and a Wifi Network in the sketch; hence, in the textual representation, the Home object has three links annotated as @containment (lines 12, 16 and 20). The Home overlaps with a Cable Modem in the sketch, being the Home icon bigger; hence, the Home object is added a link annotated as @overlapping (line 8). Finally, the Router has two adjacent Ports to the bottom side; since there are multiple ports, the Router is added a link annotated as @adjacency (line 24). The side parameter of this annotation could be removed in case the side of the adjacency is irrelevant to the domain.

In addition to creating explicit links for the detected spatial relationships, our importer heuristically adds @composition annotations to the created links (see lines 7, 11, 15, 19 and 25). This helps in organizing and realising only a *sufficient* set of spatial relationships. For example, both Ports are contained in the Home, but this relation is not made explicit because they are already adjacent to the Router, which is inside the Home. In this case, we use the @composition annotation of the abstract syntax to infer that they are indirectly contained in Home objects.

Figure 6 shows the resulting meta-model after processing this second fragment, including the annotations for style properties and spatial relationships. The new features with respect to Fig. 3 appear gray-shaded.

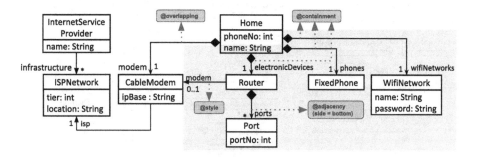

Fig. 6. Updated meta-model after processing the fragment of Listing 2.

5   Generation of Graphical Modelling Environments

Our approach to synthesize the graphical editor proceeds in two steps: we first convert the information gathered from the sketches into a technology-neutral graphical representation, and then, this representation is translated into a technology-specific editor specification. We currently target Sirius [17], but other technologies like EuGENia [11] could be easily targeted as well. Figure 7 outlines this process, where three transformations take place: one generates the meta-model with the abstract syntax of the DSL, another takes care of the concrete syntax and synthesizes the modelling environment, and the last one converts the provided sketches into models conformant to the induced meta-model. Next, we describe the main features of the *GraphicRepresentation* neutral meta-model and how it is used to produce a modelling environment for the DSL.

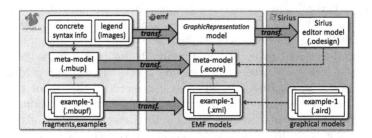

Fig. 7. Technical process: generating a (Sirius) graphical editor from examples.

Figure 8 shows the meta-model we have developed to represent graphical concrete syntaxes. It is an extended version of the one presented in [4], where we have added further features like layers, spatial relationships, reutilization through node inheritance, abstract nodes, and support for figures and edge styles.

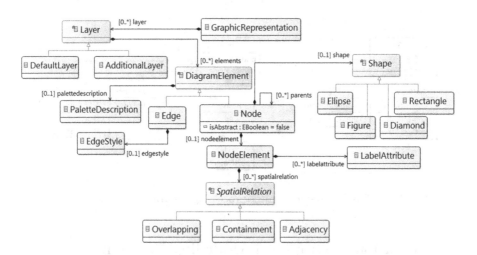

Fig. 8. Excerpt of the neutral *GraphicRepresentation* meta-model.

Thus, we convert the concrete syntax information induced from sketches into this intermediate meta-model to be independent from the target technology, but also, to be able to refine this information, e.g., by specifying palette information, organize elements in layers, or select labels for nodes. Graphical elements are organized into layers (abstract class Layer). A graphical representation has one DefaultLayer where all graphical elements belong by default, and zero or more AdditionalLayers. Layers contain graphical elements, which can be either Node-like or Edge-like. In both cases, they hold a PaletteDescription with information on how the element is to be shown in the palette. Nodes may be represented as geometrical shapes (Rectangle, Ellipse, etc.) or as image figures (class Figure). They can also display a label either inside or outside the node, being possible to configure its font style (class LabelAttribute). In addition, some nodes may need to be displayed in a relative position with respect to other nodes in the diagram, like being adjacent to (class Adjacency) or being contained in (class Containment) other nodes. Edges can specify a line style like solid, dash, dot or dash-dot (class EdgeStyle). Finally, we enable the reuse of graphical properties by means of relation parents and attribute isAbstract in class Node, so that graphical properties defined for a node are inherited by its children nodes.

The generation of the modelling environment requires establishing a correspondence between the abstract syntax meta-model of the DSL and the concrete syntax meta-model in Fig. 8. Node-like elements have a direct correspondence (e.g., meta-classes are mapped to a Node and a Shape). References are mapped into Edges, while their concrete syntax annotations are mapped into an EdgeStyle. Both Nodes and Edges keep a cross-reference to the corresponding class or reference in the abstract syntax meta-model (omitted in the figure). In addition, if the references are annotated with @containment, @adjacency or @overlapping, they get assigned a Containment, Adjacency or Overlapping object respectively. All created elements are included in the default layer and receive a PaletteDescription.

To generate the modelling environment, we first synthesize an ecore meta-model with the definition of the DSL abstract syntax, and then, we transform the obtained *GraphicRepresentation* model into a Sirius model (*.odesign) describing the graphical syntax and its correspondence to the ecore meta-model. This latter transformation is implemented using ATL.

6   Tool Support

The architecture of our solution encompasses the drawing tool yED, and two Eclipse plug-ins: *metaBup* [12] and *EMF Splitter* [4]. While *metaBup* supports the whole bottom-up abstract syntax construction process, we provide a specific *metaBup* exporter that wraps the resulting meta-model and passes it to *EMF Splitter*, which produces a fully operational graphical modelling environment from it. In the following, we explain how these two tools are integrated to support the presented approach, as well as the extensibility mechanisms of the tools.

6.1   Tool Support for the Generation Process

Domain experts can create sketches with yED as shown in Fig. 9. Once an initial set of examples is ready, the modelling expert creates a new *metaBup* project. This will initially contain a blank meta-model file with *mbup* extension, and empty *fragments* and *legend* folders. The yED sketches are imported one by one, and converted into text fragment models in the shell console of *metaBup*. Once parsed, the modelling expert can modify the fragments if needed. The revised fragments are fed to the meta-model induction process, which may trigger refac-

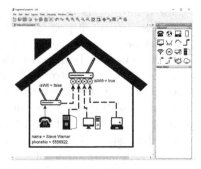

Fig. 9. Sketch drawn in yED.

torings on the meta-model. Figure 10 shows the tool once the sketch of Fig. 9 has been parsed, and the current meta-model (accessible on the second tab of the editor). Technically, we need to copy the images used in the yED palette (right side of Fig. 9) into our *legend* folder.

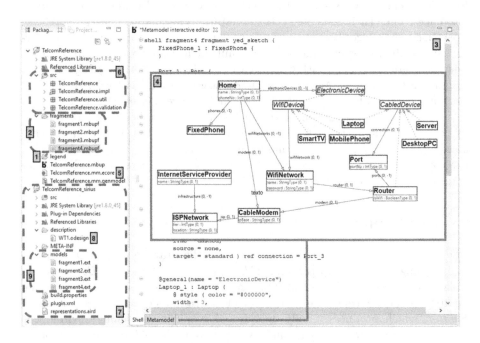

Fig. 10. *metaBup* tool: (1) Legend folder, (2) Fragments folder, (3) Parsed sketch in textual format, (4) Current version of meta-model, (5) Generated Ecore meta-model, (6) Java code generated from Ecore meta-model, (7) Generated Sirius project, (8) Sirius editor model, (9) Models transformed from the initial sketches.

After each iteration (i.e., addition of a fragment), a text version of the drawing is stored in the *fragments* folder of the project. These fragments are validated upon each meta-model change, so that they will be error-flagged if they become inconsistent after a meta-model modification.

After processing all sketches, the modelling expert can produce the Sirius-based editor by just clicking on a button. In this way, first some necessary EMF artefacts are automatically generated, like the *ecore* and *genmodel* files (label 5 in Fig. 10), and the generated meta-model Java classes (label 6). These resources contain the equivalent representation to our working meta-model in EMF. The modelling expert is prompted to type a file extension for the models built with the new editor ("ext" in our example).

Then, a new Sirius *Viewpoint Specification* project is automatically created by internally using *EMF Splitter* (label 7 in Fig. 10). This created project includes two key elements: (i) an *odesign* file, the core resource of a Sirius editor, describing the DSL concrete syntax and its mapping to the DSL abstract syntax, and (ii) a folder named *models* containing models equivalent to those in the *fragments* folder, but now in *xmi* format. These files actually serve as validation units, since they are expected to be represented in the new editor similarly to the original sketches. The generated Sirius project can then be run, and Fig. 11 shows the resulting editor with one model coming from an initial sketch.

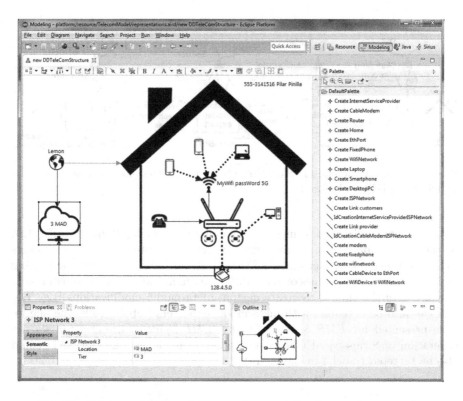

Fig. 11. Sirius graphical modelling environment for the running example.

Altogether, for the running example, we synthesized a graphical DSL using 4 fragments, with 13 object types, 4 edge styles and using 3 spatial relationships (containment, overlapping and adjacency, but not alignment). The system automatically induced a meta-model with 16 classes, 16 attributes, 13 references and 8 inheritance relationships. Finally, the generated Sirius *odesign* model contains 178 objects. The details of this case study, and some other examples, are available at http://miso.es/tools/metaBUP.html.

6.2   Extension Mechanisms

Our tools can be extended (via Eclipse extension points) in different parts of the process, as shown in Fig. 12. First, there is the possibility to contribute new fragment importers (label *1*). For this purpose, we provide a platform-independent "pivot" meta-model to represent sketch information [12], from which we produce the internal textual representation shown in the paper. We currently have importers from Dia and yED, but other drawing tools could be supported as well. Additionally, we provide a meta-model for modelling the graphical properties explained in Sect. 4 (see Fig. 4). As spatial relationships between objects are automatically inferred from fragments, it is necessary to save object locations (attributes width, height, x and y in Fig. 4).

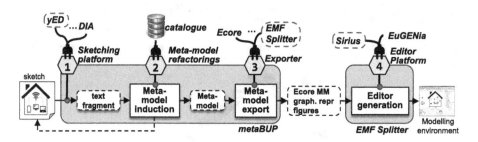

Fig. 12. Extension points: (1) Sketching platform, (2) Meta-model refactorings, (3) Exporter, (4) Editor platform.

New meta-model refactorings can be added to *metaBup* (label *2* in Fig. 12). As the meta-model grows, the modelling expert is suggested suitable refactorings to be performed on the meta-model. We natively cover basic rules like pluralizing multi-target reference names or generalizing common features to abstract classes, but also give the chance to create custom meta-model modifications [12]. The tool can also be extended with meta-model exporters (label *3*), like the one we have presented for *EMF Splitter*. Finally, *EMF Splitter* currently targets the generation of Sirius-based editors, but other technologies like EuGENia could also be targeted (label *4* in the figure).

7 Related Work

While MDE is founded on the ability to process models with a precisely defined syntax, some authors have recognised the need for more flexible and informal ways of modelling. This is useful in the early phases of system design [14,16,18], or as a means to promote an active role of domain experts in DSL development [2, 19], as we advocate in this paper. Next, we review works aiming at both goals.

There are two orthogonal design choices enabling flexible modelling in DSL development: (i) the use of examples to drive the construction process, and (ii) the explicit generation of a meta-model and a modelling tool different from the drawing tool used to build the initial examples.

Regarding the first design choice, "by-demonstration" techniques have been applied to several MDE artefacts, like model transformations [8], but their use is not so common to describe graphical modelling environments. The closest work to ours is [2], which describes a system atop Microsoft Visio to derive DSLs by demonstration. Given a single example, the system derives the concrete syntax from the icons in the palette, and some abstract syntax constraints, e.g., concerning the connectivity of elements. This information is recorded and used within Microsoft Visio. Instead, we derive an explicit meta-model, infer spatial relationships like containment and overlapping, and generate a modelling tool. Moreover, our induced meta-model supports modelling concepts like abstract classes, inheritance, compositions and attributes, which are not found in [2].

The approach in [19] uses yED to draw examples of the DSL. Types are assigned to elements on the basis of labels, and some predefined functions check for shape overlapping, colour or proximity. All modelling is performed within yED, and no meta-model or dedicated modelling environment are generated.

We believe that creating a meta-model and a modelling environment on top of a meta-modelling framework has some benefits. First, it guides the user in filling slot values, which otherwise should be done via tags in a diagramming tool like Visio. Moreover, slots and links have a type, which enables type-checking. Second, the created models can be manipulated by standard model management languages for model transformation or code generation.

Some tools for DSL development are based on generating an external modelling tool. For instance, EuGENia live [15] is a tool for designing graphical DSLs that runs on the browser. The tool supports on-the-fly meta-model editing while the user is editing a sample model and its concrete syntax. The tool can export an Ecore meta-model enriched with concrete syntax annotations, which can be used to generate an Eclipse GMF-based environment.

Finally, some modelling tools promote flexibility in the early phases of system design by offering sketching capabilities similar to pen-and-paper drawing. For instance, SKETCH [16] provides an API to enable sketch-based editing on Eclipse. Calico [14] is a sketching tool designed for electronic whiteboards, where the sketched elements can be scrapped and reused in other parts of the diagrams. FlexiSketch [18] derives simple meta-models from sketches, but the extracted meta-model does not support conceptual modelling elements like class inheritance, abstract classes or different association types (e.g., compositions).

Altogether, our approach is novel as it enables the creation of graphical DSL editors based on drawings produced by domain experts, generating a meta-model and a dedicated modelling environment. This approach helps in transitioning from informal modelling in a diagrammatic tool, to formal modelling in a modelling tool, where models are amenable to automated manipulation.

8   Conclusions and Future Work

This paper has presented our approach to the example-based generation of graphical modelling environments. In our approach, domain experts contribute with sketches built with diagramming tools, and our system induces a meta-model and a graphical modelling environment, currently based on Sirius. The paper has shown the advantages of the approach, like: (i) there is no need to code or create editor specifications; (ii) it lowers the barrier to build graphical environments, which is a highly technical task requiring expert knowledge; (iii) it bridges the gap between drawing tools (likely used by domain experts in early phases of the development) and modelling tools (useful for automated model manipulation); and (iv) drawings can be transformed into models and be manipulated using MDE technology (transformations and code generators).

In the future, we plan to perform a user study to evaluate the construction process and the generated editor. To facilitate the validation of the final editor by the domain experts, we plan to integrate our mmXtens language [13], which is able to generate "interesting" example models using constraint solving. We also plan to improve our support for the editor evolution. For instance, a common scenario might be the manual modification of the Sirius editor model. To avoid overriding these manual changes, we may employ techniques similar to [11], where manual changes are described as a program that is reapplied when re-generation occurs.

Acknowledgements. Work supported by the Spanish Ministry of Economy and Competitivity (TIN2014-52129-R), the Madrid Region (S2013/ICE-3006), and the EU Commission (FP7-ICT-2013-10, #611125).

References

1. Bak, K., Zayan, D., Czarnecki, K., Antkiewicz, M., Diskin, Z., Wasowski, A., Rayside, D.: Example-driven modeling: model = abstractions + examples. In: ICSE, pp. 1273–1276. IEEE/ACM (2013)
2. Cho, H., Gray, J.G., Syriani, E.: Creating visual domain-specific modeling languages from end-user demonstration. In: MiSE@ICSE, pp. 22–28 (2012)
3. de Lara, J., Vangheluwe, H.: AToM^3: a tool for multi-formalism and meta-modelling. In: Kutsche, R.-D., Weber, H. (eds.) FASE 2002. LNCS, vol. 2306, pp. 174–188. Springer, Heidelberg (2002)
4. Garmendia, A., Pescador, A., Guerra, E., de Lara, J.: Towards the generation of graphical modelling environments aided by patterns. In: Sierra-Rodríguez, J.-L., Leal, J.-P., Simões, A. (eds.) SLATE 2015. CCIS, vol. 563, pp. 160–168. Springer, Heidelberg (2015). doi:10.1007/978-3-319-27653-3_16

5. Graphiti. https://eclipse.org/graphiti/
6. Gronback, R.C.: Eclipse Modeling Project: A Domain-Specific Language (DSL) Toolkit. Addison-Wesley Professional, Reading (2009)
7. Hutchinson, J., Whittle, J., Rouncefield, M.: Model-driven engineering practices in industry: social, organizational and managerial factors that lead to success or failure. Sci. Comput. Program. **89**, 144–161 (2014)
8. Kappel, G., Langer, P., Retschitzegger, W., Schwinger, W., Wimmer, M.: Model transformation by-example: a survey of the first wave. In: Düsterhöft, A., Klettke, M., Schewe, K.-D. (eds.) Conceptual Modelling and Its Theoretical Foundations. LNCS, vol. 7260, pp. 197–215. Springer, Heidelberg (2012)
9. Kelly, S., Pohjonen, R.: Worst practices for domain-specific modeling. IEEE Softw. **26**(4), 22–29 (2009)
10. Kelly, S., Tolvanen, J.: Domain-Specific Modeling - Enabling Full Code Generation. Wiley, New Jersey (2008)
11. Kolovos, D.S., Rose, L.M., Abid, S.B., Paige, R.F., Polack, F.A.C., Botterweck, G.: Taming EMF and GMF using model transformation. In: Petriu, D.C., Rouquette, N., Haugen, Ø. (eds.) MODELS 2010, Part I. LNCS, vol. 6394, pp. 211–225. Springer, Heidelberg (2010)
12. López-Fernández, J.J., Cuadrado, J.S., Guerra, E., de Lara, J.: Example-driven meta-model development. Softw. Syst. Model. **14**(4), 1323–1347 (2015)
13. López-Fernández, J.J., Guerra, E., de Lara, J.: Example-based validation of domain-specific visual languages. In: SLE, pp. 101–112. ACM (2015)
14. Mangano, N., Baker, A., Dempsey, M., Navarro, E.O., van der Hoek, A.: Software design sketching with calico. In: ASE, pp. 23–32. ACM (2010)
15. Rose, L.M., Kolovos, D.S., Paige, R.F.: Eugenia live: a flexible graphical modelling tool. In: XM, pp. 15–20. ACM (2012)
16. Sangiorgi, U.B., Barbosa, S.D.: SKETCH: modeling using freehand drawing in eclipse graphical editors. In: FlexiTools @ ICSE (2010)
17. Sirius. https://eclipse.org/sirius/
18. Wuest, D., Seyff, N., Glinz, M.: Flexisketch team: collaborative sketching and notation creation on the fly. In: ICSE, vol. 2, pp. 685–688 (2015)
19. Zolotas, A., Kolovos, D.S., Matragkas, N.D., Paige, R.F.: Assigning semantics to graphical concrete syntaxes. In: XM@MoDELS. CEUR Workshop Proceedings, vol. 1239, pp. 12–21. CEUR-WS.org (2014)

UML and Meta-modeling

Associations in MDE:
A Concern-Oriented, Reusable Solution

Céline Bensoussan[✉], Matthias Schöttle, and Jörg Kienzle

School of Computer Science, McGill University, Montreal, Canada
{Celine.Bensoussan,Matthias.Schoettle}@mail.mcgill.ca,
Joerg.Kienzle@mcgill.ca

Abstract. Associations play an important role in model-driven software development. This paper describes a framework that uses Concern-Oriented Reuse (CORE) to capture many different kinds of associations, their properties, behaviour, and various implementation solutions within a reusable artifact: the *Association* concern. The concern exploits aspect-oriented modelling techniques to modularize the structure and behaviour required for enforcing uniqueness, multiplicity constraints and referential integrity for bidirectional associations. Furthermore, it packages different collection implementation classes that can be used to realize associations. For each implementation class, the impact of its use on non-functional qualities, e.g., memory consumption and performance, has been determined experimentally and formalized. We show how the class diagram notation, i.e., its metamodel and visual representation, can be extended to support reusing the *Association* concern, and present enhancements to automate feature selection and customization mappings to maximally streamline the reuse process in modelling tools.

1 Introduction

Model-Driven Engineering (MDE) [6] is a unified conceptual framework in which software development is seen as a process of *model production, refinement,* and *integration.* To reduce the accidental complexity and the effort needed to move from a problem domain to a software-based solution, MDE advocates the use of different modelling formalisms, i.e., modelling languages, to represent and analyze the system from *multiple points of view.* For each level of abstraction, the modeller uses the best formalism that concisely expresses the properties of the system that are important to that level. During development, high-level specification models are refined or combined with other models to include more solution details, such as the chosen architecture, data structures, algorithms, and finally even platform and execution environment-specific properties. The manipulation of models is achieved by means of model transformations, ideally automated by model transformations tools [8].

In the context of MDE, *associations* play an important role. During the requirements engineering phase, they are used at a high level of abstraction to formalize relationships among domain concepts in so-called *domain models.*

© Springer International Publishing Switzerland 2016
A. Wąsowski and H. Lönn (Eds.): ECMFA 2016, LNCS 9764, pp. 121–137, 2016.
DOI: 10.1007/978-3-319-42061-5_8

In later development phases, as the architecture of the software and the solution it implements begin to take form, properties are attached to the associations, e.g., *ordering, uniqueness, multiplicity,* and *navigability.* Finally, during the implementation phase, concrete data structures, such as *arrays, linked lists* or *hash tables,* are used to realize associations with multiplicity greater than one.

Because associations are widely used in MDE, modelling tools with code generators have to generate code from models that contain associations. However, most current code generators do not provide adequate support for associations [2,4,9,11,12]. For example, the properties of associations specified in the model, e.g., multiplicity constraints and bidirectionality, are rarely enforced in the generated code. Furthermore, there are many ways of implementing associations with multiplicity greater than one using different collection data structures. Each data structure has different run-time behaviour, and therefore affects the non-functional qualities of the software that is being developed, such as performance and memory use. Current modelling tools, however, shield the modeller from implementation details. As a result, they do not document or quantify the impact on non-functional qualities that underlying implementations for associations have. As a result, code generators typically resort to default implementation strategies for associations that do not take into account high-level goals and non-functional requirements of the application that is being built.

In this paper we describe a framework for dealing with associations in the context of MDE. We show how we used Concern-Oriented Reuse (CORE) [3] to capture many different kind of associations, their properties, behaviour, and various implementation solutions within a reusable artifact: the *Association* concern. The *Association* concern encapsulates models for many association variants, and exploits aspect-oriented modelling techniques to modularize the structure and behaviour required for enforcing uniqueness, multiplicity constraints and referential integrity for bidirectional associations. Furthermore, it packages several collection implementation classes that can be used to realize associations. For each provided implementation class, the impact of its use on memory consumption and performance has been experimentally determined and formalized within the concern.

The remainder of the paper is structured as follows. Section 2 reviews the essential background on CORE. Section 3 describes how we designed the *Association* concern. Section 4 presents how to streamline the reuse of the *Association* concern within a modelling tool. Section 5 discusses related work, and the last section draws our conclusions.

2   Background on Concern-Oriented Reuse

CORE [3] is a new software development paradigm inspired by the ideas of multi-dimensional separation of concerns [22]. It builds on the disciplines of MDE, software product lines (SPL) [18], goal modelling [13], and advanced modularization techniques offered by aspect-orientation [15,19] to define flexible software modules that enable broad-scale model-based software reuse called *concerns.*

A CORE *concern* is a unit of reuse that groups together software artifacts (models and code, henceforth called simply models) that address a recurring domain of interest in software development. The models encapsulated within a concern capture in a *generic* way the structural properties and behaviour of all relevant variations and ways of dealing with the domain of interest at all relevant levels of abstraction. Building a concern is a non-trivial, time consuming task, done by the *concern designer*, who is an expert of the concern's domain. Deep understanding of the nature of the concern is required to be able to identify its user-relevant features, to model the common properties and differences of all features of a concern at all relevant levels of abstraction, and to express the impact of the different variants on high level stakeholder goals and qualities. This is ensured by creating requirements, design and implementation models that (i) realize the features of the concern using the most appropriate modelling notations and programming languages, and (ii) are eventually refined into executable specifications.

2.1   The CORE Reuse Process

The concern designer elaborates *three interfaces* [3] for a concern:

- The *Variation Interface* describes the available variations of the concern and the impact of different variants on high-level stakeholder goals, qualities, and non-functional requirements. The variations are typically represented with a *feature model* [14] that specifies the individual, user-relevant features that a concern offers, as well as their dependencies, e.g., *optional, alternative, requires,* and *excludes*. The impact of choosing a feature is specified with impact models, which are based on GRL [13].
- The realization of each variant of a concern is described as generally as possible to increase reusability. Therefore, some model elements are only *partially* specified and need to be complemented with concrete modelling elements stemming from the application models that intend to reuse the concern. These generic elements are exposed in the *Customization Interface*.
- The *Usage Interface* describes how the application can finally access the structure and behaviour provided by the concern, similar to what the set of public operations represents for a class in the object-oriented paradigm.

The *concern user* reuses an existing concern through three simple steps:

1. The *concern user* first *selects the set of feature(s)* (called a *configuration*) with the best impact on relevant stakeholder goals and system qualities *from the variation interface* of the concern based on impact analysis provided by the CORE tool. Using this configuration, the CORE tool then composes the models that realize the selected features to yield new models of the concern corresponding to the desired configuration.
2. Next, the *concern user adapts* the generated realization *models to the application context by mapping customization interface elements* to application-specific model elements. Again, the CORE tool helps to establish correct

mappings based on the signatures of the model elements that have to be customized, and subsequently generates customized realization models.

3. Finally, *the concern user uses the functionality exposed in the usage interface* of the customized realization models within his application models.

To demonstrate our framework, we use TouchCORE[1] [21], a multi-touch enabled, software design modelling tool that supports feature and impact models, as well as realization models expressed using class, sequence, state diagrams, and Java implementations.

3   Designing the Association Concern

In this section we present the design of the *Association* concern, which encapsulates all relevant variants of dealing with *unidirectional, binary associations* between two entities in MDE[2]. We start by describing the variation, customization and usage interfaces of the concern, follow up with an overview of the structural and behavioural realization models encapsulated within the concern, and finally describe the experiments that we ran to determine the impact of different association realization on memory use and performance.

3.1   Association Variation Interface

Coming up with a variation interface for a concern requires (i) breaking down the domain into distinct *features*, i.e., modules that provide well-defined *user-relevant* structure, functionality and/or properties, and organizing the features and their relationships in a feature model, and (ii) identifying the non-functional qualities that the realizations of the features might impact. Usually, the variation interface of a concern is not elaborated in a top-down manner. Rather, the expert domain knowledge of a concern designer typically allows her to sketch an initial variation interface, which is then refined as more insight is gained while realizing the features. Figure 1 shows the final variation interface of the *Association* concern.

Structure: The first mandatory sub-feature, *Structure*, differentiates between an association with a maximum multiplicity of *One* (single object) and associations with a multiplicity of more than one, i.e., *Many* (collection of objects). The feature *One* is therefore used for multiplicities of 0..1 and 1..1. Among the associations with multiplicity *many*, there are qualified associations, where objects in the association are retrieved using a key (feature *KeyIndexed*), and *Plain* associations, which can be *Ordered* or *Unordered*. The leaf features finally encapsulate different data structures and algorithms that implement the collections with the corresponding properties, namely *ArrayList*, *LinkedList* and *Stack*

---

[1] http://touchcore.cs.mcgill.ca.

[2] Bidirectional associations are supported as well by using two unidirectional associations between the same elements in opposite direction.

for *Ordered* collections, *HashSet* and *TreeSet* for *Unordered* ones, and *HashMap* and *TreeMap* for *KeyIndexed*.

Association Properties: Associations are *Bidirectional* when they are navigable in both directions, in which case referential integrity must be enforced. For associations with multiplicity *Many*, it makes sense to decide whether the same element can be part of the association more than once or not. The optional feature *Unique* ensures that adding an object to an association is only allowed if the object is not already part of the association. Since the implementation data structures that we use for unordered collections—*HashSet* and *TreeSet*— do not support duplicate insertion of the same object (i.e., they implement *Sets* and not *Bags*), we specified the constraints that *TreeSet* requires *Unique,* and *HashSet* requires *Unique* within the feature model. Finally, the *Minimum* and *Maximum* features constrain the behaviour of *insertion/removal* operations to enforce minimum and maximum multiplicity constraints. They are sub-features of *Plain*, because they cannot be used in combination with qualified associations.

Impacts: The different variations of association implementations encapsulated inside the *Association* concern have an impact on memory use and performance. We modelled the impacts with the following goals: *Minimize Memory Footprint, Increase Insertion Performance, Increase Iteration Performance, Increase Access Performance* and *Increase Removal Performance*, as shown on the right side of Fig. 1. To determine the weights that drive the evaluation of the impacts based on a feature selection, we ran an extensive set of experiments that are described in Subsec. 3.6.

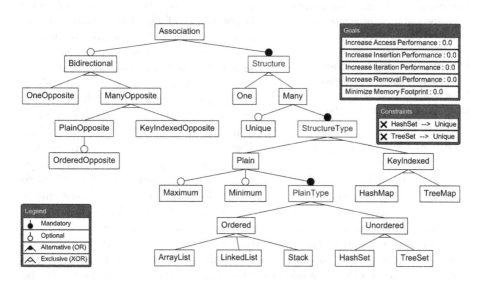

Fig. 1. Screenshot of variation interface of the *Association* concern

3.2 Customization Interface

The *customization interface* of a concern exposes the model elements that define only partial structure/behaviour. They need to be adapted by the concern user to the reuse context by mapping them to concrete model elements in the application model. To easily identify model elements that have to be customized by a concern user, the names of these *public partial* model elements are prefixed with a vertical bar ("|").

In a directed association, partial structural elements are the class of origin, i.e., the class that holds the association end, and the destination class. We named the class of origin |Data and the destination class |Associated as shown in Fig. 2 on the right. For qualified associations, the customization interface includes an additional partial |Key class as shown in Fig. 2 on the left.

Fig. 2. Customization interface for feature *KeyIndexed* (left) and others (right)

3.3 Usage Interface

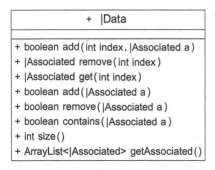

Fig. 3. Usage Int. for *ArrayList*

The *usage interface* is defined by the public elements in the concern that can be used by the application. In the case of the *Association* concern, the *usage interface* is composed of the |Data class and its *public operations*. The features of the concern do not have a common *usage interface,* as the operations of |Data vary with the properties of the collection. When |Data holds a single object reference (feature *One*), the *usage interface* consists of a *getter* and a *setter* operation. When |Data holds a collection (feature *Many*), it provides operations to *add* and *remove* elements. For ordered associations (feature *Ordered*), additional operations to *add* and *remove* at a specific index are provided. For example, the usage interface for the feature *ArrayList* is shown in Fig. 3. For qualified associations, the *add* and *remove* operations take as an additional parameter a key.

Since |Data is part of the customization interface, it is mapped by the user to the class holding the association. As a result, the operations belonging to the usage interface of |Data are added to the mapped class, ready to be used. The operations, though, are not part of the customization interface, i.e., they *do not have to be* mapped. However, the user *may want to rename* the operations for better usability, for example, rename add to addUser.

3.4 Structural Realization of Associations

In CORE, each feature is associated with realization models that describe its structural and behavioural properties at different levels of abstraction using different modelling formalisms. When a concern user makes a feature selection, the CORE tool incrementally composes all realization models associated with the selected features to create user-tailored realization models. In this subsection, we describe class diagrams encoding different structural variations of the *Association* concern.

The realization model of the root feature of the concern simply defines the two classes |Data and |Associated that we already introduced above. The realization model of the feature *One*, which is used when the upper multiplicity bound of an association end is *1*, declares a reference myAssociated pointing from |Data to |Associated. It also defines a *getter* and a *setter* operation for this reference. On the other hand, the realization model for the feature *Many*, which is used when the upper bound of the association is greater than *1*, defines a |CollectionOfAssociated class that is contained in the class |Data. It is marked as *concern partial* with a discontinuous vertical bar ("¦"), which means that it is incomplete just like model elements that are part of the customization interface of the concern. However, it has to be completed *within the concern*, i.e., by other realization models. The realization model of *Many* also defines the operations *contains*, *size* and *getAssociated*.

The structure is further refined by the realization model of feature *Plain*, which defines operations to *add* and *remove* elements to/from the ¦CollectionOfAssociated class. Continuing, the realization model of *Ordered* adds operations to *add*, *remove* and *get elements* at a certain index. Finally, the realization model for features representing concrete implementation data structures map the ¦CollectionOfAssociated class to a concrete Java class, e.g., ArrayList.

3.5 Behavioural Realization

We modelled the behaviour of operations using sequence diagrams. Figure 4 shows the add operation defined in *Plain*, which calls add of the contained collection.

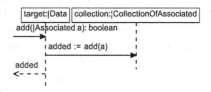

Fig. 4. Base behaviour of add

Some features of the *Association* concern may affect the behaviour of other features. For example, the feature *Unique* affects the behaviour of *insertion* operations: before adding, a check is performed to determine whether the element is already in the collection. *Maximum* also impacts insertion operations: if the maximum is already reached, the operation returns false and the addition is not performed. *Minimum* impacts *removal* operations: if the collection already contains the minimum number of elements, it returns `false` and the element is not removed. *Bidirectional* ensures referential integrity. It impacts *constructors*, *setters*, *insertion* and *removal* operations. When an element is added to a collection and the association is bidirectional, depending on whether the opposite side is one or many, the element needs to be set or added on the opposite side.

CORE uses aspect-oriented techniques to augment the behaviour of other realization models. For example, Fig. 5 shows how *Maximum* extends the behaviour of Fig. 4 to verify that the maximum has not been reached before executing the original behaviour of `add` (represented by a white box containing a "*").

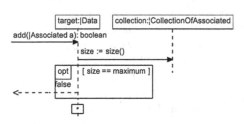

Fig. 5. Aspect sequence diagram *Maximum*

Additional complexity stems from the fact that there are some behavioural feature interactions inside the *Association* concern that need to be taken care of. For example, the behaviour of the feature *Bidirectional* requires that before a new object is associated with a current object, the object might first need to be removed from other associations, and the current object has to be added to the opposite association of the new object, and only then the new object can be added to the association of the current object. However, the operations that need to be called to deal with the opposite end of the association depend on the multiplicity constraints on the opposite end. In certain cases, *setter* operations should be invoked, in other cases, *add/remove* operations. These different behaviours had to be specified in so-called feature interaction resolution realization models, which are linked to the features they deal with, so that the CORE tool can apply them automatically when needed.

For example, Fig. 6 shows the feature interaction resolution model for *Plain* and *OneOpposite*, which ensures that for bidirectional `0..1 <-> 0..*` associations a new `|Associated` object a is only then added to the collection in the `target` object `|Data`, if `target` was successfully set as the opposite associated object of `a`. To ensure that this resolution is combined in the correct order with the behavioural modification that realizes *Maximum*, as shown previously, an additional feature interaction model has to be defined that first applies *Plain/OneOpposite*, and then *Maximum*.

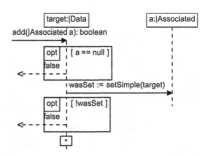

Fig. 6. Interaction Res. *Plain/OneOpposite*

3.6   Determining the Impacts of Association Realizations

In order to provide the modeller with guidance on which of the association features to choose, we conducted a series of experiments to determine the impact that the different realizations have on memory use and performance.

Experimental Setup: We ran our experiments on a machine with a 2,4 GHz Intel Core i5 processor and 16 GB 1600 MHz DDR 3 memory. The machine was running Mac OS X 10.9.5. The Java SE Runtime (v1.8.0_20-b26) was configured with 384 MB heap space. The model that was used for the experiment was the simplest possible model, i.e., a model with a directed association myB with multiplicity 0..* between classes A and B.

Impact on Memory Use: To determine the amount of memory used by the different realizations, we created n instances of B ($n = 10$ (small), $n = 100$ (medium), $n = 1,000$ (large) and $n = 10,000$ (extra-large), and added them to the association between A and B by successively calling a.addMyB(b_i). We used the Heap Walker of JProfiler [7] to determine the amount of memory used by the collection implementation class realizing the association. The results are shown on the left side of Fig. 7.

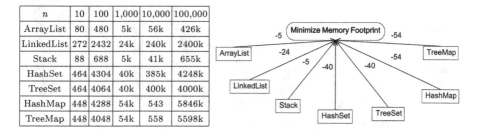

n	10	100	1,000	10,000	100,000
ArrayList	80	480	5k	56k	426k
LinkedList	272	2432	24k	240k	2400k
Stack	88	688	5k	41k	655k
HashSet	464	4304	40k	385k	4248k
TreeSet	464	4064	40k	400k	4000k
HashMap	448	4288	54k	543	5846k
TreeMap	448	4048	54k	558	5598k

Fig. 7. Memory usage in bytes and corresponding impact model

The relative measured memory use is approximately consistent across different orders of magnitude of number of elements. We therefore used the measured number of KB for 1000 elements directly as negative contribution values in the corresponding CORE impact model (see the right side of Fig. 7). This means that *ArrayList* and *Stack* (with contribution *-5*) are from a memory use point of view the best choice, whereas *HashMap* and *TreeMap* (with contribution *-54*) are the worst choice, i.e., they use approximately 10 times more memory.

Impact on Performance: To measure the impact on performance, we used an approach similar to the one described in Ahuja [1]. Again, we ran experiments with associations of different orders of magnitude (#elements = n), and measured the time t it took to execute each operation op n times from within a loop. Measuring Java performance is not trivial, because of various factors involving the virtual machine, the garbage collector, actual heap size at runtime and associated non-determinism [10]. To minimize external influences, we refrained from measuring the first runs to avoid accounting for time spent loading/initializing code, and then collected measurements of 50 runs. From those runs we calculated the *median* as well as the *10th and 90th percentile* to minimize effects of the garbage collector.

The performance measurements for *adding/appending n* objects to an association are shown in Fig. 8[3]. Some implementations perform consistently well, e.g., *ArrayList* and *LinkedList*, and others consistently bad, e.g., *TreeSet*. However, the relative performance of some varies depending on the order of magnitude of the number of elements in the association. For example, *HashSet* and *HashMap* perform well for a small number of elements, but then performance worsens for larger associations. We therefore decided to create separate impact models for each order of magnitude using the median values from the experiments as negative weights for the impact models.

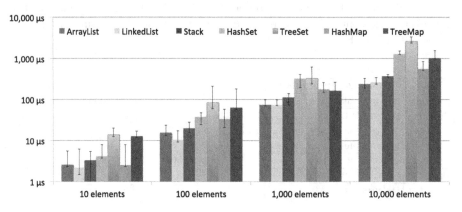

Fig. 8. Insertion performance of different collection implementations (Color figure online)

Discussion: Impact models in CORE are currently exclusively specified using the goal modelling notation [13]. Goal models work well in the context of CORE, because they allow vague, hard-to-measure system qualities to be evaluated, e.g., *user convenience* or *security*, in addition to more quantifiable qualities, e.g., *cost* and *number of messages exchanged*. Unfortunately, impact models as they are defined currently can not be parameterized with dynamic information from the reuse context. As a result, our impact models can not be used for predicting the actual memory use or the actual performance of the final application. Rather,

---

[3] The results for the other operations, i.e., access performance, iteration, and removal, are not shown for space reasons. They are available in [5], which also describes additional experiments that we ran to compare performance on different Java execution platforms.

they are intended to help the modeller make design decisions by quantifying the impacts that one selection has over another *relatively speaking*. There exist dedicated performance modelling languages that offer advanced performance simulation and prediction capabilities [17], but how to exploit these in the context of CORE is out of the scope of this paper.

3.7 Association Concern Design Summary

In the end, the *Association* concern we designed encapsulates 26 features, specifies 5 impacts, contains 10 class diagrams, and 25 sequence diagrams (3 of which are feature interaction resolution models). The feature model allows for 225 possible selections, from which the TouchCORE tool can create 225 different user-tailored realization models by combining the corresponding realization models in different ways to suit the exact needs of the concern user.

4   Using the Association Concern

The complexity of associations (different variations and implementation classes, impacts, behaviour ensuring maximum, minimum, uniqueness, and bidirectionality,and additional behaviour addressing feature interactions) is now encapsulated behind the variation, customization and usage interface of the *Association* concern and ready to be reused.

The standard CORE reuse process, outlined in Subsect. 2.1 and implemented in the TouchCORE tool, is general, i.e., it is applicable when reusing *any concern*. It can therefore also be used for reusing the *Association* concern. Unfortunately, due to its general nature, the process is unnecessarily tedious for *Association*. In TouchCORE, it involves the following effort for the modeller:

1. The modeller first needs to indicate the desire to reuse *Association*. This involves searching through the reusable concern library to find the *Association* concern, which typically involves navigating down the folder hierarchy.
2. When the *Association* variation interface is displayed, the modeller must make a selection of the desired variant. The feature model of *Association* is large, in particular because of the features that deal with ensuring the correct behaviour for bidirectional associations. It takes cognitive effort to visually browse through it and make the desired selection.
3. When the *customization interface* is displayed, the modeller has to manually establish the mappings of the source and destination classes of the association: |Data and |Associated have to be mapped, as well as |Key in case of qualified associations. The mappings of the operations are not required, but in case the modeller desires to rename the generic names of operations to more specific names, e.g., *add* to *addUser*, mappings have to be specified for each operation that is to be renamed.

Finally, a bidirectional association requires reusing the *Association* concern *twice*. This not only constitutes a duplication of effort, but it is also a potential source of inconsistencies. In order to avoid errors, the modeller must make sure to select the right sub-feature of *Bidirectional* that correctly represents the type of the opposite association (one, many, ordered, or key-indexed).

In light of these usability issues, we devised a domain-specific language (DSL) inspired by the concrete syntax for associations defined in UML to streamline the reuse of the *Association* concern for modellers. The DSL minimizes the effort involved and eliminates any risk of mis(re)use. We then integrated this DSL into the TouchCORE tool in order to facilitate the reuse of the *Association* concern while modelling with class and sequence diagrams.

4.1   DSL for Applying the Association Concern

UML already defines a visual notation for associations [16]. A line that connects two classes represents an association, arrowheads on the association ends depict navigability, and inclusive intervals of non-negative integers on the association ends specify a lower bound and a (possibly infinite) upper bound for multiplicities. The default properties for associations in UML are *unique* and *unordered*. It is possible to specify deviations from the default by annotating the association ends with textual constraints, i.e., {*ordered*} and/or {*nonunique*}. For qualified associations, the UML syntax dictates that the type of the model element used for lookup is specified in a rectangular box at the border of the originating class.

Since the graphical notation in UML already covers our features *Bidirectional*, *Minimum*, *Maximum*, *Unique*, *Ordered*, *Unordered*, and *KeyIndexed*, we simply defined additional textual constraints to allow the modeller to specify the concrete implementation classes, i.e., *ArrayList*, *LinkedList*, *Stack*, *HashSet*, *TreeSet*, *HashMap* and *TreeMap*. This list is automatically extended whenever additional implementation classes are added to the *Association* concern.

4.2   Modifications to the Class Diagram Metamodel

In the CORE metamodel [20], the *COREReuse* class represents reuses. From a *COREReuse* one can get to the *COREConfiguration*, i.e., the set of selected features of the reuse. The *CORECompositionSpecification*, i.e., the set of customization mappings can be retrieved through the *COREModelReuse*, which specifies the compositions of a reuse for a particular model. To use the *Association* concern consistently, every navigable association end has to have a corresponding model reuse of the *Association* concern. Hence, a directed association between *AssociationEnd*, i.e., the class that represents association ends in the class diagram metamodel, to *COREModelReuse* is needed. The backend of TouchCORE was updated to create a *COREReuse* and *COREModelReuse* (for the design model) whenever an association end between two classes becomes navigable.

4.3   Automated and Consistent Feature Selections

TouchCORE was adapted in such a way that whenever the modeller manipulates the graphical representation of an association, e.g., by changing the multiplicity or navigability, the selected features of the reuse of *Association* are *updated automatically* as follows:

- When the upper multiplicity bound is 1, *One* is selected, otherwise *Many*.
- When the upper multiplicity bound is greater than 1 and not many (*),
  Maximum is selected.
- When the lower bound is 1 or greater and the upper bound is greater than
  1, *Minimum* is selected.
- When the association is navigable in both directions and the upper bound on
  the multiplicity of the opposite end is 1, *OneOpposite* is selected.
- When the association is navigable in both directions and the upper bound
  on the multiplicity of the opposite end is greater than 1, *ManyOpposite* is
  selected.

Additionally, the GUI of TouchCORE was extended to display textual constraints, e.g., {*ordered*} or {*ArrayList*} on association ends. If the modeller clicks on the textual constraint, they are presented with a simplified variation interface of the *Association* concern. All automatically selected features are not shown, so the modeller can maximally focus on exploring the impact of the available implementation classes and to eventually select the most appropriate one.

4.4 Generation of Mappings and Operation Renaming

When a modeller draws a directed, navigable association from class `Source` to class `Destination`, the customization mappings for the *Association* concern are automatically created. |`Data` is mapped to `Source`, and |`Associated` to `Destination`. For qualified associations, TouchCORE displays a rectangular box at the association end that allows the modeller to specify the qualifier type. Based on the modeller's input, the corresponding mapping for |`Key` is created.

Additionally, for every operation that is in the usage interface of |`Data`, a mapping is created that renames the operation by appending the name of the association end specified by the modeller. For instance, for a directed association from class `User` to class `Account` with multiplicity `0..*` named `myAccounts`, the `add` operation would be renamed to `addToMyAccounts`.

5 Related Work

To our knowledge, the concern-orientated reuse paradigm is currently the only modelling approach that supports the encapsulation of different structural and behavioural designs and implementations and their impacts within one reusable model. As a result, most modelling tools provide only basic, "UML-like" support for modelling with associations. However, there is a substantial amount of related work on code generation optimized for and dedicated to associations.

5.1   Existing Code Generation Approaches for Associations

Harrison describes a technique for generating Java implementation code from UML diagrams [12]. The authors suggest generating an interface for dealing with the behaviour of associations (creating, deletion) in a manner transparent to the user. They propose the creation of an interface and its implementation for each association end. The interface extends both the destination class and the association class, if one was modelled. It ensures referential integrity and multiplicity constraints, but does not provide support for different collection implementation data structures. A similar approach is adopted by Gessenharter [11], who proposes that associations be implemented as classes. To implement an association between A and B, a class AB is created which holds a list of AB links. Both class A and B have an **addB** and **addA** operation, respectively, that call a static method in AB to establish a new link.

Génova presents some principles for mapping UML associations to Java code [9]. They demonstrate that it is unreasonable to ensure the minimum multiplicity constraint at any moment on a mandatory association end as it reduces usability. Therefore, they make the user responsible for initializing the system to a consistent state, and for maintaining it. Akehurst introduces Java code generation patterns from UML models with dedicated support for associations [2].

5.2   MouseTrap

Motorola has developed its own automatic code generation tool suite called *Mousetrap* [23]. The *Mousetrap* tool suite takes as input design models using SDL, UML, ASN.1, and ISL (a proprietary protocol language) and produces highly optimized C code customized for a product platform and a set of performance constraints. Mousetrap is a rule-based code transformation system driven by a vast programming knowledge base.

Section 5.4 of [23] on Abstract Data Types (ADT) is most related to our work. In their approach, code generation for associations involves the selection of a concrete implementation of an ADT. Where most code generators simply pick a default implementation, theirs analyzes the behaviour of the model and determines the specific ADT that leads to a better tradeoff between memory usage and performance. For example, if the collection is often being iterated over, the system would favour a linked list, as linked lists have superior iteration performance due the lack of repeated indexing, a fact that our own benchmark measurements confirmed.

5.3   UMPLE

UMPLE (UML Programming Language) is a textual design modelling tool supporting class diagrams and state diagrams [4]. It has a powerful code generator that handles multiplicity constraints and referential integrity for associations just like we do.

From a user's point of view, the main differences between UMPLE and Touch-CORE with the *Association* concern is that UMPLE always translates a *many* association to a fixed implementation data structure (*ArrayList* in Java, a *Vector* in C++, an *array* in Ruby) without determining the best fit or letting the user decide. As a result, UMPLE does not provide the property *unique,* and all generated association implementations are *ordered* (since they all translate to a list in the code). However, UMPLE does provide sorted associations, and allows the modeller to specify the attribute that is to be used for sorting.

5.4 Discussion

One could argue that an advantage of the code generator approach over the CORE approach is that it clearly separates design decisions, which are made at the model level, from implementation decisions, which are made by the code generator (or by a platform expert that configures code generation options before running the code generator). However, this is not the case here, as the CORE reuse process allows a modeller to make partial selections. For example, it is acceptable for a designer to choose the feature *Ordered,* and *defer the decision* of which mandatory child feature from the XOR group—*ArrayList, LinkedList* or *Stack*—should be used in the realization. This decision can be made at a later point, potentially by a different developer, e.g., a platform expert. Ideally, the decision could even be automated based on some user-defined optimization criteria. Currently, though, the developer has to perform his own tradeoff analysis and opt for faster execution time or decreased memory usage depending on his preference. In the near future we are planning to build an automated reasoning system into the TouchCORE tool that exploits the impact information from the concern's variation interface to perform automated optimization of non-functional requirements according to the developer's priorities.

In the end, the main difference between addressing associations at the modelling level as done in CORE compared to dealing with associations during code generation is that if one desires to change the way that associations are handled or to support new association implementations, the latter approach requires understanding and modifying the code generator. In contrast, in our CORE approach the modeller can simply update the structural and/or behavioural realization models of existing features of the *Association* concern, or add new features and new realization models, if needed. There is no need to modify the code generation, nor modify any code in the TouchCORE tool.

Finally, while the code generators discussed in this section address the maximum, minimum, uniqueness and bidirectionality properties of associations just as well as we do, they typically do not support qualified associations as we do through the feature *KeyIndexed*. Finally, with the exception of *Mousetrap,* they do not take into account the non-functional impacts of different concrete data structure implementations.

6   Conclusion

In this paper we described a framework for dealing with associations in the context of MDE. We designed a reusable CORE concern named *Association* that encapsulates design models for different association variants, and exploits aspect-oriented modelling techniques to modularize the structure and behaviour required for enforcing uniqueness, multiplicity constraints, and referential integrity for bidirectional associations. Furthermore, it supports the use of different collection implementation classes used to implement associations and documents their impacts on memory consumption and performance. We showed how class diagrams, i.e., the metamodel and visual notation used in the Touch-CORE tool, can be extended to support reusing the *Association* concern, and presented enhancements to automate feature selection and customization mappings to maximally streamline the reuse process.

References

1. Ahuja, K.V.: Technical Whitepaper: Performance Evaluation | Java Collections Framework (2008). http://scrtchpad.files.wordpress.com/2008/10/java-collections-performance-evaluation.pdf
2. Akehurst, D., Howells, G., McDonald-Maier, K.: Implementing associations: UML 2.0 to Java 5. Softw. Syst. Model. **6**(1), 3–35 (2006)
3. Alam, O., Kienzle, J., Mussbacher, G.: Concern-oriented software design. In: Moreira, A., Schätz, B., Gray, J., Vallecillo, A., Clarke, P. (eds.) MODELS 2013. LNCS, vol. 8107, pp. 604–621. Springer, Heidelberg (2013)
4. Badreddin, O., Forward, A., Lethbridge, T.C.: Improving code generation for associations: enforcing multiplicity constraints and ensuring referential integrity. In: Lee, R. (ed.) SERA 2013. SCI, vol. 496, pp. 129–149. Springer, Heidelberg (2013)
5. Bensoussan, C.: Associations in MDE: A Concern-Oriented, Reusable Solution. M.Sc. Thesis, School of Computer Science, McGill University, March 2016
6. Schmidt, D.C.: Model-driven engineering. IEEE Comput. **39**, 41–47 (2006)
7. EJ Technologies: JProfiler. https://www.ej-technologies.com/products/jprofiler/overview.html
8. France, R., Rumpe, B.: Model-driven development of complex software: a research roadmap. In: Future of Software Engineering, pp. 37–54. IEEE (2007)
9. Génova, G., del Castillo, C.R., Llorens, J.: Mapping UML associations into Java code. J. Object Technol. **2**(5), 135–162 (2003)
10. Georges, A., Buytaert, D., Eeckhout, L.: Statistically rigorous java performance evaluation. SIGPLAN Not. **42**(10), 57–76 (2007)
11. Gessenharter, D.: Mapping the UML2 Semantics of associations to a java code generation model. In: Czarnecki, K., Ober, I., Bruel, J.-M., Uhl, A., Völter, M. (eds.) MODELS 2008. LNCS, vol. 5301, pp. 813–827. Springer, Heidelberg (2008)
12. Harrison, W., Barton, C.: Mapping UML designs to Java. In: OOPSLA, pp. 178–188. ACM Press (2000)
13. International Telecommunication Union (ITU-T): Recommendation Z.151: User Requirements Notation (URN) - Language Definition, October 2012
14. Kang, K., Cohen, S., Hess, J., Novak, W., Peterson, S.: Feature-Oriented Domain Analysis (FODA) Feasibility Study. Technical report. CMU/SEI-90-TR-21, SEI, CMU, November 1990

15. Kienzle, J. (ed.): Transactions on Aspect-Oriented Development VII, Special Issue on a Common Case Study for Aspect-Oriented Modeling. Springer, Heidelberg (2010)
16. Object Management Group: Unified Modeling Language (UML) Superstructure, v. 2.5, pp. 32–35, March 2015
17. Object Management Group (OMG): UML Profile for MARTE: Modeling and Analysis of Real-Time Embedded Systems, June 2011
18. Pohl, K., Böckle, G., van der Linden, F.J.: Software Product Line Engineering: Foundations, Principles and Techniques. Springer, New York (2005)
19. Filman, R., Elrad, T., Clarke, S., Akşit, M.: Aspect-Oriented Software Development. Addison-Wesley, Reading (2004)
20. Schöttle, M., Alam, O., Kienzle, J., Mussbacher, G.: On the modularization provided by concern-oriented reuse. In: Modularity in Modelling Workshop - MOMO 2016, MODULARITY Companion 2016, pp. 184–189. ACM (2016)
21. Schöttle, M., Thimmegowda, N., Alam, O., Kienzle, J., Mussbacher, G.: Feature modelling and traceability for concern-driven software development with Touch-CORE. In: Companion Proceedings of MODULARITY, pp. 11–14. ACM (2015)
22. Tarr, P., Ossher, H., Harrison, W., Sutton Jr., S.M.: N Degrees of separation: multi-dimensional separation of concerns. In: International Conference on Software Engineering - ICSE, pp. 107–119. IEEE (1999)
23. Weigert, T., Weil, F., van den Berg, A., Dietz, P., Marth, K.: Automated code generation for industrial-strength systems. In: COMPSAC 2008, pp. 464–472 (2008)

Automated Metamodel/Model Co-evolution Using a Multi-objective Optimization Approach

Wael Kessentini[1]($\boxtimes$), Houari Sahraoui[1], and Manuel Wimmer[2]

[1] DIRO, University of Montreal, Montreal, Canada
kessentw@iro.umontreal.ca
[2] Business Informatics Group, Vienna University of Technology, Vienna, Austria

Abstract. We propose a generic automated approach for the metamodel/model co-evolution. The proposed technique refines an initial model to make it as conformant as possible to the new metamodel version by finding the best compromise between three objectives, namely minimizing (*i*) the non-conformities with new metamodel version, (*ii*) the changes to existing models, and (*iii*) the loss of information. Consequently, we view the co-evolution as a multi-objective optimization problem, and solve it using the NSGA-II algorithm. We successfully validated our approach on the evolution of the well-known UML state machine metamodel. The results confirm the effectiveness of our approach with average precision and recall respectively higher than 87 % and 89 %.

Keywords: Metamodel/model co-evolution · Model migration · Coupled evolution · NSGA-II

1 Introduction

Models are considered as first-class artifacts in the Model-Driven Engineering (MDE) paradigm. Available techniques, approaches, and tools for MDE support a huge variety of activities, such as model creation, model transformation, and code generation. However, there is still limited support available for model evolution. Like other software artifacts, metamodels are subject to many changes during the evolution of software modeling languages and language maintenance projects, especially for domain-specific languages [13]. Thus, models have to be updated for preserving their conformance with the new metamodel version.

Recently, several approaches emerged with the aim of tackling the metamodel/model co-evolution (e.g., [10,13,14,25]). Most of the automated co-evolution approaches focus on the detection of differences between the metamodel versions. Then, they find a set of generic rules to transform the initial models into revised ones, which conform to the new metamodel [12]. Nevertheless, the following challenges remain. The migration rules have to be defined manually for the change types which are detectable at the metamodel level, and they are difficult to generalize for all potential changes of metamodels. The definition of these rules may require a high level of expertise/knowledge from

© Springer International Publishing Switzerland 2016
A. Wąsowski and H. Lönn (Eds.): ECMFA 2016, LNCS 9764, pp. 138–155, 2016.
DOI: 10.1007/978-3-319-42061-5_9

the designer regarding both the previous and new versions of the metamodel. In addition, the detection of changes at the metamodel level is complex due to the graph isomorphism problem where different transformation possibilities are equivalent. Finally, existing approaches produce exactly one solution for a metamodel/model co-evolution scenario, while other solutions might be possible and may be more suitable in a particular context. Due to these challenges, developers are, sometimes, reluctant to migrate to a new metamodel version, considering the high effort required to adapt existing models.

To address these challenges, we propose to tackle the co-evolution of models without the need of computing differences between the metamodel versions. In particular, we view the metamodel/model co-evolution as an automated multi-objective optimization process that searches for a good combination of edit operations, at the model level, by minimizing (i) the number of constraints the revised model violates with respect to the new metamodel version, (ii) the number of changes applied on the initial model to produce the revised model, and (iii) the deviation (dissimilarity) between the initial and revised models. These three objectives are the heuristics that allow us to approximate the evolution of models without an explicit knowledge on the differences between the two metamodel versions and the rules to apply to migrate the models. The first objective ensures that the modified model conforms to the new metamodel. As changes in the metamodel are generally limited to a small subset of its elements, the second objective is used to reflect this property at the model level. Finally, the third objective allows us to limit the loss of information when migrating a model.

To implement our multi-objective approach, we adapt the NSGA-II [5] algorithm to search for solutions that offer the best trade-off between the three aforementioned objectives. We evaluate our approach on the evolution of the UML state machine metamodel. In addition, to study the proposed transformations to the considered state machine models, we compare our approach to a random search algorithm, a mono-objective algorithm, and an existing approach in which the migration rules are manually defined after finding the changes between the initial and revised metamodels. The obtained results provide evidence that our proposal is, in average, efficient with more than 92 % of manual precision achieved for the studied metamodel evolution.

The remainder of this paper is structured as follows. Section 2 provides the background of model co-evolution and presents a motivating example. In Sect. 3, we detail our approach. Section 4 discusses an empirical evaluation of our approach. After surveying the related work in Sect. 5, a conclusion is provided in Sect. 6.

2 Background and Motivating Example

This section introduces the necessary background for this paper, namely the basic notions of metamodels and models, including their *conformsTo* relationship, as well as a motivating example to demonstrate the challenges related to the metamodel/model co-evolution problem.

2.1   Metamodels and Models

In MDE, metamodels are the means to specify the abstract syntax of modeling languages. For defining metamodels, there are metamodeling standards (such as MOF, Ecore) available which are mostly based on a core subset of the UML class diagrams, i.e., classes, attributes, and references. Theoretically speaking, metamodels give the intentional description of all possible models of a given language. In practice, metamodels are instantiated to produce models which are, in essence, object graphs, i.e., consisting of objects (instances of classes) representing the modeling elements, object slots for storing values (instances of attributes), and links between objects (instances of references). The object graphs are often represented as UML object diagrams and have to conform to the UML class diagram describing the metamodel. This means, for a model to conform to its metamodel, a set of constraints have to be fulfilled. This set of constraints is normally referred to as *conformsTo* relationship [11, 22].

To make the *conformsTo* relationship more concrete, we give an excerpt of the constraints concerning objects in models and their relationship to classes in metamodels. Objects are instantiated from classes. Thus, for each referred type of an object in a given model, a corresponding class must exist in the metamodel (name equivalence), and the corresponding class must not be abstract. Such constraints may be formulated in the following way using OCL:

```
context M!Object
  inv typeExists: MM!Class.allInstances() ->
    exists(c|c.name = self.type and not c.abstract)
```

Example model versions and corresponding metamodel versions are shown in Figs. 1a and 2a, respectively. This simple language allows to define state machines consisting of states having a name as well as predecessor/successor states.

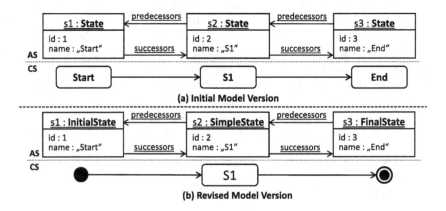

Fig. 1. Example model evolution

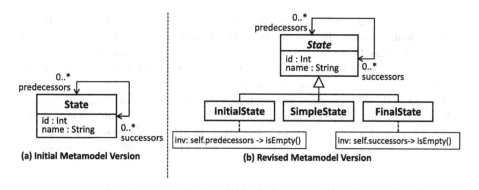

Fig. 2. A simplified metamodel evolution example

2.2 Metamodel/Model Co-evolution: A Motivating Example

While some metamodels, such as UML, are standardized and changed rarely, metamodels for Domain-Specific Modeling Languages (DSMLs), representing concepts within a certain domain, are frequently subject to change [13].

As most of the current metamodeling frameworks are strict in the sense that only fully conformant models can be used, metamodel evolution requires to co-evolve already existing models, which may no longer conform to the new metamodel version. In such cases, model migration scripts have to be provided in current tools [10] to re-establish the conformance between models and their metamodels. However, finding the best migration scripts to co-evolve models is left to the user of such tools or default migration scripts are provided. The exploration of the actual co-evolution space is considered as an open challenge.

Figure 2 shows an example of a simplified metamodel evolution, based on the simple state machine language. The metamodel evolution comprises three steps: extract sub-classes for *State* class resulting in *InitialState*, *SimpleState*, and *FinalState*, make class *State* abstract, and refine the cardinalities of the predecessor/successor references for the subclasses. This results in the fact that, besides other constraints violations, the constraint shown previously is violated when considering the initial model shown in Fig. 1a and its conformance to the new metamodel version in Fig. 2b.

To re-establish conformance for the given example, assume for now that only two operations on models are used in this context. Non-conforming objects may either be retyped (reclassified as instances of the concrete classes) or deleted. Thus, the potential solution space for retyping or deleting non-conforming elements contains $(c + 1)^O$ solutions (with c = number of candidate classes + 1 for deletion, o = number of non-conforming objects). This means, in our given example, we would end up with 64 possible co-evolutions while one (probably the preferred one) of these is shown in Fig. 1b. This one seems the preferred one due to the following reasons: (*i*) number of changes introduced, (*ii*) amount of information loss, and (*iii*) number of violated conformance constraints. In fact, designers may prefer solutions that introduce the minimum number of changes to the initial model while maximizing the conformance with the target meta-model. When applying changes to the initial model, some model elements could be deleted leading to a better conformance with the new metamodel version but it will reduce the design consistency with the initial model. Thus, these three preferences of the designers are conflicting.

To this end, we consider the metamodel/model co-evolution problem as a multi-objective one which corresponds to finding the best sequence of edit operations. This provides a balance between the consistency of the new model with the previous version of the model as well as with the new metamodel version.

3   Model Co-evolution: A Multi-objective Problem

We describe in this section our proposal and, in particular, how we can formulate the model co-evolution as a multi-objective optimization problem.

3.1   Overview

The goal of our approach is to generate a new version of an existing model, which conforms to a new version of its metamodel. We view this derivation as a search in the space of all possible sequences of edit operations on the initial model. The search is guided by three objectives, which aims at minimizing (i) the number of non-conformities with the new version of the metamodel, (ii) the number of the changes to the initial model, and (iii) the consistency between the initial model and the revised one.

In other words, the revised model has to be similar, as much as possible, to the initial model while conforming to the new metamodel version. Therefore, we implemented our idea in the form of a multi-objective optimization algorithm that derives an optimal sequence of edit operations finding the best trade-off between the three objectives. More concretely, our algorithm takes as input the revised version of the metamodel, the initial model to update and a list of possible edit operations that can be applied to this model. It generates as output a sequence of edit operations that should be applied to the initial model to migrate it to the new metamodel version. The space of all possible sequences of operations can be large, especially when dealing with large models. An exhaustive search method cannot be applied within a reasonable timeframe. To cope with the size of the search space, we use a heuristic search with a multi-objective evolutionary algorithm, namely NSGA-II [5].

3.2   Adapting NSGA-II for Model Co-evolution

Multi-objective Optimization and NSGA-II. To better understand our contribution, we present some definitions related to multi-objective optimization.

Definition 1 (MOP). A multi-objective optimization problem (MOP) consists in minimizing or maximizing an objective function vector $f(x) = [f_1(x), f_2(x),$

$..., f_M(x)]$ of M objectives under some constraints. The set of feasible solutions, i.e., those that satisfy the problem constraints, defines the search space Ω. The resolution of a MOP consists in approximating the whole Pareto front.

Definition 2 (Pareto optimality). In the case of a minimization problem, a solution $x^* \in \Omega$ is Pareto optimal if $\forall x \in \Omega$ and $\forall m \in I = \{1, ..., M\}$ either $f_m(x) = f_m(x^*)$ or there is at least one $m \in I$ such that $f_m(x) > f_m(x^*)$. In other words, x^* is Pareto optimal if no feasible solution exists, which would improve some objective without causing a simultaneous worsening in at least another one.

Definition 3 (Pareto dominance). A solution u is said to dominate another solution v (denoted by $f(u) \preceq f(v)$) if and only if f(u) is partially less than f(v), i.e., $\forall m \in \{1, ...M\}$ we have $f_m(u) \leq f_m(v)$ and $\exists m \in \{1, ..., M\}$ where $f_m(u) < f_m(v)$.

Definition 4 (Pareto optimal set). For a MOP f(x), the Pareto optimal set is $P^* = \{x \in \Omega | \neg \exists x' \in \Omega, f(x') \preceq f(x)\}$.

Definition 5 (Pareto optimal front). For a given MOP f(x) and its Pareto optimal set P^* the Pareto front is $PF^* = \{f(x), x \in P^*\}$.

NSGA-II [5] is one of the most-used multi-objective evolutionary algorithms (EAs) in tackling real-world problems. It begins by generating an offspring population from a parent one by means of variation operators (crossover and mutation) such that both populations have the same size. After that, it ranks the merged population (parents and children) into several non-dominance layers, called fronts, as depicted by Fig. 3. Non-dominated solutions are assigned a rank of 1 and constitute the first layer (Pareto front). After removing solutions of the first layer, the non-dominated solutions form the second layer and so on and so forth until no non-dominated solutions remain. After assigning solutions to fronts, each solution is assigned a diversity score, called crowding distance [5], inside each front. This distance defines a partial ranking inside the front which aims, later, at favoring diverse solutions in terms of objective values. A solution is then characterized by its front and its crowding distance inside the front.

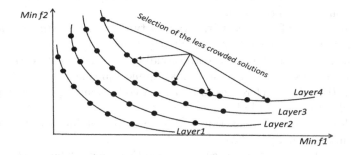

Fig. 3. NSGA-II selection mechanism for a two-objective problem.

To finish an iteration of the evolution, NSGA-II performs the environmental selection to form the parent population for the next generation by picking half of the solutions. The solutions are included iteratively from the Pareto front to the lowest layers. If half of the population is reached inside a front than the crowding distance is used to discriminate between the solutions. Figure 3 shows an example of the selection process for two objectives. The solutions of the three first layers are included but not all those of the 4th one. Some solutions of the 4th layer are selected based on their crowding distance values. In this way, most crowded solutions are the least likely to be selected; thereby emphasizing population diversification. To sum up, the Pareto ranking encourages convergence towards the near-optimal solution while the crowding ranking emphasizes diversity.

Problem Formulation. The model co-evolution problem involves searching for the best sequence of edit operations to apply among the set of possible ones. A good solution s is a sequence of edit operations to apply to an initial model with the objectives of minimizing the number of non-conformities $f_1(s) = nvc(s)$ with the new metamodel version, the number of changes $f_2(s) = nbOp(s)$ applied to the initial model, and the inconsistency $f_3(s) = dis(s)$ between the initial and the evolved models such as the loss of information.

The first fitness function $nvc(s)$ counts the number of violated constraints w.r.t. the evolved metamodel after applying a sequence s of edit operations. We consider three types of constraints, as described in [17]: related to model objects, i.e., model element (denoted by O.*), related to objects' values (V.*), and related to objects' links (L.*). We use in our experiments the implementation of these constraints inspired by Schoenboeck et al. [22] with slight adaptations. We use the following constraints:

O.1 For an object type, a corresponding class must exist (name equivalence).

O.2 Corresponding class must not be abstract.

V.3 For all values of an object, a corresponding attribute in the corresponding class (or in its superclasses) must exist (name equivalence).

V.4 For all (inherited) attributes in a class, a corresponding object must fulfil minimal cardinality of values.

V.5 For all (inherited) attributes in a class, a corresponding object must fulfil maximum cardinality of values.

V.6 For all values of an object, the value's type must conform to the corresponding attribute's type (Integer, String, Boolean).

L.7 For all links of an object, a corresponding reference in its corresponding class (or in its superclasses) must exist (name equivalence).

L.8 For all (inherited) references in a class, a corresponding object must fulfil minimal cardinality of links.

L.9 For all (inherited) references in a class, a corresponding object must fulfil maximum cardinality of links.

L.10 For all links of an object, the target object's type must be the class defined by the reference (or its subclasses).

For the second fitness function, which aims at minimizing the changes to the initial models, we simply count the number of edit operations $nbOp(s)$ of a solution s (size of s). The third fitness function $dis(s)$ measures the difference between the model elements in the initial and revised model. As the type of a model element may change because of a change in the metamodel, we cannot rely on elements' types. Alternatively, we use the identifiers to assess whether information was added or deleted when editing a model. Let Id_i and Id_r be the sets of identifiers present respectively in the initial (i) and revised (r) models. The inconsistency between the models is measured as the complement of the similarity measure $sim(s)$ which is the proportion of common elements in the two models. Formally:

$$dis(s) = 1 - sim(s) \text{ and } sim(s) = \frac{|Id_i \cap Id_r|}{Max(|Id_i|, |Id_r|)}$$

NSGA-II Application. To adapt NSGA-II to our problem, we define (i) how to represent a co-evolution solution, (ii) how to derive new solutions from existing ones, and (iii) how to evaluate a solution.

Solution Representation. To represent a candidate solution (individual), we use a vector containing all the edit operations to apply to the initial model. Each element in the vector represents a single operation (with links to the model elements to which it is applied) and the order of operations in this vector represents the sequence in which the operations are applied. Consequently, vectors representing different solutions may have different sizes, i.e., number of operations. Table 1 shows the possible edit operations that can be applied to model elements. These operations are inspired by the catalog of operators for the metamodel/-model co-evolution in [9].

Table 1. Model edit operations

Operations	Description
Create/delete	Add/remove an element in the initial model.
Retype	Replace an element by another equivalent element having a different type.
Merge	Merge several model elements of the same type into a single element.
Split	Split a model element into several elements of the same type.
Move	Move an attribute from a model element to another

Figure 4 depicts an example of a solution that can be applied to revise the initial model of Fig. 1. The solution consists of 10 different edit operations to apply:

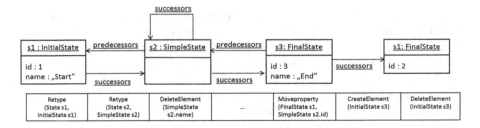

Fig. 4. Example of a solution representation

Retype(State s1, InitialState s1), Retype(State s2, SimpleState s2), Dele-teElement(SimpleState s2.name), Retype(State s3, FinalState s3), CreateElement(SimpleState s2, SimpleState s2, successors), CreateElement(FinalState s1), MoveElement(FinalState s1, SimpleState s2.id), CreateElement(FinalState s3, FinalState s1, successors), CreateElement(InitialState s3), DeleteElement(InitialState s3). The proposed algorithm first generates a population of random operation sequences (solution candidates), which are used in the subsequent iterations to produce new solutions.

Solution derivation. In a search algorithm, the variation operators play a key role of moving within the search space with the aim of driving the search towards better solutions. In each iteration, we select *population_size/2* individuals from the population pop_i to form population pop_{i+1}. These (*population_size/2*) selected individuals will produce other (*population_size/2*) new individuals using a crossover and mutation operators. To select parents for reproduction, we used the principle of the roulette wheel [5]. According to this principle, the probability to select an individual for crossover and mutation is directly proportional to its relative fitness in the population. We use a one-point crossover operator. For our problem, this operator split each parent operation sequence $S1$ (resp. $S2$) into two subsequences $\{S1_1, S1_2\}$ (resp. $\{S2_1, S2_2\}$) according to a cut position k. Then, it combines the subsequences to create two sibling solutions $\{S1_1, S2_2\}$ and $\{S2_1, S1_2\}$. Our crossover operator could create a child sequence that contains conflict operations. In this case, it will be penalized by the component *nvc* of the fitness function. The mutation operator consists in randomly selecting one or two operations in a solution vector and modifying them. Two modifications are used: (*i*) swapping the two selected operations in the sequence or (*ii*) replacing an operation by a randomly created one. When applying both change operators, we are using a repair operator to detect and fix possible redundancies between the model elements. When a redundancy is detected, we remove one of redundant model elements from the solution (vector).

Solution Evaluation. As mentioned in the problem formulation, a solution is evaluated according to three objectives. Thus, for each solution s, we calculate $nvc(s)$, $nbOp(s)$, and $dis(s)$. These values are used later to establish the dominance relation between solutions. Based on the example of the solution of Fig. 4, the value of the fitness functions are the following: $f_1(S) = 1$ (a final state should not have a successor), $f_2(S) = 10$ (10 operations) and $f_3(S) = 1 - (9/Max(15, 13))$ since the intersection between the ids of the initial model of Fig. 1 (State.s1, s1.id, s1.name, s1.successors, State.s2, s2.id, s2.name, s2.successors, s2.predecessors, State.s3, s3.id, s3.name, s3.predecessors) and the ids of the revised one of Fig. 4 (InitialState.s1, **s1.id**, **s1.name**, **s1.successors**, InitialState.s2, **s2.successors**, **s2.predecessors**, FinalState.s3, **s3.id**, **s3.name**, **s3.predecessors**, s3.successors, FinalState s1, **s2.id**) is 9 (bold elements in the revised model), the size of the initial model of Fig. 1 is 13 and the size of the revised one of Fig. 4 is 15.

4   Validation

In order to validate our metamodel/model co-evolution approach, we conducted a set of experiments[1] based on a well-known evolution case of UML Metamodel for State Machine from v1.4 to v2.0 [1].

4.1   Research Questions

The validation study was conducted to quantitatively and qualitatively assess the completeness and correctness of our co-evolution approach when applied to realistic settings and to compare its performance with an existing deterministic approach [26]. More specifically, we aimed at answering the following research questions:

- **RQ1: Sanity check:** *To what extent the obtained results are attributable to our search strategy and to the large number of solutions that we explore?*
- **RQ2: Correctness:** *To what extent can the proposed multi-objective approach co-evolve models to make them comply with a new metamodel version (in terms of correctness and completeness of proposed edit operations)?*
- **RQ3:** *How does the multi-objective metamodel/model co-evolution approach perform compared to a mono-objective one?* We use a genetic algorithm with a fitness function that represents the average of the normalized scores of the three objectives.
- **RQ4:** *How does our approach perform compared to an existing co-evolution approach* [26] *not based on metaheuristic search?*

4.2   Experimental Setting

Studied Metamodels and Models. To answer the four research questions, we considered the evolution of UML State Machine Metamodel from version 1.4 to 2.0 [1]. This is a very interesting case since it represents a real metamodel evolution and was studied in other contributions [26]. Therefore, the two versions

---

[1] The data of the experiments can be found in https://sites.google.com/site/datapaperswaelkessentini/data.

were manually analyzed to determine the actually applied changes. We also used
10 models from version 1.4 and evolved them manually to version 2.0 to create
new models from the initial ones using the edit operations.

As described in Table 2, the manually defined sequences for the selected models are used as baseline sequences for the calculation of precision and recall scores. Table 2 shows for each model, the number of expected edit operations and the size in terms of elements.

Table 2. The models studied

Models	SM1	SM2	SM3	SM4	SM5	SM6	SM7	SM8	SM9	SM10
Number of expected edit operations	8	11	12	11	12	9	20	14	10	21
Number of model elements	34	38	72	64	46	37	82	56	47	94

Evaluation Metrics. To compare our approach with the other alternatives, we use precision and recall measures. For an operation sequence corresponding to a given solution, precision indicates the proportion of correct edit operations (w.r.t. the baseline sequence) in a solution. Recall is the proportion of correctly identified edit operations among the set of all expected operations. Both values range from 0 to 1, with higher values indicating good solutions. The baseline sequences do not represent unique evolution solutions for the used models. Indeed, more than one alternative can be possible to evolve a given model. Thus, in addition to automatic precision (AC-PR) and recall (AC-RE), we calculated a manual correctness (MC). To this end, we manually checked the solutions to determine the accuracy of their operations.

Based on the example of the solution of Fig. 4 the value of the results are the following: AC-PR=0.3 (the set of correct edit operations which is 3, divided by the set of all actually applied operations which is 10), AC-RE=1 (the set of correct edit operations which is 3, divided by the set of all expected operations which is 3), MC=0.37 (when we check the solution operation by operation, we found that the sequence of the 2 operations: CreateElement(InitialState s3), DeleteElement(InitialState s3) can be considered correct since the InitialState s3 was created and then deleted). In addition to the three above-mentioned metrics, we report the number of operations (NO) per solution and the computation time (CT). Finally, it is worth noting that the mono-objective GA and the deterministic [26] approaches produce a unique co-evolution solution, while NSGA-II generates a set of non-dominated solutions (Pareto front). In order to have meaningful comparisons, we select the best solution for NSGA-II using a knee point strategy [5].

Statistical Tests. Since the used metaheuristic algorithms (NSGA-II and GA) are stochastic by nature, different executions may produce different results for the same model with the same execution parameters. For this reason, our experimental study is performed based on 30 independent simulation runs and the obtained results by the alternative approaches are compared using the Wilcoxon rank sum test [2] with a 95 % confidence level ($\alpha = 5\,\%$).

4.3   Results

Results for RQ1. We do not dwell long in answering the first research question (RQ1) that involves comparing our approach based on NSGA-II with random search. Figures 5 and 6 confirm that using NSGA-II (as well as the GA and the deterministic algorithm) produce results by far better (and statistically significant) than just randomly exploring a comparable number of solutions. NSGA-II has precisions (AC-PR and MC) and recall (AC-RE) more than twice higher than the ones of random search as shown in Fig. 5 ($\sim 89\,\%$ vs $\sim 43\,\%$). Moreover, these results were obtained with smaller operation sequences in the 10 models (Fig. 6) comparing to random search. The slight difference in execution time in favor of random search (Fig. 7), due to the crossover and mutation operators, is largely compensated by quality of the obtained results.

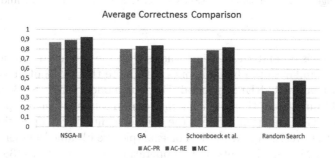

Fig. 5. Average correctness results of NSGA-II, GA, Schoenboeck et al. and Random Search. (Color figure online)

To formally answer **RQ1**, we state that *there is an empirical evidence that the quality of the co-evolution results obtained are due to our multi-objective approach and not to the number of explored solutions.*

Results for RQ2. We evaluated the averages of NO, AC-PR, AC-RE and MC scores for non-dominated co-evolution solutions proposed by NSGA-II. Figure 6 shows that our NSGA-II adaptation was successful in generating good co-evolution solutions that minimize the number of operations. The number of suggested operations seems very reasonable if we consider the high number of changes applied at the metamodel of State Machine during the evolution from v1.4 to v2.0. In fact, 23 edit operations were recommended for the largest model (SM10) with an average of 16 operations for the remaining models.

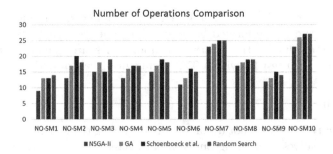

Fig. 6. Average number of suggested operations of NSGA-II, GA, Schoenboeck et al. and Random Search. (Color figure online)

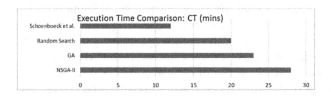

Fig. 7. Average execution time of NSGA-II, GA, Schoenboeck et al. and Random Search.

For the precision and recall, Fig. 8 shows that the produced solutions using NSGA-II are similar to the baseline ones with more than 85 % of precision and recall (AC-PR and AC-RE) in general. For four models (SM1, SM3, SM5, and SM8), we obtained more than 90 % for the recall. From another perspective, we did not observe a correlation between the size or the number of operations of the models and the precision and recall. For example, we obtained higher precision and recall for SM7 (82 elements and 20 operations) than for SM2 (38 elements and 11 operations). This means that the correctness of the results is not degraded as the size of the models or the size of necessary modifications increase. For the manual correctness, the results are even better. Except for SM2, SM3 and SM9

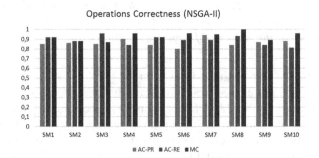

Fig. 8. Correctness results of NSGA-II. (Color figure online)

all the MCs are higher than 90 % with a perfect score for SM8. Here again, the scalability in terms of correctness is valid for MC. Indeed MC increases from 88 % (SM2) to 95 % (SM10) while the size of the model (resp. operation sequence) goes from 38 to 94 (resp. 11 to 21).

To formally answer **RQ2**, we state that *the multi-objective co-evolution approach allows to migrate models with higher precision and recall and with a limited number of edit operations. This achieved without any explicit knowledge on the specific changes that occurred on the metamodel.*

Results for RQ3 and RQ4. For the recall and the automatic and manual precisions, Fig. 5 shows that the solutions of NSGA-II have the highest scores compared to the other algorithms. The same observation holds for the manual precision, for which NSGA-II is the only algorithm that has an average score higher than 91 %. These differences in favor of NSGA-II are all statistically significant according to the Wilcoxon tests. Additionally, Fig. 6 shows that, for all the models, NSGA-II produces higher scores with smaller operation sequences compared to those of the two contender algorithms.

Regarding the execution time (Fig. 7), considering that the model evolution happens rarely (not a daily activity), the time magnitude (minutes) for all the algorithms is reasonable. Our NSGA-II approach takes more time than [26] (28 vs 12 min). We believe that this difference is acceptable knowing that for [26], we do not count the time of metamodel comparison and rules writing. The slight difference with the mono-objective algorithm is also acceptable if we consider the improvement in accuracy.

To formally answer **RQ3** and **RQ4**, we state that *there is an empirical evidence that the multi-objective algorithm outperforms the mono-objective and deterministic algorithms for AC-PR, AC-RE and MC. This must be mitigated by the fact that these good results come at the cost of more execution time.*

4.4 Threats to Validity

We used the Wilcoxon rank sum to test if significant differences exist between the scores of the co-evolution algorithms. This test makes no assumption on the data distribution, especially for small samples. We are then confident that our observations are valid. Another possible threat is related to the parameter tuning of our multi-objective algorithm. Further experiments are required to evaluate the impact of the parameters setting on the quality of the solutions.

To ensure that the results are attributable to our multi-objective algorithm and not to chance, we performed 30 independent simulation runs for each model. This makes it unlikely that the observed differences are due to the probabilistic decisions of the algorithms. Another threat is related to our choice of taking the average of the three objective functions in the mono-objective algorithms. Other forms of combination, e.g., weighted average, may give different results.

With respect to generalizability of our findings, we performed our experiments on a single evolution scenario (state machine metamodel from v1.4 to v2.0).

Future replications of this study are necessary to confirm these findings, in particular, with industrial settings. In addition, the comparison of the performance of NSGA-II to the state of the art is limited to the approach in [26]. The decision was made as the concerned tool was easily accessible to us.

5   Related Work

Co-evolution has been subject for research since several decades in the database community [18], and especially, the introduction of object-oriented database systems [3] gave rise to the investigation of this topic. However, metamodel/model co-evolution introduces several additional challenges mostly based on the rich modeling constructs for defining metamodels, and consequently, it has to be dealt with the specific *conformsTo* relationship between models and metamodels. Thus, in the last decade, several approaches emerged which aim to tackle metamodel/model co-evolution from different angles using different techniques (cf. e.g., [13,20,21] for an overview).

In one of the early works [23], the co-evolution of models is tackled by designing co-evolution transformations based on metamodel change types. In [4,7], the authors compute differences between two metamodel versions which are then input to adapt models automatically. This is achieved by transforming the differences into a migration transformation with a so-called higher-order transformation (HOT). Going one step further concerning the nature of change types is presented in [24], where ideas from object-oriented refactoring and grammar adaptation are presented to provide the basis for metamodel/model co-evolution. In [8], a conservative copying algorithm is presented: for each initial model element for which no transformation rule is found, a default copy transformation rule is applied. This algorithm has been developed in a model migration framework Epsilon Flock [19] and in the framework described in [15]. In order to avoid copy rules at all, co-evolution approaches which base their solution on in-place transformations (i.e., transformations which are updating an input model to produce the output model) have been proposed [10,12–14,26]. In such approaches, the co-evolution rules are specified as in-place transformation rules by using a kind of unified metamodel representing both metamodel versions.

Although the main goal of all discussed approaches is similar to ours, there are several major differences. We tackle co-evolution of models without the need of computing differences on the metamodel level. Instead, we reason on the consistency of the models by following a similar research line as presented in the visionary paper by Demuth et al. [6]. In particular, we search for transformation executions on the model level, which fulfil multiple goals expressed as our fitness functions. By this, the critical and challenging task of finding proper co-evolution rules of the model level is automated which allows exploring a much larger space of possible solutions which is possible when manually developing co-evolution transformations. To sum up, none of the existing approaches allows the exploration of different possible co-evolution strategies. On the contrary, only one specific strategy is either automatically derived or manually developed from the calculated set of metamodel changes.

The only work we are aware of discussing metamodel/model co-evolution using some search-based techniques is [25]. In this paper, the authors discuss the idea of using search-based algorithms to reason about possible model changes, but in contrast to our approach, they rely again on metamodel differences which have to be computed (probably using a search-based approach) before the co-evolution of models can be performed. We use a different approach by using an explicit definition and formalization of the *conformsTo* relationship which can be used as basis to formulate fitness functions for reasoning about the quality of a certain model co-evolution strategy. To the best of our knowledge, this approach is unique compared to previous approaches and outperforms logic-based approaches for repairing models [22]. Furthermore, we are not dependent on the quality of metamodel change detection algorithms. By this, we allow the automatic exploration of the model co-evolution space given a certain metamodel evolution and we developed formal quality characteristics to assess the quality of model co-evolutions.

6   Conclusion

This paper proposes a multi-objective approach for the co-evolution of models by finding the best operation sequence that generates, from the initial model, a new model version conforming as much as possible to the evolved metamodel. Therefore, a generated revised model should minimize the number of inconsistencies (with the new metamodel), the number of changes made to the initial model and the dissimilarity with the initial model. The experiment results indicate clearly that the best generated models have a precision and recall of more than 86 % and a manual precision of more than 92 %.

Although our approach has been evaluated with a real-world scenario with a reasonable number of applied operations and models, we are working now on larger metamodels and models with larger lists of operations to apply. This is necessary to investigate more deeply the applicability of the approach in practice, but also to study the performance of our approach when dealing with very large models. Moreover, we will further evaluate the performance of NSGA-II with several other multi-objective algorithms as well as compare our approximate approach with exact approaches [16]. More generally, we plan to extend this work by evolving model transformation rules when the metamodels were revised.

References

1. Object Management Group, Unified Modeling Language Specification v1.4 and v2.0. http://www.omg.org
2. Arcuri, A., Briand, L.: A practical guide for using statistical tests to assess randomized algorithms in software engineering. In: Proceedings of ICSE (2011)
3. Banerjee, J., Kim, W., Kim, H.J., Korth, H.F.: Semantics and implementation of schema evolution in object-oriented databases. In: Proceedings of SIGMOD (1987)
4. Cicchetti, A., Ruscio, D.D., Eramo, R., Pierantonio, A.: Automating co-evolution in model-driven engineering. In: Proceedings of EDOC (2008)

5. Deb, K., Agrawal, S., Pratap, A., Meyarivan, T.: A fast elitist non-dominated sorting genetic algorithm for multi-objective optimization: NSGA-II. In: Deb, K., Rudolph, G., Lutton, E., Merelo, J.J., Schoenauer, M., Schwefel, H.-P., Yao, X. (eds.) PPSN 2000. LNCS, vol. 1917, pp. 849–858. Springer, Heidelberg (2000)
6. Demuth, A., Lopez-Herrejon, R.E., Egyed, A.: Co-evolution of metamodels and models through consistent change propagation. In: Proceedings of ME Workshop (2013)
7. Garcés, K., Jouault, F., Cointe, P., Bézivin, J.: Managing model adaptation by precise detection of metamodel changes. In: Paige, R.F., Hartman, A., Rensink, A. (eds.) ECMDA-FA 2009. LNCS, vol. 5562, pp. 34–49. Springer, Heidelberg (2009)
8. Gruschko, B.: Towards synchronizing models with evolving metamodels. In: Proceedings of MoDSE Workshop (2007)
9. Herrmannsdoerfer, M., Vermolen, S.D., Wachsmuth, G.: An extensive catalog of operators for the coupled evolution of metamodels and models. In: Malloy, B., Staab, S., Brand, M. (eds.) SLE 2010. LNCS, vol. 6563, pp. 163–182. Springer, Heidelberg (2011)
10. Herrmannsdoerfer, M.: COPE – a workbench for the coupled evolution of metamodels and models. In: Malloy, B., Staab, S., Brand, M. (eds.) SLE 2010. LNCS, vol. 6563, pp. 286–295. Springer, Heidelberg (2011)
11. Iovino, L., Pierantonio, A., Malavolta, I.: On the impact significance of metamodel evolution in MDE. J. Object Technol. **11**(3), 1–33 (2012)
12. Mantz, F., Lamo, Y., Taentzer, G.: Co-transformation of type and instance graphs supporting merging of types with retyping. ECEASST **61**, 1–24 (2013)
13. Meyers, B., Vangheluwe, H.: A framework for evolution of modelling languages. Sci. Comput. Program. **76**(12), 1223–1246 (2011)
14. Meyers, B., Wimmer, M., Cicchetti, A., Sprinkle, J.: A generic in-place transformation-based approach to structured model co-evolution. In: Proceedings of MPM Workshop (2010)
15. Narayanan, A., Levendovszky, T., Balasubramanian, D., Karsai, G.: Automatic domain model migration to manage metamodel evolution. In: Schürr, A., Selic, B. (eds.) MODELS 2009. LNCS, vol. 5795, pp. 706–711. Springer, Heidelberg (2009)
16. Olaechea, R., Rayside, D., Guo, J., Czarnecki, K.: Comparison of exact and approximate multi-objective optimization for software product lines. In: Proceedings of SPLC (2014)
17. Richters, M.: A precise approach to validating UML models and OCL constraints. Technical report (2001)
18. Roddick, J.F.: Schema evolution in database systems: an annotated bibliography. SIGMOD Rec. **21**(4), 35–40 (1992)
19. Rose, L.M., Kolovos, D.S., Paige, R.F., Polack, F.A.C.: Model migration with epsilon flock. In: Tratt, L., Gogolla, M. (eds.) ICMT 2010. LNCS, vol. 6142, pp. 184–198. Springer, Heidelberg (2010)
20. Rose, L.M., Paige, R.F., Kolovos, D.S., Polack, F.A.C.: An analysis of approaches to model migration. In: Proceedings of MoDSE-MCCM Workshop (2009)
21. Rose, L., Herrmannsdoerfer, M., Mazanek, S., Van Gorp, P., Buchwald, S., Horn, T., Kalnina, E., Koch, A., Lano, K., Schätz, B., Wimmer, M.: Graph and model transformation tools for model migration. SoSyM **13**(1), 323–359 (2014)
22. Schoenboeck, J., Kusel, A., Etzlstorfer, J., Kapsammer, E., Schwinger, W., Wimmer, M., Wischenbart, M.: CARE: a constraint-based approach for re-establishing conformance-relationships. In: Proceedings of APCCM (2014)
23. Sprinkle, J., Karsai, G.: A domain-specific visual language for domain model evolution. J. Vis. Lang. Comput. **15**(3–4), 291–307 (2004)

24. Wachsmuth, G.: Metamodel adaptation and model co-adaptation. In: Ernst, E. (ed.) ECOOP 2007. LNCS, vol. 4609, pp. 600–624. Springer, Heidelberg (2007)
25. Williams, J.R., Paige, R.F., Polack, F.A.C.: Searching for model migration strategies. In: Proceedings of ME Workshop (2012)
26. Wimmer, M., Kusel, A., Schoenboeck, J., Retschitzegger, W., Schwinger, W.: On using inplace transformations for model co-evolution. In: Proceedings of MtATL Workshop (2010)

Enabling OCL and fUML Integration by Transformation

Massimo Tisi[1], Frédéric Jouault[2(✉)], Zied Saidi[1], and Jérome Delatour[2]

[1] AtlanMod team (Inria, Mines Nantes, LINA), Nantes, France
{massimo.tisi,zied.saidi}@mines-nantes.fr
[2] TRAME team (ESEO), Angers, France
{frederic.jouault,jerome.delatour}@eseo.fr

Abstract. Until the recent adoption of fUML, UML has lacked standard execution semantics. However, parts of UML models have always been executable: OCL expressions. They may notably be used to express contracts (i.e., invariants, pre- and post-conditions), to define side-effect free operations, and to specify how to compute derived features. Nonetheless, although fUML is partly inspired by OCL (notably for primitive behaviors), its specification does not consider interoperability with OCL expressions. Moreover, the semantics of OCL is specified independently of (f)UML, and their implementations are separate execution engines, hampering all global activities (e.g., analysis, optimization, debugging). This paper explores a possible integration approach of OCL and fUML: by transforming (i.e., compiling) OCL expressions into fUML activities we obtain a unified executable model. With this approach, operations specified in OCL can be called, and getters can be generated for derived features. Preconditions (resp. postconditions) can be automatically executed before (resp. after) the execution of their contextual operations. A precise semantics for invariant evaluation can be specified in fUML. Thanks to this work, OCL may also be seen as a functional counterpart to Alf.

1 Introduction

Foundational UML (fUML) [1] is the ongoing effort by the Object Management Group (OMG) for providing standard execution semantics to UML models. Executable models may be beneficial in Model-Driven Engineering (MDE) when a higher degree of precision is required at the modeling level (e.g., for critical systems), and for allowing users to simulate and analyze the system behavior before the actual implementation. fUML acts as the cornerstone of this vision, by providing, in its current version, standard execution semantics for a core subset of UML Activity Diagram and Class Diagram. Extensions are in progress for Statechart Diagram (Precise Semantics of UML State Machines, PSSM [2]) and Composite Structure Diagram (Precise Semantics of UML Composite Structures PSCS [3]). The Action Language For Foundational UML (Alf) [4] is a textual language that executes by translation towards fUML activities, and that is designed as a convenient alternative to complex diagrams.

© Springer International Publishing Switzerland 2016
A. Wąsowski and H. Lönn (Eds.): ECMFA 2016, LNCS 9764, pp. 156–172, 2016.
DOI: 10.1007/978-3-319-42061-5_10

Before the introduction of fUML, UML users could provide precise executable semantics only to a limited part of their models. Common practice was (and still is) to express executable contracts, side-effect free operations and computation of derived features by using the Object Constraint Language (OCL) [5], a purely functional language standardized by OMG. Moving to executable modeling by fUML/Alf does not lower the need for contracts, functional operations and derived features. However fUML does not include a built-in support for these tasks, that could constitute a viable alternative to OCL.

The specifications of OCL and fUML do not directly reference each other, and the interaction between the two languages passes through standard UML mechanisms: e.g., OCL expressions can call UML operations implemented in fUML activities and fUML activities can use UML value specifications computed by OCL expressions. Also the execution environment of the two languages is generally separated: OCL evaluators and fUML interpreters are separated tools, interacting at runtime on the same modeling platform (e.g., Java and the Eclipse Modeling Framework). This makes global optimization extremely difficult and hampers the possibilities of global analysis and simulation promised by the executable modeling approach.

In this paper we propose a mechanism for compile-time integration of OCL and fUML. We use a translational approach by providing a compiler able to transform a model including both OCL expressions and fUML activities into a pure fUML model. The resulting model is semantically equivalent to the original one, meaning that the OCL semantics for contracts, derived features, operation bodies, etc. has been implemented as fUML activities.

The paper contribution is twofold: (1) we provide a translation from OCL expressions to equivalent fUML activities; (2) we use fUML to provide a default semantics for under-specified parts of the OCL standard, e.g. timing of feature derivation. We also validate the feasibility of the approach by developing a proof-of-concept implementation of our mapping in the form of a compiler transformation, publicly available[1].

The paper is structured as follows: Sect. 2 introduces a running example in order to exemplify the problem of integrating OCL and fUML; Sect. 3 provides an intuitive look on our solution by describing its application to the example; Sect. 4 describes the mapping rules between OCL and fUML; Sect. 5 gives implementation details on our proof-of-concept compiler; Sect. 6 analyzes design decisions, limitations and alternative applications of the approach; Sect. 7 discusses related work and Sect. 8 concludes the paper.

2   Interaction Between fUML and OCL by Example

As an example of the joint use of OCL constraints and fUML behavior we adapt the Company example from the OCL specification [5, pp. 7–29]. The class diagram is presented in Fig. 1.

---

[1] https://github.com/atlanmod/OCL2fUML.

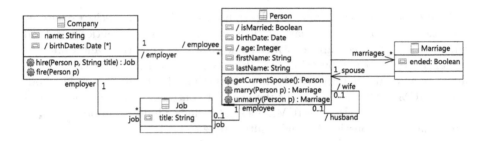

Fig. 1. Excerpt of the Company class diagram (adapted from [5, p. 7])

In this model a `Person` is described by her `firstName`, `lastName` and `birthDate`. The `age` of each `Person` is derived from her `birthDate`. A `Person` may be involved in one or more `Marriages`, but among them at most one is not currently `ended`[2]. To simplify access to marriage information, the `Person` class includes the `isMarried`, `husband` and `wife` derived features, and the `getCurrentSpouse()` operation whose precondition (i.e., the person is currently married) and function body (i.e., get the spouse of the only marriage that is not ended) are shown in Listing 1.1. Since the operation is free from side-effects its body can be expressed in OCL. According to the UML specification a call to `getCurrentSpouse()` returns the evaluation of the body only if the precondition is satisfied, otherwise the behavior is undefined.

Listing 1.1. getCurrentSpouse operation [5, p. 9]

```
context Person :: getCurrentSpouse () : Person
  pre: self.isMarried = true
  body: self.marriages->select( m | m.ended = false ).spouse
```

The operations `marry(p: Person)` and `unmarry(p: Person)` are used to simplify model updates in case of marriage and divorce (avoiding the need to manually perform model element edits). Husbands and wives are adults, as specified by the OCL invariant in Listing 1.2. According to the OCL semantics, any update to the model, e.g., by the `marry` and `unmarry` operations, may trigger the re-verification of this invariant and the re-computation of the above-mentioned derived features. For instance, the evaluation of the invariant to false at the end of the operation execution results in an undefined behavior. The moment in which derived features are re-evaluated is not precisely specified by OCL, but computation will be performed before the subsequent access to the feature.

Listing 1.2. Wives and husbands are adults [5, p. 20]

```
context Person inv:
  (self.wife->notEmpty() implies self.wife.age >= 18) and
  (self.husband->notEmpty() implies self.husband.age >= 18)
```

Each `Person` may have a `Job` in a `Company`, which is identified by a `name` and cannot have less than 50 employees, as imposed by the invariant in Listing 1.3.

---

[2] For space reasons we can not provide here the code of all OCL contracts, derived features and fUML activities mentioned in this section.

Listing 1.3. Companies have at least 50 employees (adapted from [5, p. 20])

```
context Company inv:
  self.employee->size() >= 50
```

Derived features `employer` and `employee` simplify navigation between `Companies` and `Persons`. A derived attribute `birthDates`, computed as shown in Listing 1.4, gathers the birthdates of all `employees`.

Listing 1.4. birthDates derived attribute [5, p. 29]

```
context Company::birthDates : Bag(Date)
  derive: self.employee->collect( person | person.birthDate )
```

Start and end of work contracts are handled by the operations `hire(Person p, String title)` and `fire(Person p)`, both implemented as fUML activities. In particular in Fig. 3 we show the fUML activity diagram for `fire`. In the next section we will describe the fUML semantics by example. Then it will be clear that the `fire` activity selects the `Job` of the given `employee` among all `Jobs` in the current `Company`, and deletes it. Since a call to `fire` may change the list of `employees`, it will generally trigger the re-computation of both invariant and derived feature in Listing 1.3 and 1.4.

Figure 2 gives an overview of the relations between the languages we mentioned so far. The set of UML concepts (or metaclasses) can notably be divided into structural concepts (e.g., `Class`, `Property`, `Operation`, `Interface`), and behavioral ones (e.g., `Activity`, `Action`, `StateMachine`). Associations between structural and behavioral concepts enable jointly modeling both aspects. fUML considers only subsets of these structural and behavioral parts (e.g., excluding `Interface`, and `StateMachine`). Alf and OCL are two textual languages that are defined outside of UML, but that can be integrated in it using `OpaqueBehavior` and `OpaqueExpression`. Additionally, Alf specifies a transformation from its textual syntax to fUML elements, and a reverse transformation from fUML elements to Alf textual syntax. This enables usage of a textual syntax instead of relatively verbose diagrams.

A model of Company uses these languages for a precise executable specification of its semantics. Global analysis on Company could for instance detect that the `fire` activity does not impact the invariant in Listing 1.2. Optimization could avoid checking the invariant in this case. However such cross-language activities are not available in current executable modeling. In the following sections we introduce a translational approach, represented in Fig. 2 as the dashed arrow from OCL to fUML, that addresses this problem and others.

3   Integrating OCL in fUML by Translation

In this paper we propose a compilation strategy and a prototype compiler that takes as input an executable model, written by the joint use of fUML and OCL, and returns an OCL-free fUML model, where the OCL part has been translated into fUML behavior. To give a first view over our objective, this section illustrates the result of the compilation of the Company model from the previous section.

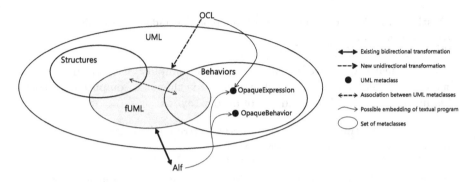

Fig. 2. Overview of relations between UML, fUML, Alf, and OCL

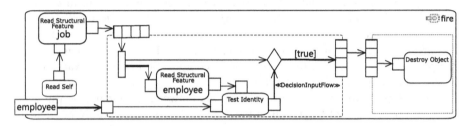

Fig. 3. The `fire` fUML activity

Bodies and pre/postconditions of OCL operations become side-effect free fUML activities. For instance the precondition of the `getCurrentSpouse()` OCL operation becomes the fUML activity in Fig. 4. The structure of an fUML activity is given by object flows that propagate object tokens from inputs to outputs and control-flow edges that force an execution order by passing control tokens. The activity in Fig. 4 makes exclusive use of object flows: the `result` of the activity comes from the comparison by a `TestIdentityAction` of (1) a constant value `true` provided by a `ValueSpecificationAction` and (2) the feature `isMarried` of the current object, obtained by a `ReadStructuralFeatureAction` over the output of a `ReadSelfAction`.

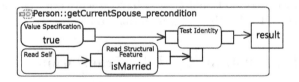

Fig. 4. `getCurrentSpouse` precondition activity (corresponding to Listing 1.1)

The body of `getCurrentSpouse()` becomes the activity in Fig. 5. Here the activity has to iterate through all the `marriages` to find the one that is not ended. This is done in fUML by an `ExpansionRegion` (the dashed rectangle). An `ExpansionRegion` expects a collection as input (represented in the fUML semantics as a sequence of object tokens flowing on the link) and the content of the region is executed once for each element of the collection. The expansion node of the `ExpansionRegion` passes the elements of the input collection one by one through its outgoing object flow. The result of all iterations is gathered by the output node of the `ExpansionRegion`. In Fig. 5 each `marriage m` flows through a `fork` that passes it to (1) a flow that accesses the `ended` attribute and compares it to the constant `false`, and (2) a `DecisionNode` (the diamond) that will let the marriage pass through only if the result of the previous test is `true`. The output node of the expansion region will gather the expected result, i.e. the `marriage` that is not `ended`, and the `spouse` of this `marriage` will be returned to the caller.

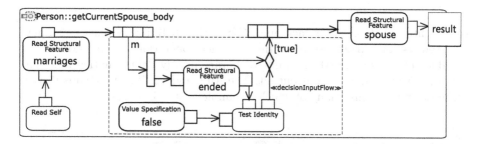

Fig. 5. `getCurrentSpouse` body activity (corresponding to the operation body in Listing 1.1)

The translation of the OCL expressions for precondition and body does not complete the translation of the `getCurrentSpouse()` operation to fUML. We still need to represent the implicit precondition semantics: the body is evaluated only if the precondition is satisfied, otherwise the behavior is undefined. We propose to describe this semantics in fUML by providing a wrapper for the operation, as shown in Fig. 6. The wrapper method starts by launching the evaluation of the precondition using a `CallOperationAction`. Depending on the result of the precondition, one of two possible `StructuredActivityNodes` (shown as dashed rectangles sub-activities) is executed: (1) if the precondition is true, the activity representing the operation body is called and its result returned, (2) if the condition is false, the missed precondition is reported (e.g., using a logger or the standard output through the `WriteLine` operation of the standard fUML library), and no result token is returned. An alternative (undefined) behavior would be to terminate the execution. However, fUML does not support exceptions, and does not provide means to terminate the execution engine. Note that this wrapping approach can also be used for post-conditions.

The translation of the invariants in Listing 1.2 (i.e., spouses are adults) and 1.3 (i.e., companies are big) are respectively shown in Figs. 7 and 8. The structure

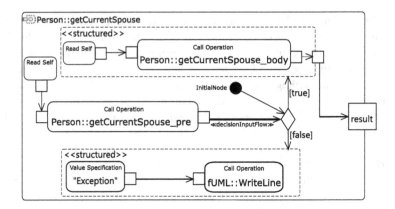

Fig. 6. getCurrentSpouse main activity (corresponding to Listing 1.1)

is straightforward, since for each operation of the OCL library (e.g., `notEmpty`, `implies`, `>=`, `and`, `size`) we reuse the equivalent operation in the fUML or Alf standard libraries. The fUML standard library mostly defines native functions for primitive types, and input-output. The Alf standard library extends it with higher-level functions, many of which are implemented in fUML.

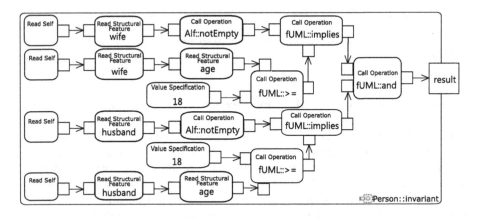

Fig. 7. Invariant on Person (corresponding to Listing 1.2)

Figure 9 is the result of the compilation of the derived feature in Listing 1.4 (`birthDates`). In this case we produce a getter operation for the derived feature, that performs the attribute (re-)computation. The OCL `collect` is compiled as an `ExpansionRegion` that iterates on `employees` and gathers their `birthDates`. As fUML does not support derived features, we propose to turn them into getters without backing fields. This also requires replacing every action accessing a derived property into a call to the corresponding getter. The approach works

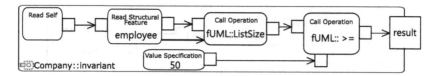

Fig. 8. Invariant on Company (corresponding to Listing 1.3)

in fUML because property values are not observable (while it could fail in UML where `ChangeEvents` can be leveraged to observe property values).

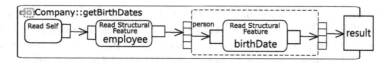

Fig. 9. getBirthDates activity (corresponding to Listing 1.4)

We have now considered the translations of all OCL examples from the previous section. Their interaction with regular fUML activities like `fire(p : Person)` from Fig. 3 can now be explained. Because it has side-effects, `fire(p : Person)` must be wrapped in a way similar to what was done for `getCurrentSpouse()`. This takes care of checking the invariant from Listing 1.3 after each change to the list of employees. The getter created from the `birthDates` derived feature does not need a special treatment, since it will return an updated value the next time it is accessed.

Finally, we quickly consider some uses of OCL in other parts of a UML model. It can notably be used everywhere a `ValueSpecification` can be used. We only have space to mention three possibilities here:

1. **Activity simplification.** A `ValueSpecificationAction` could actually contain an OCL expression instead of a constant literal. Figure 10 shows how the `fire(p : Person)` activity from Fig. 3 can be simplified by leveraging this possibility. The purely side-effect free part of the activity has been expressed as an OCL expression embedded in a `ValueSpecificationAction`. Given this new fUML+OCL activity, deriving the pure fUML version is simply a matter of compiling the OCL expression in the same way we compile bodies, pre- and post-conditions, invariants, and derive expressions.
2. **Default values of properties** can be specified in OCL with the `init` kind of expression, or with `Property.defaultValue` from the UML metamodel. They could be compiled into actions that initialize the corresponding properties from within constructors.
3. **Default values of parameters** can similarly be expressed in OCL. These OCL expressions could be compiled, and leveraged to generate alternative versions of a given operation, in which parameters with default values would disappear, and be computed instead.

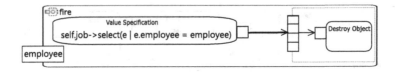

Fig. 10. A variant of the fire(p : Person) activity (Fig. 3) simplified using OCL

4   Compiling OCL to fUML

To obtain the result outlined in the previous section we defined a compilation scheme of OCL to fUML, that we describe in this section. The mapping is specified as an ATL transformation and we outline here its points of interest. We address three problems: mapping operations from the OCL standard library to the fUML or Alf standard libraries (Sect. 4.1), defining translation patterns for OCL expressions (Sect. 4.2), and translating the fUML extensions for embedding OCL code into pure fUML (Sect. 4.3).

4.1   Mapping the OCL Library to fUML

Table 1 summarizes the main correspondences between operations for OCL data types and fUML/Alf[3]. We can identify three kinds of correspondence:

- Operations on **OclType and OclAny** are directly translated into specific fUML actions, properly parametrized.
- Operations on **primitive data types** (`Boolean`, `String`, `Integer`, `Real`) translate into calls to primitive behaviors in the fUML standard library.
- Operations on **collections** translate into calls to behaviors in the Alf standard library. Note that this mapping does not include iterators. Alf does not include support for lambda expressions, so its library cannot include an implementation of general iterators. We therefore support iterators by statically compiling them to fUML patterns.

4.2   Translating OCL Expressions

In Figs. 11, 12, 13, and 14 we illustrate some examples of compilation patterns for OCL. These patterns are analogous to those given in the fUML specification [1, Appendix A] for Java to fUML translation.

The pattern in Fig. 11 is generated for all OCL conditional expressions. The compiled condition propagates its boolean result through an object flow to a `DecisionNode`. Depending on the boolean value, two control-flow edges

---

[3] The complete mapping for the OCL standard library is available at the project repository https://github.com/atlanmod/OCL2fUML.

Table 1. Mapping the OCL standard library to fUML

Context	OCL operation	Generated fUML
OclType	allInstances	ReadExtentAction
OclAny	=	TestIdentityAction
	<>	TestIdentityAction
		CallBehaviorAction(fUML::Not)
	oclIsKindOf	ReadIsClassifiedObjectAction
Boolean	[and | or | xor | not | implies]	CallBehaviorAction(fUML::[And | Or | Xor | Not | Implies])
String	[concat | size | substring]	CallBehaviorAction(fUML::[Concat | Size | Substring])
Integer,Real	[+ | - | * | / | >|<|≥|≤]	CallBehaviorAction(fUML::[+ | − | * | / | >|<|≥|≤])
Collection	size()	CallBehaviorAction(fUML::ListSize)
	[includes | excludes | including | excluding | count | isEmpty | notEmpty | union | intersection | at | first | last | union | includesAll | excludesAll | insertAt]	CallBehaviorAction(Alf::[includes | excludes | including | excluding | count | isEmpty | notEmpty | union | intersection | at | first | last | union | includesAll | excludesAll | insertAt])

pass the control token (coming from an initial node) to the compiled expression from the **then** or **else** part. Thanks to the use of control flows the part that does not receive the control token is not evaluated at all. Finally a `MergeNode` gathers the result of the active part (**then** or **else**).

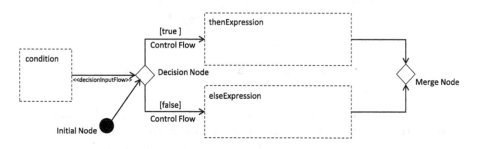

Fig. 11. Compilation pattern for OCL `if`

OCL iterators are generally compiled to fUML expansion regions, as we show in the following examples. For clearly understanding the correspondence a key point is remembering that collections in the fUML semantics are represented as sequences of object tokens that flow consecutively over an object flow. The expansion region considers the tokens one by one, and for each token it may compute a result and propagate it to the object flow outgoing from its output node.

Compiling the `collect` iterator is straightforward, since the default behavior of fUML expansion regions corresponds to a functional map semantics. As shown in Fig. 12 from each `collect` we generate an expansion region that takes the input collection as a sequence of object tokens through the object flow coming from the source. The expansion region directly includes the compilation result from the body of the collect. We only add a `ForkNode` to simplify the distribution of the iterator in case it is used multiple times in the body.

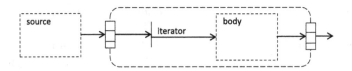

Fig. 12. Compilation pattern for OCL `collect`

The pattern in Fig. 13 represents the translation of an OCL `select` iterator. In this case the compiled body returns a boolean value that is used as decision input of a `DecisionNode`. If the boolean is `true` then the current value of the iterator is passed to the output node, otherwise it is discarded (because there is no `false` outgoing edge).

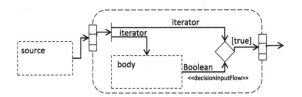

Fig. 13. Compilation pattern for OCL `select`

We compile an OCL `exists` iterator to the pattern in Fig. 14 that chains the `select` pattern of Fig. 13 with a `CallBehaviorAction` to the `notEmpty` behavior of the Alf library. In conformance to the OCL semantics the body of the `exists` is evaluated for the whole collection (the evaluation is not short-circuited when an element satisfying the body is found). When the entire collection has been evaluated a control flow launches the `notEmpty` behavior that returns the final result.

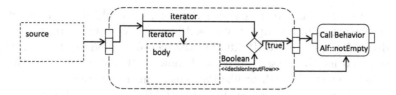

Fig. 14. Compilation pattern for OCL `exists`

4.3   Translating fUML Extensions

OCL expressions are included in our fUML models using mechanisms that are not part of the fUML specification, but are imported from UML. These mechanisms need to be translated into fUML elements to be executable. Depending on the role of the OCL expression, we generate a different fUML scaffolding:

- **body:** If the corresponding operation is missing from the fUML class model, we create a new operation. A wrapper activity with structure analogous to Fig. 6 is attached to the operation. We create also a separate private operation for the body, and we attach to it the activity generated from the OCL expression. The wrapper has a `CallOperationAction` towards the body operation.
- **pre, post, inv:** For each constraint we generate a new auxiliary operation associated with a side-effect free fUML activity that returns a boolean. Bodies of other operations in the model are wrapped in activities that check pre- and post-conditions of the operation and invariants of the class.
- **derive:** We create a getter operation (e.g., `get<FeatureName>`). We attach the fUML activity generated from the OCL expression to the getter. We replace all read accesses to the feature (`ReadStructuralFeature`) by calls (`OperationCallAction`) to the getter.
- **def:** We create a new operation and associated method.
- **init:** We add an `AddStructuralFeatureValueAction` to the class constructor to set the value of the property to the result of the compilation of the OCL expression.

5   Proof-of-Concept Implementation

In order to evaluate the feasibility of the approach presented in this paper, we partially implemented it. All OCL examples given in the previous sections have been translated into fUML using this implementation, and executed using an fUML execution engine. The present section describes this implementation.

We decided to use Moka[4] [2] as an fUML engine because (1) it is based on the reference implementation but (2) provides more tooling. Thanks to (1) we have confidence in its conformity to the fUML specification. And (2) means that activities like debugging are simpler than with the reference implementation.

---

[4] https://wiki.eclipse.org/Papyrus/UserGuide/ModelExecution.

Also, because Moka is integrated into Papyrus, we could use it to create the diagrams presented in this paper[5]. We used Moliz [6] in previous work [7] because we needed xMOF [8] (i.e., fUML lifted to the metametamodel). However, xMOF is not required for the present work, and showing that the approach can work with a full-featured UML editor like Papyrus seems more relevant.

The translation of OCL expressions into fUML is performed in two steps:

1. **Text-to-model parsing** yields a model representation of textual OCL expressions. We used the ATL parser for this purpose. This is possible because ATL expressions are written in a variant of OCL 2.0, which we call ATL-OCL. An additional shortcut consisted in writing OCL expressions in a separate file to simplify parsing. Parsing OCL expressions actually embedded in a UML model (in `OpaqueExpressions`) would not present significant issues.

2. **Model transformation** integrates the OCL model resulting from parsing into an fUML model. This transformation is written in ATL refining mode, which enables in-place updates. It takes as inputs both an extended fUML model, as well as an ATL-OCL model, and gives as output an updated version of the fUML model. The resulting fUML model contains the elements generated from the translation of all OCL expressions given as input. Additionally all fUML extensions have been integrated and removed.

Several other existing OCL parsers could have been reused. Notably, in an actual tool, leveraging Eclipse OCL would make more sense, because it closely follows the current OCL specification. The choice of ATL-OCL was motivated by the two following considerations: (1) familiarity with ATL-OCL enabled reduced development time (we have already worked on several ATL transformations that process ATL-OCL [9]); (2) reusability of ATL code helps amortize development cost. We already had an ATL-OCL to fUML transformation for a small subset as part of previous work on an ATL to fUML transformation [7]. Furthermore, we also intend to integrate the new transformation (extended to a larger subset of OCL) into the ATL to fUML transformation.

For the OCL to fUML model tranformation, we used only declarative ATL, which means that the rules are very close to a mapping specification. Each rule translates an OCL metaclass into a set of fUML elements. To connect the different fUML elements that are generated by different rules, we use a solution that can be summarized in two steps. The first step creates from each OCL expression, a set of fUML elements that should include one *result* element and may contain a set of *input* elements. The *result* and *input* elements can be represented by the input node, output nodes, the fork nodes, the join nodes, the input expansion region or output expansion region according to the corresponding source element. The second step aims to generate for each *input* element an object flow coming from the appropriate *result* element, e.g. the one generated from the parent OCL expression.

---

[5] The diagrams have nonetheless been modified manually in Inkscape (https://inkscape.org/), mostly to improve whitespace usage.

Our compiler supports most OCL constructs with the following notable exceptions: (1) tuples and iterate expressions could be added with relatively little work, (2) introspection of previous values of object properties, as well as of all messages sent by an operation in post-conditions would require detailed bookkeeping, and is likely to have a significant overhead, (3) `oclIsInState` is not relevant because fUML does not include state machines yet, at least until PSSM is standardized.

6 Discussion

A tool based on the OCL to fUML approach has two main *usage scenarios*:

1. *Synchronization* from OCL to fUML activities could be used to simplify the definition of fUML activities. Users would write a couple of OCL expressions, then run the transformation to translate them into fUML. Then, they would continue working on the resulting model, and iterate the process. This is similar to what can be done with Alf, except that Alf can also go back from fUML activities into code.
2. *As a pre-processor* for an fUML execution engine. Users would express significant parts of their model in OCL. They would only use the transformation to fUML before loading their model into an fUML engine (e.g., for simulation), but would never modify the resulting model. Then, they would continue working on the original model, and iterate the process.

A combination of these two scenarios is also possible. Parts of the OCL expressions may be used to specify fUML activities, and therefore be translated as soon as possible into fUML. Other parts could be left as OCL expressions (e.g., preconditions, invariants), and only translated to fUML before execution.

The synchronization scenario is likely to require more complex tooling. Whereas a pre-processor may be invoked transparently (or as a command line tool), synchronization between code and fUML is non trivial and requires a well-designed user interface, as the integration of Alf into Papyrus shows [10]. Additionally, later modifications may be more difficult. For instance, removing an OCL precondition simply consists of removing the link between operation and constraint. However, removing a precondition compiled to fUML requires editing an activity.

We observe that the OCL to fUML transformation is similar to the Alf to fUML transformation (see Fig. 2). Therefore, users could use *OCL in place of Alf* to textually specify some fUML activities: those that are side-effect free. This is even possible on UML models that contain more than just fUML and the relatively simple extensions compiled in our work, although fUML execution may not be possible. Some users may prefer OCL because it is a purely functional language. For instance, it is not possible to inadvertently insert side-effects in query operations written in OCL. However, the missing fUML to OCL reverse transformation would make OCL less convenient than Alf for this purpose. Moreover, this missing transformation would necessarily be partial because fUML activity with side-effects would not be translatable into OCL expressions.

Since OCL has been in use for quite some time (OCL 1.1 published in 1997), some users are likely to know it much better than Alf (version 1.01 published in 2013), and fUML (version 1.0 published in 2011). Being able to translate OCL expressions into fUML could help them getting started with fUML. Also, even if they do not write OCL expression in order to generate fUML activities, playing with an OCL to fUML compiler could be a significant learning aid.

Our integration solution is based on a compilation approach: OCL expressions are translated into fUML activities. An alternative approach would be to evaluate OCL expressions using an *interpreter written in fUML*. Although both approaches have pros and cons, we preferred the compilation one because it avoids double interpretation of OCL (i.e., interpretation of OCL by an fUML interpreter itself interpreted by an fUML engine). Current implementations of fUML (the reference implementation, as well as Moka and Moliz, which are based on it) are all interpreters. Another possibility would be to extend the fUML interpreter with support for OCL interpretation. This could be done by coupling it with an existing black-box OCL interpreter, but then one would lose the fine grained control over execution provided by the fUML interpreter.

While working on the translation presented here, we considered the following *possible extensions to fUML*:

1. *Integration with State Machines.* Ongoing work at OMG on a state machine extension to fUML could make use of our OCL to fUML translation approach. Transition guards can notably be specified in OCL.
2. *Built-in support for pre- and post-conditions.* The previous sections presented one possible integration of pre- and post-conditions into fUML. However, other integrations are possible, notably with respect to when they are evaluated. One possible way to support several integration strategies would be to add options to the compiler. Another way would be to extend fUML with a strategy similar to the existing `DispatchStrategy`, and `ChoiceStrategy` (among others), which respectively enable plugging alternative operation dispatch algorithms, and alternative algorithms to select which action to perform next among those activated.
3. *Anonymous Functions.* Translation of OCL iterator expressions such as *select* and *collect* does not leverage a generic library but rather always generates expansion regions. If fUML supported anonymous functions, using a library approach could be quite simple. Alternatively, we could have used classes as function wrappers, like in Java, or even implemented defunctionalization.
4. *Exceptions.* Violations to pre-, post-conditions and invariants encoded in fUML (Sect. 3), cannot result in fail-fast terminations, but rather in undefined behaviors. Exceptions are one UML feature which would be particularly useful to integrate in fUML for this purpose. An alternative would be to add a native function to the fUML execution engine that would terminate its execution (similarly to what `System.exit(1)` does in Java).

7   Related Work

Approaches like [11] focus on UML model validation with respect to OCL pre- and post-conditions, as well as invariants. In contrast, our approach focuses on model executability. For instance, we also integrate OCL in places where its execution is part of the execution of the model (e.g., operation bodies, derived features), not just to validate it. However, our integration of the pre- and post-conditions is weaker, and closer to what can be achieved with asserts in Java.

In [12], the authors extend OCL with the capability to perform side effects (e.g., assign values to properties, create instances). They then use this extended OCL as an action language for an executable UML. To support UML actions, they further define a mapping from actions to extended OCL expressions. This is basically the opposite of the mapping we propose from OCL to UML actions.

Several UML editors, like Papyrus, provide execution of OCL. However, this execution is typically supported using a dedicated interpreter. Tools that also integrate fUML do not necessarily provide the capability to call OCL from fUML. When they do they typically exhibit a problem mentioned in Sect. 6: the OCL and fUML interpreters are only loosely connected.

The Alf specification can also be considered as a related work, but its relation to our work has already been described in Sect. 6. Another aspect of our approach is that it enables evaluation of OCL expressions in tools that do not support OCL but only fUML. We then see fUML as a kind of virtual machine. This aspect and corresponding related work is described in our papers [7,13].

8   Conclusion

In this work, we have presented a compiler to generate a fully executable fUML model from a user-specified model containing both fUML activities and OCL constraints. We discussed the practical advantages of building executable models using both languages, and having them executed at the same level of abstraction. In previous work we already used the analogy of fUML as a modeling virtual machine, a common platform for execution of modeling tools. This paper is a step in this path, by showing the integration of constraint checkers and query languages in fUML. Since OCL is integrated as expression language in several other MDE tools, this work may be leveraged to port them to fUML as well.

References

1. Object Management Group (OMG): Semantics of a Foundational Subset for Executable UML Models (fUML), v1.2.1, January 2016
2. Guermazi, S., Tatibouet, J., Cuccuru, A., Seidewitz, E., Dhouib, S., Gérard, S.: Executable modeling with fUML and alf in papyrus: tooling and experiments. In: 1st International Workshop on Executable Modeling, pp. 3–8 (2015)
3. Object Management Group (OMG): Precise Semantics Of UML Composite Structures (PSCS), v1.0. http://www.omg.org/spec/PSCS/1.0/, October 2015

4. Object Management Group (OMG): Concrete Syntax For A UML Action Language: Action Language For Foundational UML (ALF), v1.0.1. http://www.omg.org/spec/ALF/1.0.1/, October 2013
5. Object Management Group (OMG): Object Constraint Language (OCL), v2.4. http://www.omg.org/spec/OCL/2.4/, February 2014
6. Mayerhofer, T., Langer, P.: Moliz: a model execution framework for UML models. In: Proceedings of the 2nd International Master Class on Model-Driven Engineering: Modeling Wizards. MW 2012, pp. 3: 1–3: 2. ACM, New York (2012)
7. Tisi, M., Jouault, F., Delatour, J., Saidi, Z., Choura, H.: fUML as an assembly language for model transformation. In: Combemale, B., Pearce, D.J., Barais, O., Vinju, J.J. (eds.) SLE 2014. LNCS, vol. 8706, pp. 171–190. Springer, Heidelberg (2014)
8. Mayerhofer, T., Langer, P., Wimmer, M., Kappel, G.: xMOF: executable DSMLs based on fUML. In: Erwig, M., Paige, R.F., Wyk, E. (eds.) SLE 2013. LNCS, vol. 8225, pp. 56–75. Springer, Heidelberg (2013)
9. Tisi, M., Jouault, F., Fraternali, P., Ceri, S., Bézivin, J.: On the use of higher-order model transformations. In: Paige, R.F., Hartman, A., Rensink, A. (eds.) ECMDA-FA 2009. LNCS, vol. 5562, pp. 18–33. springer, Heidelberg (2009)
10. Seidewitz, E., Tatibouet, J.: Tool Paper: Combining Alf and UML in Modeling Tools - An Example with Papyrus. In: Brucker, A.D., Egea, M., Gogolla, M., Tuong, F. (eds.) OCL@MoDELS. vol. 1512 of CEUR Workshop Proceedings, CEUR-WS.org, pp. 105–119 (2015)
11. Gogolla, M., Büttner, F., Richters, M.: USE: A UML-based specification environment for validating UML and OCL. Sci. Comput. Program. **69**(1), 27–34 (2007)
12. Jiang, K., Zhang, L., Miyake, S.: Using OCL in executable UML. In: Proceedings of the Workshop Ocl4All: Modeling Systems with OCL at MoDELS 2007. vol. 9, Electronic Communications of the EASST (2008)
13. Tisi, M., Jouault, F., Delatour, J., Saidi, Z., Choura, H.: fUML as an assembly language for model transformation. In: Combemale, B., Pearce, D.J., Barais, O., Vinju, J.J. (eds.) SLE 2014. LNCS, vol. 8706, pp. 171–190. Springer, Heidelberg (2014)

Isolating and Reusing Template Instances in UML

Matthieu Allon[1(✉)], Gilles Vanwormhoudt[1,2],
Bernard Carré[1], and Olivier Caron[1]

[1] University of Lille, CRIStAL Lab. (UMR CNRS 9189), Villeneuve-d'ascq, France
Matthieu.Allon@etudiant.univ-lille1.fr,
{Gilles.Vanwormhoudt,Bernard.Carre,Olivier.Caron}@univ-lille1.fr
[2] Mines-Telecom Institute, Villeneuve-d'ascq, France

Abstract. In MBE, design of systems can be improved and accelerated thanks to reusable models which are made available in model repositories or libraries. One answer for designing reusable models is parameterization as offered by UML templates and their binding relationship. The standard aims at embracing under the same constructs two distinct kinds of template usages, namely template instantiation and aspectual binding. Template instantiation is concerned with the capacity of UML templates to model generic components (like C++ templates or Java generics) and produce new models from their binding. Aspectual binding is much more concerned with the capacity of UML templates to specify functionalities to inject into models of systems (contexts) which must conform to a required parameter model. In this paper, we focus on the generative interpretation of UML template binding. On the basis of a deep analysis of the standard, it will be shown that template binding consists in template instantiation plus context merging. This allows to isolate the capacity of instantiating templates (under their generative view) to get reusable models coming from applicative contexts. Then the possibility of partial instantiation inspired by partial binding as promoted by the standard is studied. At a practical level, related functionalities are offered within Eclipse.

Keywords: UML templates · Aspectual templates · Template binding · Partial binding · Template instantiation

1 Introduction

In Model-based Engineering, model reuse is a big challenge that aims to facilitate the capitalization of technology independent design efforts and logics ("off-the-shelves" model components libraries [8]) then to accelerate system design and improve their quality via early checking, by the reuse of proved models. Besides the composition of model pieces [10,16], another way to face this challenge is model parameterization [3,9], that is the capacity for a model to expose some of its elements as parameters, then produce other models through parameter

© Springer International Publishing Switzerland 2016
A. Wąsowski and H. Lönn (Eds.): ECMFA 2016, LNCS 9764, pp. 173–187, 2016.
DOI: 10.1007/978-3-319-42061-5_11

substitution. This allows to capitalize models of a higher kind which capture recurrent structure, so that they can be applied (reused) in multiple modeling contexts.

The UML standard answer to this need is the "template construct" and its binding relationship. This construct is general enough to support MBE reuse practices ranging from the representation at a model level of generic software components (such as C++ templates or Java generics) to the weaving of reusable functionalities into models, mainly the way aspect-, pattern- and view-oriented modeling do. In our prior work [18], we contributed to this research by enhancing the semantics of UML Templates for their aspectual interpretation. This leads to so called "aspectual templates" whose parameters must form a model of systems in which to inject the functionalities. This semantics enhancement ensures the "parameters as a model" requirement and its consistency throughout substitution and composition mechanisms, notably when binding is partial. Thanks to this enhancement, UML templates can be better controlled for their aspectual usage, particularly in case of complex assembly.

In this paper, we concentrate on template instantiation which underlies MBE practices related to their generative usage, that is the creation of new models from their generic modeling structure. This calls for the isolation of template instantiation from standard binding. Given this, consequences on template parameters, particularly when they form a model, need to be examined and we do so by the proper identification of template constituents as submodels. It will be shown that instantiation can be applied on any templates being aspectual or not. Similarly to partial binding, partial instantiation is provided when not all parameters are substituted. A study of this feature is offered and its interest for producing models with pieces from multiple contexts is presented. More generally, the isolation of template instances as stated here contributes to increase UML templates reusability and to enrich template-based MDE facilities [1].

The rest of the paper is structured as follows. After providing background on UML templates, we present an analysis of template binding in Sect. 3. This analysis will lead to the isolation of template instantiation. Then, Sect. 4 examines how instantiation relates to template parameters. Partial instantiation is studied in Sect. 5. Section 6 describes application of the results in modeling tools. Before concluding with perspectives, Sect. 7 discusses template instantiation in existing works.

2   Background on UML Templates

In this section, a reminder on UML templates and their aspectual enhancement [18] are presented to ground the study.

2.1   UML Template and the Binding Relationship

In UML [13], a template is a model which exposes some of its model elements as formal parameters using a signature (list of formal parameters). Examples are class or package templates. Graphically, the signature is contained in a small dashed rectangle on the top right-hand corner of the template symbol. Templates can be applied, and thus reused to produce other models thanks to parameter substitution, through the standard *binding relationship*[1]. It links a *bound model* to a template (from which it was obtained) via a parameter substitution set that associates *formal parameters of the template* to *actual elements of the bound model*. Constraints of the standard only impose that the type of each actual model element must be a subtype of the corresponding formal parameter.

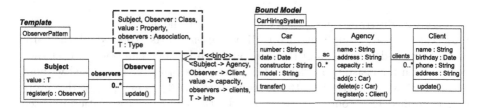

Fig. 1. UML package template example

Figure 1 shows an example of UML template and its binding for extending the model of a system. It shows a package template used to model the *observer* pattern parameterized by the *Subject* and *Observer* classes, the *value* property, the *T* type and the *observers* association. The system where the pattern must be applied represents a car rental agency with its clients and cars. In the figure, the *ObserverPattern* template is used to introduce the observer functionality between *Agency* and *Clients* for capacity observation by clients. This design choice is specified by the binding relationship between the *CarHiringSystem* model and the *ObserverPattern* template with the specified set of substitutions. As a result of the binding, *CarHiringSystem* includes the model structure of the *ObserverPattern* with respect to substitutions.

Finally, UML allows partial binding. Partial binding occurs when not all formal template parameters are substituted. For that, the UML specification states that the unsubstituted formal template parameters are formal template parameters of the bound element, which is itself a template as a consequence. Partial binding will be specifically studied in Sect. 5.

2.2 Parameters as a Model

Regarding template parameters, the standard does not require any structuring between them. The only constraint imposed by UML is the inclusion of the set of parameters into the set of template elements. Although this choice is permissive, it is underspecified to capture structuring constraints expected from candidate models to correctly apply the template functionality.

---

[1] Informally specified in [13], p. 650.

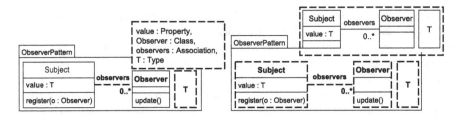

Fig. 2. Set of parameters vs model of parameters

Figure 2 illustrates the issue. On the left of the figure, a variant of the Observer template compliant with UML is presented. As expected, all the parameters are model elements of the template core but one can observe that they do not form a consistent model. Indeed, the *value* property is exposed without its owning class whereas the latter is required to enable its mapping with a property contained in a context class. Similarly, the *observers* association exposed as parameter is underspecified because one of its ends (the *Subject* class) is not declared as a parameter.

In our previous work [18], we deeply studied the aspectual interpretation of UML templates with the requirement that parameters have to form a well formed modeling structure to which candidate models must have to conform. Following this requirement, we stated a semantical enhancement of UML templates which consists in enforcing templates to have a full model as parameter. Its aim is to improve the consistency of templates, notably for aspectual usages, but also to better specify the model of systems to which the functionalities will apply. Following this enhancement, the (partial) binding mechanism has been adapted to enable substitution of the model parameter by a conforming substructure of the base model.

Right of Fig. 2 gives the enhanced version of the Observer template. One can observe that the template parameters (see the superimposed dashed box) form a full model. One can also verify that the structure of this model parameter is well preserved by the substituted elements of the binding in Fig. 1.

3   Towards Explicit Template Instantiation

In this section, we analyze template binding. We will see that template binding underlies template instantiation. This analysis will serve to motivate our proposal which consists in isolating template instantiation separately from template binding. Constraints that template instantiation imposes on the parameters and the specific case of partial template instantiation will be studied in the next sections.

In UML, the semantics of the binding relationship is specified as follows:

"The presence of a TemplateBinding relationship implies the same semantics as if the contents of the template owning the target template signature were copied into the bound element, substituting any elements exposed as a formal template parameter by the corresponding elements specified as actual parameters in this binding." ([13], p. 650)

Following this semantics, the bound model resulting from a template binding can be seen as the merging of an applicative context with the content of the template after substitutions were made. Figure 3 presents this construction principle on the scenario presented in Fig. 1. It makes explicit (upper-right in the figure) the applicative context (car agency) to which both the template and the intermediate model apply, instance of the template (*ObserverPatternInstance* upper-left). It is the context that provides actual elements for the binding.

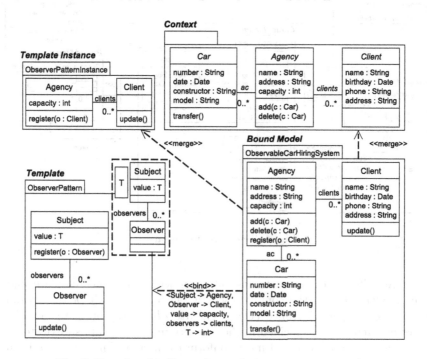

Fig. 3. Template binding = instantiation + context merging

As represented in Fig. 3, the bound model (*ObservableCarHiringSystem*) contains all the content of the template instance plus the content of the context. This can be captured using the standard "merge" relationship from the bound model to the template instance and the context:

$$template\ binding = instantiation + context\ merging$$

Following this, once template instances have been isolated, they can be promoted as valuable artifacts of their own and then be reused. This new capacity is of interest when designers are much more concerned by the construction of new models from templates instead of enriching existing ones. This calls for giving a much more active role to template instantiation in the modeling space and its related processes.

As a consequence, we propose to isolate template instantiation from template binding. For representing template instantiation, we use a relationship named *instantiate*. Like the binding relationship, this relation requires a template, a source modeling context plus a set of parameter substitutions. Its semantics consists in copying the content of the template and replacing the parameters by corresponding copies of actual elements from the source model.

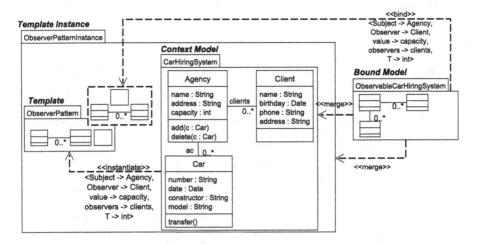

Fig. 4. Template instantiation

Figure 4 illustrates template instantiation with the same template and a source model equal to the context used in Fig. 3. The result of this instantiation is the template instance (*ObserverPatternInstance*) presented in Fig. 3. Regarding substitution specified in the instantiate relationship, substituted elements from the context model must conform to the modeling structure formed by the parameters. In Fig. 4, one can verify that it is actually the case.

Finally, to isolate the instantiate relationship, we showed the treatment of template with a well formed parameter model. More generally, how instantiation relates to the structure of templates needs to be deeply examined. It is the intent of the next section.

4   Instantiation Regarding Kinds of Templates

To study how instantiation relates to template structure, we decompose a template into two complementary constituents: its *parameter* and its *specific sub-models*. Main questions are: which constituent provides the template structure

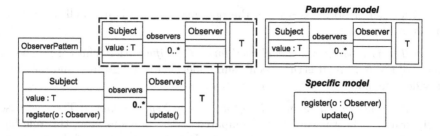

Fig. 5. Template model = parameter + specific submodels

and what are the requirement on template parameters when instantiation is considered ?

Consider a template with a well formed parameter submodel. It is this submodel which provides the modeling structure of the template core. This is illustrated in Fig. 5. In this situation, the lack of well-formedness for the specific model is due to the fact that classes owning the *register* and *update* methods are parameters, so are not part of the specific model.

The observation regarding the well-formedness of template constituents raises the question of alternative cases. It can be questioned whether a parameter submodel that is not well formed (respectively a specific model that is well formed) is of interest and what are the specific usages. Indeed, depending on the well-formedness or not of each template constituent, other cases can be considered in addition to the previous one, whether the parameter submodel

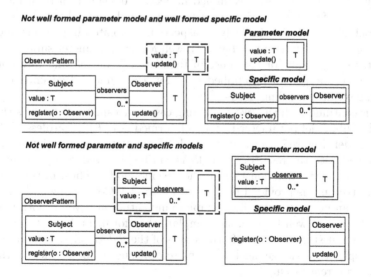

Fig. 6. Possible forms of template constituents

is well formed or not. Cases when the parameter model is not well formed are shown in Fig. 6.

Not well formed parameter model, well formed specific model: This case is shown on top of Fig. 6. Here, it is the specific submodel that is well formed and therefore provides the modeling structure of the template.

Not well formed parameter model, not well formed specific model: This last case is illustrated in bottom of Fig. 6. Compared to the previous case, this one has both submodels which are not well formed. Here, the structure of the template content is in the template in its entirety.

Table 1 gives a summary of all possible cases of template constituents.

Table 1. Possible forms of template constituents

		Specific Model	
		well formed	not well formed
Parameter Model	well formed	Case 1	Case 2
	not well formed	Case 3	Case 4

These cases being identified, they can be analyzed with regard to template instantiation. It is done in the following.

Let us consider cases 1 and 2 corresponding to a well formed parameter submodel. The situation was examined in Sect. 3. It leads to a resulting model where the well-formedness of its structure is brought by substituted elements of the context model. So, similarly to aspectual template binding, instantiation can be applied to any template having a well formed parameter submodel. This is an interesting result for the reuse of templates. It means that any template having this property can be applied both for aspectual and generative usages depending on the modeling needs.

Let us continue with the two remaining cases corresponding to the situations where the submodel parameter is not well formed (Fig. 6), regardless of its specific submodel. Figure 7 shows an example of template instantiation for case 3, accompanied with the resulting model. As can be observed, the parameter submodel is not well formed contrary to the specific model. Thus, in this case, the template structure is provided by the specific model. Concerning case 4, similar comments can be made regarding template instantiation. Even if both template submodels are not well formed, the template they form can be instantiated. To be convinced, it suffices to modify the status of the *Subject* class as parameter in Fig. 7. Despite this change, such a template continues to be applicable through an *instantiate* relationship.

The last two cases typically occur when modeling generics (e.g. C++ or Java) but also in partial template instantiation. Thus, it is important to handle them and ensure they are treated consistently through template instantiation. The

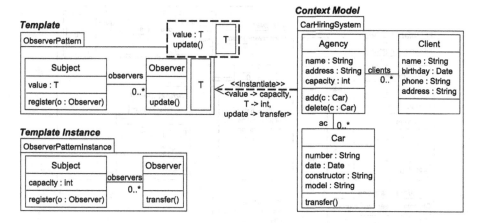

Fig. 7. Template instantiation with a not well formed parameter model

following section specifically studies partial instantiation and concludes on the comparison between aspectual binding and template instantiation.

5 Partial Instantiation

UML templates allow partial binding when not all parameters are substituted and unsubstituted ones remain parameters in the resulting model which is therefore a template. Partial binding is a powerful feature that allows modelers to obtain richer templates through the composition of templates. It was deeply studied in our preceding work [18] for aspectual templates. Following UML principles concerning parameter substitution and propagation of the unsubstituted parameters, partial instantiation can be offered to benefit from additional capacities. It gives the ability to produce new templates from instantiated ones and, thus, sequences of instantiations. It also enables instantiation in multiple contexts.

Figure 8 gives an example of a partial instantiation between the *Observer-Pattern* template and the *CarHiringSystem* model. In this example the *Subject*, *value* and *T* parameters are bound in the substitution set of the instantiate relationship while the *observers* and *Observer* parameters are unbound. This figure also shows the result of this partial instantiation which is a new template named *ObservableAgency*. For this template, the parameter model contains the unbound *observers* and *Observer*, following the propagation strategy of UML for unsubstituted parameters.

One observation can be made concerning the propagation of unsubstituted parameters in the new template. This propagation is achieved with respect to specified substitution causing adaptation of method parameters. See for example the substitution of *Observer* by *Resource* in the *register* method of the *Agency* parameter, in the *ObservableAgencyResource* template instance. Depending on

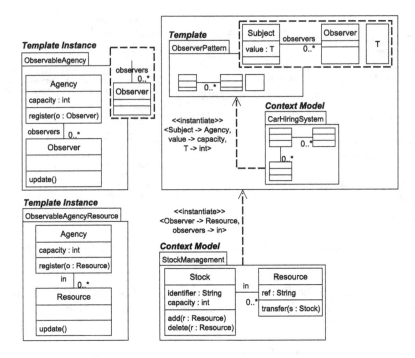

Fig. 8. Partial instantiation

the substituted parameters, the resulting template may have a well formed model as parameter or not.

Templates resulting from partial instantiation can be further applied. They can help to construct other parts of the same system or serve as valuable artifacts in order to build parts of new systems. For applying a template resulting from partial instantiation to a new context, complete or partial instantiation can be used. Additionally, such a template can also be bound for aspectual usages as long as their parameter model is well formed. In our example, only instantiation is enabled because the parameter model is not well formed. Figure 8 shows a partial instantiation of the obtained template *ObservableAgency* to get *ObservableAgencyResource*. This instantiation takes place in a new applicative context related to stock management. In this instantiation, the *Observer* and *observers* are substituted in order to produce a final model that combines ingredients from the two modeling contexts. Such a model can be useful for observing state changes between the two parts.

In this example, it is interesting to highlight that the same result could be obtained through an alternative sequence of instantiations: first, partially instantiating the *ObserverPattern* template in the *StockManagement* context and then instantiating the intermediate result in the *CarHiringSystem* context. Moreover, obtaining the same *ObservableAgencyResource* model with a complete instantiation would require merging *CarHiringSystem* and *StockManagement* models into a single model followed by a complete instantiation of *ObserverPattern* to this merged model. These equalities emphasize the compatibility between partial and complete instantiation and, thus, their consistency.

The preceding example also illustrates successive template instantiations from an initial template. Along a sequence of instantiations, the set of parameters decreases in intermediate templates. This may cause relaxation of structural constraints on the parameters. Such relaxation has the effect to enlarge the set of potential elements for substituting parameters in instantiation. This flexibility at the level of substitution is visible in the previous example. In the obtained template *ObservableAgency, Observer* and *observers* parameters form a less-constrained structure than their counterpart in the initial template. This enables mapping them on a larger set of candidate elements when compared with the initial template.

Table 2 summarizes the situations studied in this paper. It characterizes applicability and results of examined relationships depending on whether the template is aspectual or not. This table should help to have a better understanding of the UML Template modeling space, particularly in case where parameters form a model.

Table 2. Template applicability and kinds of resulting models

	Aspectual Template (Well formed Parameter Model)		Not Aspectual Template (Not Well formed Parameter Model)	
	Applicable ?	*Kind of Resulting Model*	*Applicable ?*	*Kind of Resulting Model*
Aspectual Binding	Yes	Model	No	No Resulting Model
Instantiation	Yes	Model	Yes	Model
Partial Aspectual Binding	Yes	Aspectual Template	No	No Resulting Model
Partial Instantiation	Yes	Template	Yes	Template

6 Tool Support

A software environment dedicated to template based model engineering in Eclipse was previously implemented [18]. This environment[2] is composed of plugins which are based on the official EMF (Eclipse Modeling Framework), UML and OCL plugins. These plugins offer core functionalities to specify and verify aspectual templates well-formedness but also apply their binding in a compliant way with the UML plugin thanks to a specific profile. In addition, the plugins provide general and original facilities to support other modeling tasks targeting templates or user assistance such as automatic completion of template signature and binding inference. All the plugins functionalities are reusable in modeling tools that handle model templates.

---

[2] Eclipse plugins and modeling tool snapshots are available at http://www.cristal. univ-lille.fr/caramel/MBE_Template/

Following the present work, this environment has been extended to include the capacity of instantiating templates. For that purpose, we added the following enhancements to existing plugins :

- An adaptation of OCL constraints for checking the consistency of template parameters and their substitutions when instantiation is applied. The constraints applied in that case are a subset of the ones for checking aspectual templates. These constraints mainly enforce that parameters and the substituted elements involved in a template instantiation have a compatible structure.
- An implementation of total and partial instantiation. The implemented algorithm proceeds by copying the core of the template into a new model and replacing copied parameters by substituted elements from the context model. Thanks to their compatibility with instantiation, this implementation is also applicable to aspectual templates.
- An extension of the current profile dedicated to templates with a new stereotype related to template instantiation, i.e., *InstantiationBinding*. It specializes the *TemplateBinding* UML metaclass and provides an OCL context for applying constraints due to template instantiation.

7   Related Works

This study started from UML template and showed that this concept is a general construct both for aspect-oriented and generative modeling based on parameterized models. A detailed review of related works regarding aspectual templates can be found in our previous work [18]. In these works, instantiation is sometimes mentioned as an underlying mechanism for binding aspectual templates [2, 9, 15] but it is not isolated as a full-right mechanism, as studied here. In the following, we review existing works that explicitly support template instantiation since it is the focus of this paper.

As already indicated, one motivation for template instantiation is the modeling of generic classes. [5] is a work that studies this need in UML by means of template classifier. The authors mainly focus on mechanism offered by this construct for expressing constraints on type parameters of represented generic classes and checking their substitutability in bindings. The work presented in [7] addresses the similar modeling need but aims to offer a stronger conformance for the binding of template classifiers. For that purpose, it proposes a set of well-formedness rules, additional to that of UML, to enforce the correctness of bound attributes and methods regarding their types, their membership and some of their meta-attributes. By offering generic classes similar to Java, Ecore (the metamodel of EMF) [17] can also be cited as a work dealing with this need. Thanks to this feature, models expressed in Ecore can contain declaration of generic classes or use instantiation of generic classes for typing attributes and methods. This feature also improves the capacities delivered by EMF for code generation (i.e., generate generic code).

The Catalysis approach [6] proposes model frameworks in order to design reusable packages. A model framework is a form of parameterized package containing placeholders which are names that can be substituted with actual type names when the framework is instantiated. Each instantiation of the framework provides its own substitution of the placeholders. The names of attributes and associations of placeholder types are themselves placeholders. This approach, based on string substitution, is realized in the XMF tool.

[14] studies the support of genericity in component models. This work proposes a structural pattern to extend an existing component model with concepts for genericity. With this pattern, a component model can be made generic through parametrization. Elements that can be exposed as parameters are types of input and output ports, types of component implementation and the number of nested subcomponents. This work also introduces an algorithm to instantiate a generic component model. The use of the pattern is demonstrated by extending the SCA component model.

In [11], the authors present a notion of model template and its instantiation mechanism in the context of the MetaDepth framework. In this work, a model template specifies its generic modeling structure by means of the "concept" construct which is a separate model expressing both the parameters and a set of structural requirements on these parameters. In some way, the "concept" construct is related to the notion of "parameters as a model" and has a similar purpose but it is not part of the template body. Instantiation of a model template is done by importing substituted elements from a model conforming to the concept into a new model constructed from the template body.

Compared to these works, the present contribution differs on several main points. First, only one of the existing works [5] takes place inside the scope of standard UML but only for template classifiers. Second, all these works except [11] do not consider template parameters as a fully structured model. As discussed in the paper, this requirement allows us to overcome possible inconsistencies when instantiating templates. It also provides a way to better characterize and control the usages of templates during processes. A last difference between the present work and existing ones is related to partial instantiation. To our knowledge, no existing approach offers capacities comparable to this feature. As a result, interesting capacities are enabled like instantiation of template in multiple contexts or the construction of complex assembly, mixing aspectual and generative usages of templates through partial binding and instantiation.

8 Conclusion

Starting from UML templates and their binding relationship, this work isolated instantiation of templates with "parameters as a model". As a consequence, new capacities were offered for the reuse of templates and the construction of new models from their complete or partial instantiation. This work also provided a characterization of the resulting UML Template modeling space. More generally, it contributes to enrich template-based MDE capacities.

In future work, we plan to focus on order and equivalence of instantiation sequences, the way we did in one of our works [12] for aspectual binding. Another interesting perspective to investigate is the study of alternative strategies for unsubstituted parameters, like no propagation or the use of default values for them. Lastly, we are working on the formalization of the template construct by exploiting our previous work on model inclusion and the notion of submodel [4]. We expect this formalization will help to achieve a better theoretical understanding and generalization of template for the quest of model reuse.

Acknowledgement. We would like to thank the anonymous reviewers for their work and comments in order to improve the presentation of the results.

References

1. Allon, M., Vanwormhoudt, G., Carré, B., Caron, O.: Template based MDE. In: 4ème Conférence en Ingénierie du Logiciel (CIEL 2015) (2015). https://hal.archives-ouvertes.fr/hal-01162652
2. Berg, H., Møller-Pedersen, B.: Type-safe symmetric composition of metamodels using templates. In: Haugen, Ø., Reed, R., Gotzhein, R. (eds.) SAM 2012. LNCS, vol. 7744, pp. 160–178. Springer, Heidelberg (2013)
3. Bottoni, P., Guerra, E., de Lara, J.: A language-independent and formal approach to pattern-based modelling with support for composition and analysis. Inf. Softw. Technol. **52**(8), 821–844 (2010)
4. Carré, B., Vanwormhoudt, G., Caron, O.: From subsets of model elements to submodels, a characterization of submodels and their properties. Softw. Syst. Model. **14**, 861–887 (2015)
5. Cuccuru, A., Radermacher, A., Gérard, S., Terrier, F.: Constraining type parameters of UML 2 templates with substitutable classifiers. In: Schürr, A., Selic, B. (eds.) MODELS 2009. LNCS, vol. 5795, pp. 644–649. Springer, Heidelberg (2009)
6. D'Souza, D., Wills, A.: Catalysis: Objects, Components, and Frameworks with UML. Object Technology Series. Addison-Wesley, Boston (1998)
7. Farinha, J., Ramos, P.: Extending UML templates towards computability. In: Proceedings of the 3rd International Conference on Model-Driven Engineering and Software Development (MODELSWARD 2015), pp. 122–133. SciTePress, February 2015
8. Herrmannsdörfer, M., Hummel, B.: Library concepts for model reuse. Electr. Notes Theoret. Comput. Sci. **253**(7), 121–134 (2010)
9. Klein, J., Kienzle, J.: Reusable aspect models. In: 11th Aspect-Oriented Modeling Workshop, Nashville. Citeseer (2007)
10. Whittle, J., Jayaraman, P., Elkhodary, A., Moreira, A., Araújo, J.: MATA: a unified approach for composing UML aspect models based on graph transformation. In: Katz, S., Ossher, H., France, R., Jézéquel, J.-M. (eds.) Transactions on Aspect-Oriented Software Development VI. LNCS, vol. 5560, pp. 191–237. Springer, Heidelberg (2009)
11. de Lara, J., Guerra, E.: From types to type requirements: genericity for model-driven engineering. Softw. Syst. Model. **12**(3), 453–474 (2013)
12. Muller, A., Caron, O., Carré, B., Vanwormhoudt, G.: On some properties of parameterized model application. In: Hartman, A., Kreische, D. (eds.) ECMDA-FA 2005. LNCS, vol. 3748, pp. 130–144. Springer, Heidelberg (2005)

13. OMG: Auxiliary Constructs Templates, Chap. 17. UML 2.4.1 Superstructure Specification (2011)
14. Bigot, J., Pérez, C.: Increasing reuse in component models through genericity. In: Edwards, S.H., Kulczycki, G. (eds.) ICSR 2009. LNCS, vol. 5791, pp. 21–30. Springer, Heidelberg (2009)
15. Reddy, Y.R., Ghosh, S., France, R.B., Straw, G., Bieman, J.M., McEachen, N., Song, E., Georg, G.: Directives for composing aspect-oriented design class models. In: Rashid, A., Akşit, M. (eds.) Transactions on Aspect-Oriented Software Development I. LNCS, vol. 3880, pp. 75–105. Springer, Heidelberg (2006)
16. Melnik, S., Bernstein, P.A., Halevy, A., Rahm, E.: A semantics for model management operators. Microsoft Technical report, pp. 1–12 (2004)
17. Steinberg, D., Budinsky, F., Merks, E., Paternostro, M.: EMF: Eclipse Modeling Framework. Addison-Wesley, Reading (2008)
18. Vanwormhoudt, G., Caron, O., Carré, B.: Aspectual templates in UML. In: Software and Systems Modeling, pp. 1–29 (2015). http://dx.doi.org/10.1007/s10270-015-0463-3

Experience Reports and Case Studies

MBF4CR: A Model-Based Framework for Supporting an Automated Cancer Registry System

Shuai Wang[1(✉)], Hong Lu[1], Tao Yue[1,2], Shaukat Ali[1],
and Jan Nygård[3]

[1] Simula Research Laboratory, Oslo, Norway
{shuai,honglu,tao,shaukat}@simula.no
[2] University of Oslo, Oslo, Norway
[3] Cancer Registry of Norway, Oslo, Norway
Jan.Nygard@kreftregisteret.no

Abstract. The Cancer Registry of Norway (CRN) collects medical information (e.g., laboratory results, clinical procedures and treatment) of cancer patients from different medical entities, for all cancer patients in Norway. The collected data are checked for validity and correctness (i.e., *validation*) and is the basis for the registration of cancer cases (i.e., *aggregation*) by employing more than a thousand of medical rules. However, the current practice of CRN lacks of a systematic way to capture the domain knowledge and maintain medical rules at a proper level of abstraction.

To tackle these challenges, this paper proposes a model-based framework (named as *MBF4CR*) for capturing the domain knowledge, formalizing medical rules, automating rule selection, and enabling data (cancer messages and cancer cases) validation and aggregation using Unified Modeling Language (UML) and Object Constraint Language (OCL). *MBF4CR* systematically captures domain knowledge (e.g., cancer messages) as an UML class diagram and formally specifies medical rules as OCL constraints. By associating tags to OCL constraints, *MBF4CR* enables an automated rule selection process with tool support. We employed a case study from CRN that consists of 187 medical rules to evaluate *MBF4CR* from two aspects: *Performance* in terms of selecting and executing rules, and *Correctness* in terms of producing correct validation and aggregation results. Results show that *MBF4CR* can facilitate the current practice by complying with the medical domain knowledge with an acceptable performance, while reducing the maintenance effort.

Keywords: Automated Cancer Registry System · UML · OCL

1 Introduction

In the last few generations, cancer is one of the most challenging diseases to be tackled and large amount research effort has been put on studying cancer and estimating effects of different treatments [1]. To gain sufficient input for cancer research and national report, a national cancer registry plays a key role in the research community and

© Springer International Publishing Switzerland 2016
A. Wąsowski and H. Lönn (Eds.): ECMFA 2016, LNCS 9764, pp. 191–204, 2016.
DOI: 10.1007/978-3-319-42061-5_12

society, aiming to collect information (e.g., diagnosis) for all cancer patients in a country [2]. Such information is collected from different medical entities (e.g., clinical departments) [2]. All these data require to be thoroughly checked for validity by employing more than a thousand of medical rules to ensure data quality [2].

The Cancer Registry of Norway (CRN) is making a transfer from a paper-based/manual registry system to an ICT-based Automated Cancer Registry System (ACRS). Based on the domain knowledge and discussions with medical experts (i.e., the chief medical officers and medical coders) in CRN, we learned that ACRS needs to automate three main tasks: (1) *Cancer Message Validation*: collecting cancer messages from different medical entities, and checking their validity and correctness (e.g., a female cannot have a prostate cancer); (2) *Cancer Message Aggregation*: aggregating several relevant cancer messages into a cancer case, which contains information related with a cancer such as diagnosis, treatment and morphology; and (3) *Cancer Case Validation*: validating aggregated cancer cases since errors may be introduced during the aggregation process. It is worth mentioning that the three tasks are based on more than a thousand of medical rules that have been specified by chief medical officers, implemented by programmers, and applied by medical coders over the last 60 years.

We observe that the current practice of CRN poses two key challenges: (1) *Low Level of Abstraction*: The domain knowledge (i.e., cancer messages and cancer cases) is currently captured directly at the implementation level, which makes it difficult to understand the domain. In particular, when a new medical coder starts her/his job, it requires medical coding training and it takes long time for her/him to acquire domain knowledge; and (2) *Large Effort to Maintain*: The existing rules are scattered and represented in different means, i.e., source code, database and look-up tables. There is no unique manner (e.g., a rule repository) to manage and maintain such a large number of rules. When a new rule is introduced or the existing rules are modified, programmers have to modify the implementation and consequently test the modified source code, which is time-consuming, costly, and might lead to low quality of ACRS.

Model-based engineering (MBE) has been applied in practice to address various challenges [7–9, 12–14] such as automated generation of test cases [8]. To cope with the above-mentioned challenges, this paper proposes a model-based framework for supporting ACRS, named as *MBF4CR* with tool support. *MBF4CR* first systematically captures the domain knowledge by building Unified Modeling Language (UML) models, and formally specify medical rules as Object Constraint Language (OCL) constraints [3, 4]. Furthermore, *MBF4CR* links OCL constraints with relevant attributes in UML models by associating tags to each constraint with the aim to enable automated rule selection. *MBF4CR* also consists of a set of external tools and five tools we developed for supporting capturing domain knowledge systematically, specifying rules formally, and selecting and executing relevant rules automatically. To evaluate *MBF4CR*, we employed a case study from CRN that consists of 187 medical rules and results show that *MBF4CR* can achieve an acceptable performance in terms of selecting and executing rules, and the results for data validation and aggregation returned by *MBF4CR* comply with the medical domain knowledge. We also discuss that *MBF4CR* can reduce the effort for maintaining the large number of rules.

As compared with the current practice, *MBF4CR* posts several benefits, which include: (1) The domain knowledge is captured at a high abstraction level, which can be understood more easily by medical coders without getting into implementation details; (2) All the medical rules are specified in a formal and standard way and organized in a medical rule repository (separated from the implementation of ACRS), which largely improves the maintenance of the medical rules.

The rest of the paper is organized as follows. Section 2 presents the *MBF4CR* framework followed by the evaluation (Sect. 3). An overall discussion is presented in Sect. 4. Section 5 presents the related work and Sect. 6 concludes the paper.

2   The Model-Based Framework for Cancer Registry

2.1   Modeling Methodology

An overall diagram (in UML activity diagram) is given in Fig. 1, in which the manual steps have been marked as gray. The modeling methodology of *MBF4CR* contains three parts: (1) modeling the domain knowledge as a UML class diagram; (2) specifying rules as OCL constraints; and (3) associating tags to the OCL constraints.

Modeling the Domain Knowledge as an UML Class Diagram (A1). Two key domain concepts were identified based on the domain knowledge: *Cancer Message* and *Cancer Case*. A cancer message including a set of fields (e.g., message type) records all the necessary cancer information about a cancer patient from one medical entity, e.g., pathology laboratory. A cancer case consists of a number of fields (e.g., cancer type) that are necessary for public health surveillance and cancer research. Each cancer message can only be associated with one cancer case, while one cancer case can be associated with several cancer messages. Notice that cancer messages and cancer cases share a set of common fields. For example, *DS (Diagnostic Certainty)* exist in both cancer messages and cancer cases, which is used to determine a cancer if the value of *DS* is more than 3 (lower values of *DS* indicate a pre-cancer). It is important to point it out that values of the common fields for cancer cases require to be obtained by aggregating corresponding cancer messages based on pre-defined medical rules.

As shown in Fig. 1, we first automatically converted the existing database schema of CRN (i.e., cancer patient, cancer message and cancer case) into an UML class diagram (*A1.1*) and captured them as three classes (*CancerPatient, CancerMessage* and *CancerCase*). Notice that each cancer message and cancer case should be associated with a specific cancer patient (*CancerPatient*, Fig. 2) that has associated information, e.g., *personId, age, birth* and *gender*. All the fields related with cancer messages and cancer cases are specified as attributes of *CancerMessage* and *CancerCase*. Based on the domain knowledge, we manually refined the diagram (*A1.2*, gray rectangle) and Fig. 2 shows an excerpt of the refined UML class diagram. Since cancer messages and cancer cases share a set of common fields (e.g., *DS*), we grouped them (in total 48) and specified as the attributes of a separate class (*CommonField*).

Moreover, each cancer message consists of a number of attributes, e.g., *messageId* to uniquely identify a specific cancer message and *personId* to trace a cancer message for a particular cancer patient (*CancerPatient* class in Fig. 2). Two key attributes are

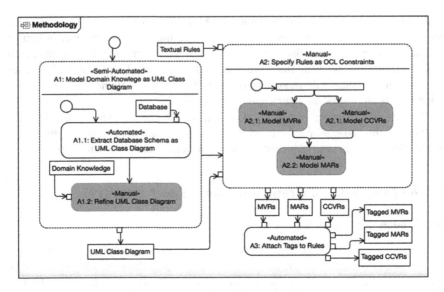

Fig. 1. An overview of the methodology

associated with each cancer message, i.e., *messageType* used to identify from which medical entity a cancer message is sent, and *cancerType* (*CommonField* class) used to identify the cancer type a particular cancer message refers to. These two attributes are used for automatically selecting relevant medical rules for validating and aggregating cancer messages in our methodology. Notice that we only list five types of cancers (e.g., prostate cancer) in Fig. 2 for illustration. In addition, an attribute called *cancerCaseId* is required for a cancer message, which is used to associate a cancer

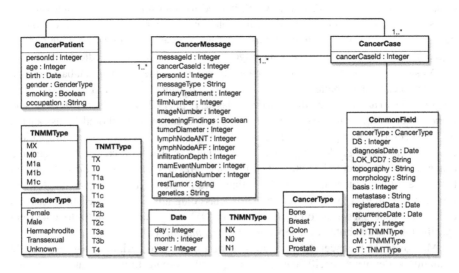

Fig. 2. An excerpt of the refined UML class diagram

message with the corresponding cancer case for aggregation. In total, 64 attributes have been included into the *CancerMessage* class, which denote all necessary medical information for a cancer patient from different medical entities, such as treatment information from clinical departments and morphology and topography from pathology laboratories. Notice that some of the attributes may have empty values when a cancer message is reported from a medical entity to CRN, e.g., the information morphology will be empty when a cancer message comes from a clinical department.

Similarly, a cancer case (*CancerCase*) also includes a number of attributes, such as *cancerCaseId* and *cancerType* (Fig. 2). In summary, there are 49 attributes in total for *CancerCase* including 48 common attributes with the *CancerMessage* class. The detailed medical meanings of other attributes of *CancerMessage* and *CancerCase* classes (Fig. 2) will not be explained since it is out of the scope of this paper.

Specifying Rules as OCL Constraints (A2). The medical rules in CRN can be classified into three categories, i.e., cancer message validation rules (*MVRs*), cancer message aggregation rules (*MARs*) and cancer case validation rules (*CCVRs*). These rules are manually modeled, shown as *A2* in Fig. 1. We first model the *MVRs* and *CCVRs* in parallel since both *MVRs* and *CCVRs* are only for the validation of values of fields. Figure 3 shows the overall classification of these rules and how they are associated with OCL constraints. We present each type of rules in detail.

Cancer Message Validation Rules (MVRs).
Definition: *MVRs* in the current practice of CRN are defined to evaluate: (1) the validity of one field value of a cancer message, e.g., the value for *DS* in a cancer message should be an integer ranging from 1 to 9; and (2) the consistency of several fields within a cancer message. For example, if the value of attribute *basis* is equal to "79" and the message type is not "*O*", the value of *surgery* can only choose either "95" or "97" (*rule 1* in Table 1).

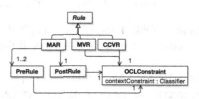

Fig. 3. Rules classification and relationship with OCL constraints

Guidelines: As shown in Fig. 3, one *MVR* is specified as one OCL constraint. The context of an OCL constraint associated with a *MVR* is always the *CancerMessage* class (Fig. 2). This guideline is specified formally in OCL as below:

context MVR **inv**: self.oclConstraint.contextConstraint = CRN::CancerMessage

Example: Table 1 provides an example of a *MVR* as *rule 1*. The result of the evaluation of a *MVR* is *true* if the constraint is satisfied and *false* otherwise.

Cancer Case Validation Rules (CCVRs). **Definition:** *CCVRs* aim to evaluate: (1) the validity of one field in a cancer case; and (2) the consistency of several fields within a

Table 1. Examples for specifying rules as OCL constraints

No	Category	Constrained fields	OCL specification
1	MVR	*Basis* *messageTypesurgery*	**context** CancerMessage inv: self.basis = 79 **and** self.messageType <> 'O' **implies** (self.surgery = 95 **or** self.surgery = 97)
2	CCVR	*Topography* *surgery*	**context** CancerCase **inv:** (self.topography = 'C70' **or** self.topography = 'C71' **or** self.topography = 'C72') **implies** self.surgery <>1
3	MAR	*DS* in cancer message, *DS* in cancer case	*Pre-rules:* **context** CancerMessage **inv:** self. DS = 2 **context** CancerCase **inv:** self. DS = 3 *Post-rule:* **context** CancerCase **inv:** self. DS = 2

cancer case. For instance, for a cancer case, *rule 2* in Table 1 constrains that the value of *surgery* cannot be 1 when the value of *topography* is C70, C71 or C72.

Guidelines: Same as for *MVR*, except that the context of a *CCVR* is class *CancerCase* (Fig. 2). This guideline is specified formally as the OCL constraint:

> **context** CCVR **inv**: self.oclConstraint.contextConstraint = CRN::CancerCase

Example: Table 1 shows an example that specifies *rule 2* as an OCL constraint. The evaluation result of a *CCVR* is *true* if the constraint is satisfied and *false* otherwise.

Cancer Message Aggregation Rules (MARs). **Definition:** This type of rules is defined to aggregate one or more cancer messages into a cancer case. For instance, there is a *MAR* (*rule 3*, Table 1) stating when a new cancer message comes, if and only if the *DS* value for the new cancer message is 2 and the current *DS* value for the cancer case is 3 (condition), the *DS* value for the cancer case will be updated to 2 (action).

Guidelines: We specify each *MAR* with one or two *PreRules* and one *PostRule* (Fig. 3). A *PreRule* specifies the condition of a *MAR* and a *PostRule* describes the action of an *MAR*. There are two possibilities for a pre-rule. First, there can be exactly one pre-rule if the condition only includes the values of the cancer message. This can be formally captured as an OCL constraint below:

> **context** MAR **inv**: self.preRule->size() =1 **implies** self.preRule-
>select(preR:PreRule|preR.oclConstraint.contextConstraint = CRN::CancerMessage)->size() =1

Second, there are two pre-rules if the condition constrains values of the cancer message and the relevant cancer case (e.g., *rule 3*, Table 1), which can be formally specified as an OCL constraint below:

context MAR inv: self.preRule->size() =2 implies self.preRule.oclConstraint-
>select(c:OCLConstraint|c.contextConstraint = CRN::CancerMessage)->size() =1 and
self.preRule.oclConstraint->select(c:OCLConstraint|c.contextConstraint = CRN::CancerCase)->size() =1

As for a post-rule (*PostRule*), there is always exactly one since the action can only be taken in the cancer case level. A post-rule is always specified on the *CancerCase* class (Fig. 3) and it is formally specified as below:

context PostRule inv: self.oclConstraint.contextConstraint = CRN::CancerCase

Example: Table 1 shows an example of *MAR* (*rule 3*) that includes two pre-rules for the value of *DS* in a cancer message (equal to 2) and the value of *DS* in the relevant cancer case (equal to 3) and one post-rule that specifies the action to be performed, i.e., the value of *DS* in the cancer case should be updated to 2.

Associating Tags to OCL Constraints (A3). Furthermore, to support automated rule selection, tags are associated with a rule based on one or more attributes that the rule constrains (*A3* in Fig. 2). Notice that the tags reuse the same names as the attributes in the domain model, which makes it easier to match specific rules with corresponding attributes in the UML class diagram. With tags, a particular rule (from *MVRs*, *MARs* or *CCVRs*) will not be selected for data validation and aggregation until the values of specific attributes related with rule tags in cancer messages or cancer cases are not empty. For instance, three tags "*basis*", "*messageType*" and "*surgery*" are associated to *rule 1* in Table 1 since *rule 1* constrains these three fields. Similarly, two tags "*to-pography*" and "*surgery*" are assigned to *rule 2* (*CCVR*) while one tag "*DS*" is assigned to *rule 3* (*MAR*). When a new cancer message is introduced for validation, *rule 1* (Table 1) will not be selected for validating the cancer message unless the fields of "*basis*", "*messageType*" and "*surgery*" of the cancer message have specified values. Notice that the process of associating tags to rules is automated, which involves parsing OCL constraints to obtain tags and automatically associating them with the rules.

2.2 Tool Support

This section presents the tool support of *MBF4CR* and the design port is shown in Fig. 4. *MBF4CR* relies on three external tools: IBM RSA, Dresden OCL [10] and EsOCL [11] (highlighted as gray rectangles in Fig. 4), and five newly developed tools: *Extraction Tool, Tagging Tool, Validation Tool, Aggregation Tool* and *Transformation Tool* (shown as black rectangles in Fig. 4).

The *Extraction Tool* (implemented in Java) first takes the existing database schema from the CRN implementation as input and automatically generates an initial version of UML class diagram (e.g., cancer messages and cancer cases). Based on the modeling methodology (Sect. 2.1), IBM RSA is used to manually refine the UML class diagram and specify the three types of rules as OCL constraints as discussed in Sect. 2.1. Notice that we implemented guidelines as OCL constraints as part of our modeling method-ology (Sect. 2.1). These OCL constraints are automatically enforced when modeling the rules. For example, a modeler will not be allowed to model a *MVR* as an OCL

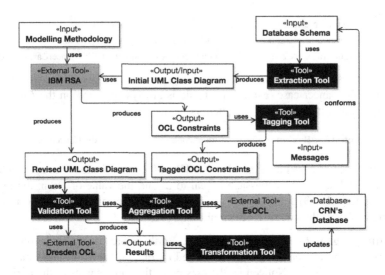

Fig. 4. The design of the *MBF4CR* tool support

constraint with the context other than the *CancerMessage* class. These OCL constraints are inputted into the *Tagging Tool* (implemented in Java) for automatically associating tags with each OCL constraint. The tool outputs a set of tagged OCL constraints (Fig. 4).

When cancer messages are introduced from various medical entities, the cancer messages, the revised UML class diagram and tagged OCL constraints will be taken as input to the *Validation Tool* for selecting and executing the *MVRs* to check the validity of the cancer messages. Notice that the *Validation Tool* is developed based on top of the Dresden OCL tool [10] for parsing and evaluating OCL constraints. If some of the selected *MVRs* are evaluated to be *false* (violated), the *Validation Tool* will return a report that specifies in which field(s) of which cancer message(s) which rule is violated, so that the cancer messages that do not comply with the *MVRs* will be returned to specific medical entities for correcting.

If all the selected *MVRs* are evaluated to be *true*, the cancer messages will be inputted to the *Aggregation Tool* that is developed based on an existing OCL solver tool called EsOCL [11] (Fig. 4) and works in two steps. First, the tool selects relevant *MARs* based on the tagged OCL constraints and use the *Validation Tool* to evaluate if the *PreRule* of a *MAR* is evaluated to be *true* using the Dresden OCL tool. Second, if the *PreRule* is evaluated to be true, the *Aggregation Tool* takes input the corresponding *PostRule* and solves it using the EsOCL solver. The EsOCL solver returns a set of values that satisfies the *PostRule*. These values are used by the *Aggregation Tool* to update the instance of a cancer case in the UML class diagram. Once the corresponding values in the cancer case are updated, the *Validation Tool* will be applied again to choose the relevant *CCVRs* for checking the validity of the cancer case. Similarly, if some of the *CCVRs* are evaluated to be *false*, a report will be returned by *MBF4CR* to medical coders in CRN. If all the *CCVRs* are evaluated to be *true*, the updated values of the cancer case will be transformed to the same format as the current CRN's practice (i.e., structured XML files) using a *Transformation Tool* (implemented in Java), which is used to update the database of CRN (Fig. 4).

3 Evaluation

To evaluate *MBF4CR*, we employed a real case study from CRN, consisting of 10 cancer messages, 6 cancer cases, 89 *MVRs*, 30 *MARs* and 68 *CCVRs*. All these rules have been formally specified using OCL based on the plain (English and Norwegian) texts of medical rules. The evaluation aims at addressing two research questions: (1) *RQ1*: Does *MBF4CR* reduce the number of medical rules to execute and is the time performance of *MBF4CR* acceptable in practice (*Performance*)? (2) *RQ2*: Does *MBF4CR* produce correct data validation and aggregation results (*Correctness*)?

3.1 RQ1 (Performance)

Tables 2 and 3 show the results of the percentage of selected rules out of the total number of rules related with each cancer message and cancer case. For instance, for *cancer message 1*, 24 out of 89 *MVRs* (27.0 %) were selected for validation, while 15 out of 30 *MARs* (50 %) were selected for aggregation (Table 2). On average, 32.8 % of *MVRs* and 63.3 % of *MARs* were selected for the 10 cancer messages. As for validating cancer cases (*CCVRs*), for instance, 25 out of 68 *CCARs* (36.8 %) were chosen for validating *cancer case 1* (Table 3). On average, 37.5 % of *CCVRs* were selected for all the 6 cancer cases.

Table 2. Results of percentage of selected *MVRs* and *MARs* for each cancer message

Cancer message	MVRs	MARs	Cancer message	MVRs	MARs
1	27.0 %	50.0 %	6	36.0 %	63.3 %
2	29.2 %	63.3 %	7	56.2 %	80.0 %
3	32.6 %	76.7 %	8	28.1 %	53.3 %
4	20.2 %	90.0 %	9	34.8 %	60.0 %
5	44.9 %	66.7 %	10	19.1 %	30.0 %

Table 3. Results of percentage of selected *CCVRs* for each cancer case

Cancer case	CCVRs	Cancer case	CCVRs
1	36.8 %	4	27.9 %
2	33.8 %	5	52.9 %
3	44.1 %	6	29.4 %

To evaluate the time performance of *MBF4CR*, we report the selection and execution time of the rules for each cancer message and cancer case. Results are shown in Tables 4 and 5. For instance, selecting the relevant *MVRs* and executing them for *cancer message 1* took 609 ms while the selection and execution time of *MARs* took 318 ms (Table 4). Similarly, the time taken by selecting and executing *CCVRs* for *cancer case 1* is only 465 ms.

Table 4. Results for selection and execution time of rules for cancer messages

Cancer message	MVRs	MARs	Cancer message	MVRs	MARs
1	609	318	6	810	386
2	654	376	7	1243	475
3	725	470	8	617	334
4	446	567	9	764	362
5	1018	421	10	435	194
Average	**MVRs per cancer message: 732.1**				
	MARs per cancer message: 390.3				
	Per MVR: 25.1, Per MAR: 20.5				

Table 5. Results for selection and execution time of rules for cancer cases

Cancer Case	CCVRs	Cancer Case	CCVRs
1	615	4	471
2	592	5	796
3	498	6	497
Average	**CCVRs per cancer case: 578,**		
	Per CCVR: 22.7		

It took on average 732.1, 390.3 and 578 ms to select and execute the *MVRs*, *MARs* and *CCVRs* for the 10 cancer messages and 6 cancer cases, respectively (Tables 4 and 5). We also report the average time of selection and execution for each type of rules, i.e., 25.1, 20.5, 22.7 ms for a *MVR*, a *MAR* and a *CCVR*, respectively (Tables 4 and 5), which is reasonable based on the discussions with medical coders. Thus, we answer RQ1 as: *MBF4CR* can largely reduce the number of rules to execute and the time performance of *MBF4CR* is acceptable in practice.

3.2   RQ2 (Correctness)

To check whether results returned by *MBF4CR* (validation and aggregation for cancer messages and cancer cases) are correct, in the sense of complying with the medical domain knowledge, we manually went through all the results produced by *MBF4CR*. More specifically, for *MVRs*, we checked if the value of a cancer message field is valid or the combinations of the values of several cancer message fields are valid if the returned result is *true*; If *false*, we also checked if the value of a cancer message field is invalid or the combinations of the values of several cancer messages are invalid; For *MARs*, we manually checked (a) when the condition of a *MAR* is evaluated to be *true*, whether its corresponding cancer case fields are updated correctly; (b) when the condition of a *MAR* is evaluated to be *false*, whether the cancer case fields are updated incorrectly. For *CCVRs*, similarly as for *MVRs*, we manually checked if the values of cancer case fields and the combinations of the values of several cancer case fields are valid or not when the returned results for *CCVRs* are *true* or *false*.

In summary, we manually checked the correctness of the results. For the 10 cancer messages, in total, there were 292 times of execution of *MVRs*, which led to the 879 field checks, and there were 190 times of execution of *MARs*, which led to the 599 field checks. For the 6 cancer cases, in total, *CCVRs* were executed 139 times, which led to 958 field checks. Based on the manual check, we observed that all the results returned by *MBF4CR* are consistent with the medical domain knowledge. This implies that the *MBF4CR* framework is correctly implemented with: (a) correct domain model, (b) correctly specified medical rules as OCL constraints, (c) correct implementation of the tagging mechanism, and (d) correct implementation of the rule execution.

3.3   Threats to Validity

One of the main *external threats* is that the experiment only included 10 cancer messages and 6 cancer cases, which may be a small sample of cancer messages and cancer cases. Notice that the 10 cancer messages we chose cover all the types of cancer messages (from different medical entities, e.g., clinic departments), and the 6 cancer cases we chose cover the most common types of cancers (e.g., lung cancer and breast cancer). Thus, the cancer messages and cancer cases we chose are representative. The main *internal threat* to validity is that one may argue that the manual check for the correctness of the results may not be always correct due to the insufficient medical domain knowledge. We need to mention such manual check also involved some of the medical coders from CRN with the aim to ensure the correctness.

4   Overall Discussion

Raising Level of Abstraction and Enabling Automation. The *MBF4CR* methodology relies on UML class diagrams and OCL constraints to specify required domain knowledge (i.e., cancer messages and cancer cases) at a higher level of abstraction than actual implementation (i.e., code). Raising the level of abstraction provides a better support in terms of facilitating communications of domain knowledge, especially medical rules, among stakeholders: e.g., chief medical officers, medical coders and programmers. In addition, training new stakeholders for the domain knowledge is limited to train them with the UML class model (Sect. 2.1) instead of going into the details of database and code. Furthermore, formalizing the domain knowledge as the UML class diagram and OCL constraints provides an opportunity to facilitate the automated process of selecting relevant medical rules for validation and aggregation, thereby significantly reducing the number of rules to execute (Sect. 3).

Systematically Maintaining Medical Rules. The current practice lacks a systematic way to maintain the more than a thousand of medical rules. Whenever a new rule is introduced, the chief medical officers need to specify it and a programmer needs to implement it into the system and medical coders will apply these rules for validation and aggregation of cancer messages and cancer cases. Similarly, when the chief medical officers request that a rule is to be deleted, a programmer has to look through the system and delete the corresponding code. When existing rules are modified, programmers have to update relevant code accordingly. Moreover, similarly as for maintaining any code, regression testing needs to be performed whenever the code is changed to ensure the quality of the implementation. Therefore, the cost of maintaining this kind of system is very expensive. With *MBF4CR*, we however provide a systematic way to maintain the rules: when a new rule is introduced, a new OCL constraint is created and added to the rule repository; when an old rule is deleted, the corresponding OCL constraint is removed; when an existing rule is modified, one only need to refine the affected OCL constraint. In summary, if any change occurs to rules, only affected OCL constraints need to be updated and there is no impact on the system implementation at all, thereby reducing the overall maintenance effort.

5 Related Work

Ensuring data quality is the core task in cancer registries, which has led to the development of a number of tools [5]. The Program established between the International Agency for Research on Cancer (IARC) and the International Association of Cancer Registries (IACR) aims to check the validity of data obtained from medical entities [6]. CanReg5[1] is an open source tool provided by IACR for inputting, checking and analyzing encoded data in a standard way. As compared to *MBE4CR*, the IARC/IACR Check Program, and CanReg5 only focus on checking data validity (i.e., cancer case validation) without considering the aggregation, which is more challenging than the validation in the context of CRN. Moreover, the domain knowledge is captured in the implementation level, which brings a challenge for understanding and all the rules are hardcoded in the program, which is difficult to manage and maintain.

GenEdit Plus[2] is a batch-mode application, developed by the Centers for Disease Control and Prevention (CDC) for checking the validity and consistency of cancer registry data. Its core part is a metafile containing data dictionary, record layout, lookup tables and validation algorithms. GenEdit Plus also provides a metafile called *NCDB*, which contains around 780 rules. Similar to *MBF4CR*, GenEdit Plus encodes all the rules in a portable way, i.e., rules are not hardcoded in the program but in a separate metafile. However, as compared with GenEdit Plus, *MBF4CR* specifies medical rules using OCL, which is a standardized notation having a number of open source and commercial tools available in the market for use. OCL also has a number of off-the-shelf

---

[1] CanReg5: http://www.iacr.com.fr/CanReg5/CanReg5-instructions.pdf.
[2] NPCR–EDITS Tools: http://origin.glb.cdc.gov/cancer/npcr/tools/edits/index.htm.

evaluators to enable automated data validation and aggregation (i.e., cancer messages and cancer cases). Moreover, GenEdit Plus does not support the aggregation of data (e.g., cancer message aggregation in our case).

6 Conclusion and Future Work

This paper proposes a model-based framework for supporting an automated cancer registry system (i.e., *MBF4CR*), which systematically models the domain knowledge (i.e., cancer messages and cancer cases) as an UML class diagram and formally specifies different types of medical rules as OCL constraints. By associating tags to each OCL constraint, an automated rule selection process is enabled. We evaluated *MBF4CR* using a case study from CRN and the results show *MBF4CR* can facilitate the current practice of CRN with an acceptable performance at the same time complying with the medical domain knowledge and reducing the maintenance effort of medical rules. In the future, we plan to evaluate *MBF4CR* with a large-scale case study involving more cancer data and medical rules. We also want to conduct a questionnaire-based study to solicit the views of medical experts for applying *MBF4CR*.

Acknowledgement. This research was supported by RFF Hovedstaden funded MBE-CR project. Shuai Wang is also supported by RCN funded Certus SFI. Tao Yue and Shaukat Ali are also supported by RCN funded Zen-Configurator project, EU Horizon 2020 project funded U-Test project, RCN funded MBT4CPS project and Certus SFI.

References

1. World Health Organization. Work Cancer Report (2014)
2. Larsen, I.K., et al.: Data quality at the Cancer Registry of Norway: an overview of comparability, completeness, validity and timeliness. Eur. J. Cancer **45**(7), 1218–1231 (2009)
3. Unified Modeling Language (UML). http://www.uml.org/
4. Object Management Group (OMG). http://www.omg.org/spec/OCL/2.2/
5. Ferlay, J., Burkhard, C., et al.: Check and conversion programs for cancer registries. International Agency for Research on Cancer (2005)
6. TR for IARC/IACR Tool. http://www.iacr.com.fr/images/doc/TechRep42.pdf
7. Joint Workshop on HCMDSS-MDPnP, pp. 156–159. IEEE (2007)
8. Wang, S., Ali, S., Yue, T., Liaaen, M.: Using feature model to support model-based testing of product lines: an industrial case study. In: QSIC Conference, pp. 75–84 (2013)
9. Wang, S., Gotlieb, A., Ali, S., Liaaen, M.: Automated test case selection using feature model: an industrial case study. In: ACM/IEEE 16th International Conference on Model Driven Engineering Languages and Systems (MODELS), pp. 237–253 (2013)
10. Dresden OCL. http://www.dresden-ocl.org/index.php/DresdenOCL
11. Ali, S., Iqbal, M.Z., Arcuri, A., Briand, L.: Solving OCL constraints for test data generation in industrial systems with search techniques. IEEE Trans. Softw. Eng. (TSE) **39**(10), 1376–1402 (2013)

12. Wang, S., Ali, S., Gotlieb, A., Liaaen, M.: A systematic test case selection methodology for product lines: results and insights from an industrial case study. Empirical Softw. Eng. (EMSE), 1–37 (2014). doi:10.1007/s10664-014-9345-5
13. Wang, S., Ali, S., Gotlieb, A., Liaaen, M.: Automated product line test case selection: industrial case study and controlled experiment. J. Softw. Syst. Model. (SOSYM), 1–25 (2015). doi:10.1007/s10270-015-0462-4
14. Wang, S., Ali, S.: Modeling BCMS product line using feature model, component family model, and UML. In: Comparing Modeling Approaches Workshop (2013)

Metamodeling vs Metaprogramming: A Case Study on Developing Client Libraries for REST APIs

Markus Scheidgen[1]([✉]), Sven Efftinge[2], and Frederik Marticke[1]

[1] Humboldt Universität zu Berlin, Berlin, Germany
{scheidge,marticke}@informatik.hu-berlin.de
[2] Typefox GmbH, Kiel, Germany
sven.efftinge@typefox.de

Abstract. Web-services with REST APIs comprise the majority of the programmable web. To access these APIs more safely and conveniently, language specific client libraries can hide REST details behind regular programming language idioms. Manually building such libraries is straightforward, but tedious and error prone. Fortunately, model-based development provides different methods to automate their development. In this paper, we present our experiences with two opposing approaches to describe existing REST APIs and to generate type-safe client side Java libraries from these descriptions. First, we use an EMF-metamodel and a code generator (external DSL). Secondly, we use the Java compatible language Xtend and its metaprogramming mechanism *active annotations*, which allows us to alter the semantics of existing Xtend constructs to describe REST APIs within Xtend (internal DSL). Furthermore, we present related approaches and discuss our findings comparatively.

1   Introduction

Many of today's data intensive web applications (e.g. most social networks: Google+, Facebook, Twitter, etc.) provide access to their data via REST APIs. The representational state transfer (REST) principles impose very little restrictions on the development of clients. Ubiquitous technologies like HTTP and JSON facilitate development in almost all programming environments. On the downside, this technology combination provides little safety. IDEs cannot determine whether a certain request is part of the used API, if a certain parameter actually exists, if arguments have the right type, or whether the response is structured as expected.

Used to the safety and comfort (e.g. code-completion) of type-safe languages and IDEs, many developers build language specific client libraries for existing REST APIs. Those libraries transparently hide the necessary HTTP and JSON processing behind type-safe programming language idioms. The development of such client libraries is a straightforward deduction of boilerplate code from API documentation. This tedious and error prone process presents an archetypical use-case for model-based development (MBD).

© Springer International Publishing Switzerland 2016
A. Wąsowski and H. Lönn (Eds.): ECMFA 2016, LNCS 9764, pp. 205–216, 2016.
DOI: 10.1007/978-3-319-42061-5_13

Following our goal to create a set of homogeneous Java libraries for social networks and their existing REST APIs, we experimented with a metamodel- and a metaprogramming-based approach (implementations are provided as an open-source Github project [15]). First, we developed a metamodel that allows developers to describe REST APIs on a high level of abstraction through the use of domain (REST) specific modeling concepts (external DSL [9]). A code generator then produces the desired libraries from these descriptions.

Secondly, we use the Java compatible language Xtend [4] to describe REST APIs (internal DSL [9]). Xtend provides a metaprogramming concept called *active annotations*. Active annotations allow developers to eXtend the Xtend compiler with specialized semantics for existing language constructs. We use this to derive client libraries from REST APIs described with annotated Xtend classes and fields.

The next section will give a short introduction to REST and defines problems that we observed while developing Java libraries for existing REST APIs. In Sects. 3 and 4, we describe the two approaches and how we used them. We complement our approaches with those found in related work in Sect. 5 and finally compare everything and draw conclusions in the closing Sect. 6.

2   REST APIs and Client Libraries

Representational state transfer (REST, often also RESTful or ReST) is a set of principles for Internet client-server architectures originally formulated by Fielding [8]. REST is tightly associated with HTTP as the client-server-communication protocol. In fact, it is believed, that Fielding, who was part of the HTTP 1.0 and 1.1 standardization process, actively aligned HTTP with his REST principle [18]. There are two REST principles that are important for clients: *communication is stateless* and there has to be a *uniform interface*. The first principle, stateless communication, means everything necessary to understand a request and a respective response has to be part of the corresponding message. This facilitates simple and scalable server-side application design and is probably the most important factor for its wide adoption. In fact, 62 % of APIs listed on *programmableweb.com* are REST APIs, compared to mere 17 % of SOAP APIs. The second principle (uniform interface) can be realized at different levels according to Richardson's maturity model [2]. Level 0, there is no interface, just a blackbox (no REST or RESTless); level 1, clients can identify specific resources on a server (i.e. through URLs); level 2, clients can also use different verbs (i.e. HTTP methods) to create, read, update, and delete (CRUD) resources; level 3, there is *hypermedia as the engine of application state* (HATEOAS). This means that resources reference each other with hyperlinks and that clients do not need to understand the full interface (i.e. resource URL path and parameters) because they simply navigate from one resource to another through contained hyperlinks. Although, HTTP allows different MIME-types, the majority of APIs use JSON to represent data. Figure 1 shows an example of REST communication.

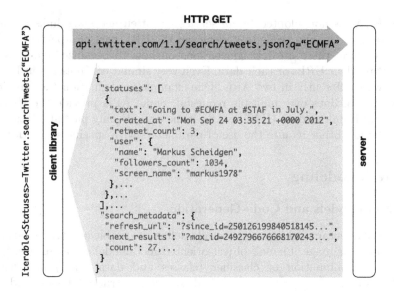

Fig. 1. Example request and response for a tweet search with Twitter's REST API. The resulting JSON is simplified; strings are abbreviated.

There are few restrictions for the development of REST clients: HTTP-, URL-, and JSON libraries exist for most programming environments; the learning curve compared to other web-service architectures, i.e. SOAP is low. But, client code becomes very verbose, since HTTP requests need to be constructed, possible errors handled, JSON needs to be parsed, etc. Furthermore, as stated earlier, there is no safety when compared to other architectures and to what most statically type-safe programming languages have to offer. Not surprisingly language specific and type-safe client libraries are in high demand. The left side of Fig. 1 shows a type-safe Java idiom that could be used to process the example request on the right side.

While the development of client libraries is pretty straightforward, we experienced a set of issues that any MBD of such libraries needs to cope with:

1. To avoid confusion, client libraries need to use the names that the original API uses. This includes names to distinct different kinds of resources in URL paths, names for URL parameters, and keys in JSON objects. But often, the existing names are not suitable for a particular programming language. Names might break naming conventions, inconveniently or illegally hide or override other names (e.g. `Class` in Java), or are outright forbidden (e.g. keywords).
2. JSON has a limited set of primitive types: boolean, strings, and numbers. This leads to non-trivial data mappings. For example, clients want to process dates as dates and not as strings that represent dates. Other examples are URLs, colors, or GPS-coordinates. Furthermore, each REST API might encode the same data differently.

3. HATEOAS is not adopted by all services or often necessary links are missing. In practice, one needs to understand the URL part of a particular API. Furthermore, there are few conventions on how to organize resources and structure their URLs or their data. Even very similar concepts might be realized very differently in two APIs. One example is pagination (i.e. providing long lists of data over multiple requests). Some APIs provide the URLs to the next chunk of data (HATEOAS), some provide only partial URLs, some provide ids, other require the use of parameters with specific semantics.

3   Metamodeling

3.1   Metamodels and Code-Generation

The goal of a metamodel is to structurally define the usable constructs (abstract syntax) of a language. Like all object-oriented metamodeling languages, Ecore provides a combination of classifier (classes and data types) and feature (attributes and references) concepts to describes constructs (classes) and their possible attributes and relationships (features). Thereby, the metamodel is not concerned with what language instances (models) mean or what the language constructs are used for.

In order to give semantics to a metamodel, one can provide a code generator: a program that takes a metamodel instance (model) as input and translates it into code (i.e. an instance of a programming language). Thereby, a code generator realizes rules; each rule determines how to translate a certain language construct and each rule gives a meaning to a metamodel class and its features. While the code generator depends on a given metamodel, the metamodel is fully independent from the code generator. In fact, one can use multiple code generators that realize different semantics for the same metamodel. This is a major factor in MBD, since it facilitates the (re-)use the same model for different things.

In order to allow language users to express themselves with the defined constructs, a concrete notation (concrete syntax) and an accompanying tool (e.g. editor) are necessary. A tuple of metamodel, code generator, and notation/editor is often referred to as an external domain specific language (external DSL).

3.2   A Metamodel for REST APIs

Figure 2 shows a simplified version of our REST API metamodel. The model contains the constructs necessary to describe all aspects of a REST APIs that are necessary to generate client libraries. The top part of the metamodel comprises core object-oriented constructs that we also find in many other languages (including UML, Java, or metamodeling itself). `Classes` can contain `Features` that describe slots for values of a certain `DataType`.

There are two specializations of these common constructs in REST APIs: `Request` classes and `ComplexDataTypes`. A `Request` class defines a set of `Parameters` (communicated through either URL path, URL parameter,

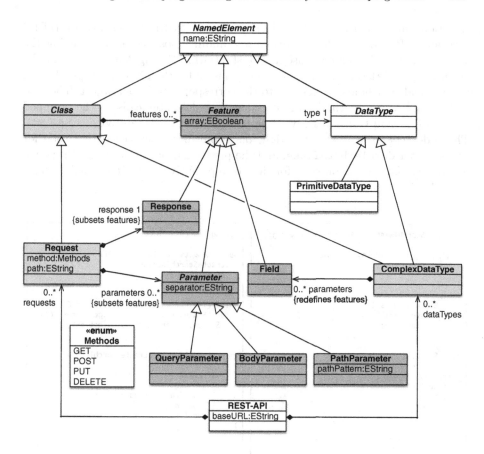

Fig. 2. Simplified metamodel for our REST client API generator.

or HTTP body) and a specific `Response`. Both have respective types. A `ComplexDataType` (i.e. a schema for JSON objects) defines `Fields` (i.e. JSON key/value-pairs) which also have a respective type. Besides complex types, predefined and custom `PrimitiveDataTypes` can be used. All `Features` can also describe `arrays` of data.

We have written a code generator that translates REST API descriptions (metamodel instances) into client libraries (Java code). Instances of all class constructs (i.e. `Request` classes and `ComplexDataTypes`) are translated into Java classes, and all instances of feature constructs (i.e. `Parameter`, `Response`, `Field`) are translated into Java properties (i.e. pairs of get- and set-methods). Properties have Java types that match the respective `DataType` in the model.

Depending on the meta-class, some semantic variations are generated. A `Parameter` can only be modified before the response is accessed. Instead of properties, we generate a fluent interface for parameters. The response's get-method contains all the code that is needed to execute the request: construction and execution of the HTTP request with the corresponding HTTP verb and URL, waiting for its response, handling possible errors, parsing the JSON contained in the response, and instantiating the right Java class for the given `ComplexDataType`. Generated Java classes for `ComplexDataTypes` have a private field that holds a reference to the corresponding JSON object. The generated field access methods contain code that delegates calls to the wrapped JSON object and translates Java data to JSON data (set) and vice-versa (get). The code generator creates the right data-conversion and delegation code for arrays, other `ComplexDataTypes`, and the predefined primitive types. Users can declare custom conversion rules for their own primitive types (refer to Sect. 6 for more details).

```
request SearchTweets path="search/tweets.json"
    response=SearchResults {
  query array q: String sperator=" "
  query since_id: long
  ...
}

data SearchResults {
  array statuses: Status
  search_metadata: SearchMetaData
}

data Status {
  text: String
  created_at: Date
  retweet_count: int
  user: User
  id: long
  ...
}

data User {
  ...
```

partial description of Twitter's API in a pseudo syntax

```java
String searchKey = "ECMFA";

SearchResults results = Twitter
    .createSearchTweets()
    .q(searchKey)
    .xResult();

while (!results.getStatuses().isEmpty()) {
  for (Status status: results.getStatuses()) {
    System.out.println(status.getText());
  }

  results = Twitter.createSearchTweets
      .q(searchKey)
      .sinceId(
        results
          .getSearchMetadata()
          .getMaxId()
      ).xResult();
}
```

use of the generated wrapper API in Java

Fig. 3. Example API description and example use of generated library.

3.3 Example

The left side of Fig. 3 exemplifies the use of the metamodel with a self explanatory concrete syntax. The example shows a description for a request class that defines the Twitter API's tweet search function that was depicted by example in Fig. 1. The description contains the appropriate path, a few parameters, and refers to a complex data type to wrap the expected response. The right side of the same figure shows how one can use the library that was generated from this partial API description. The fluent interface for request creation allows to create and configure request in a single line. The method `xResult` triggers request execution and returns the result contained in the request's response. Note that the response (as all features) has the proper Java type and the Java tooling can actually validate the proper use of these types. The rest of the example shows how to access the complex result data. You also see, how we can configure further request in typical REST fashion by passing state data from one response to the next request.

4   Metaprogramming

4.1   Xtend and Active Annotations

As a general paradigm, metaprograms are programs that transform the code of other programs or themselves into regular programs (object-programs) [16]. A specific approach to metaprogramming that Sheard [16] would classify as a homogeneous, manually annotated two staged metaprogram, is a metaprogram that uses annotations to replace idioms in the program with generated code in order to create object-programs. Readers unfamiliar with this application of metaprogramming can also think of this as a profile mechanism for programming languages, where one can define stereotypes (i.e. annotations) to assign a specialized meaning to existing language constructs.

Active annotations in Xtend provide such a metaprogramming mechanism. Xtend compiles into Java code and active annotations allow developers to inject specialized semantics into the compilation process. Syntactically, active annotations work like regular Java annotations. Semantically, Xtend provides a callback interface that hooks client code into the Xtend compiler. Developers can provide their own static semantics rules and provide further checks for the annotated elements. They can provide model-to-model transformation rules that expand the annotated elements into more complex Java structures. Finally, developers can provide code generator rules to implement the expanded annotated elements. In metaprogramming terms [16], implementations of the mentioned callback interface provide metaprograms that replace parts of a given object-program with different object-program code. The active annotations function as manual annotations to trigger the metaprograms for the intended object-program parts. The translation process only has two stages, so the generated code cannot contain further active annotations (or at least Xtend wont compile them as such). We have homogeneous metaprograms, since callback interface implementations are also Xtend programs.

4.2   A Set of Active Annotations to Describe REST APIs

As part of the REST API metamodel in Sect. 3, we observed that request classes and complex data objects have a class/feature/datatype structure. The same structure that Java classes and their member fields also have. We can use this similarity here. With active annotations, we cannot define new meta-classes; we cannot introduce new language constructs for requests or complex data types. But, we can use the existing Java/Xtend class and member field constructs to model request classes and complex data types. More concretely, we eXtend the semantics of classes and their members fields with active annotations.

The left side of Fig. 4 shows some of our annotation definitions. They are themselves annotated with annotations that describe details about the new annotations. The annotation `Active` turns a regular Java annotation into an active annotation. It also assigns the intended implementation of the before mentioned callback interface (i.e. the semantics of the annotation). We have defined two active annotations, one for request classes, called `Request` and one for complex data types, called `JSON`. When these annotations are used, they have to carry very little information, since most of the necessary information is already conveyed by the Xtend classes and their member fields. Classes already have a name, a set of member fields, and each field has a name as well as a type. The `Request` annotation has attributes for the URL path and for its response type. To denote specific characteristics of features, we add additional annotations. Fist, `Body-` and `PathParameter` to denote fields as body or path parameters (query

```
@Active(RequestCompilationParticipant)
@Target(TYPE)
annotation Request {
    String path
    HttpMethod method = HttpMethod.GET
    Response response
}

@Target(FIELD) annotation BodyParameter {
}

@Target(FIELD) annotation PathParameter {
    String value // path pattern to replace
}

@Target(FIELD)
annotation Response {
    Class<?> type
    boolean isArray = false
}

@Target(FIELD)
annotation Name {
    String value
}

@Active(JSONWrapperCompilationParticipant)
@Target(TYPE)
annotation JSON {
}

@Target(FIELD)
annotation WithConverter {
    Class<? extends Converter<?>> value
}

interface Converter<T> {
    def T toValue(String str)
    def String toString(T value)
}
```

some annotations used to describe REST APIs

```
@Request(
    path="search/tweets.json",
    response=@Response(type=SearchResults)
)
class SearchTweets {
    @Required String q
    String since_id
}

@JSON class SearchResults {
    List<Status> statuses
    SearchMetaData search_metadata
}

@JSON class Status {
    String text

    @WithConverter(TwitterDateConverter)
    Date created_at

    User user

    @Name("id_str") String id
}

@JSON User {
...
```

partial description of Twitter's API in Xtend with annotations

```
val searchKey = "ECMFA"
var results = twitter.search.tweets
    .q(searchKey).xResult

while(!results.statuses.empty) {
    results.statuses.map[it.text]
        .forEach[println(it)]

    results = twitter.search.tweets
        .q(searchKey)
        .sinceId(results.searchMetadata.maxId)
        .xResult
}
```

use of the generated wrapper API in Xtend

Fig. 4. Xtend annotation for REST API description, example use of annotations and example use of the generated library.

parameter is the default). Secondly, Name to provide different feature names in case the necessary name is not a valid Java identifier (details in Sect. 6). Thirdly, we have an annotation to describe the response (it's type or whether it is an array). Fourthly, to further describe complex data types, we can assign different names to fields or add data conversion to fields (also refer to Sect. 6).

Semantically, the active annotations work similar to the code generator in our metamodel-based approach. The difference is that corresponding Java classes and fields already exist. However, the active annotations will replace the declared member fields with get- and set-methods (properties) and implement these methods similar to the described code generator in Sect. 3.

4.3   Example

We use the example from Fig. 1 again (upper right in Fig. 4). If you compare the Xtend code used to describe the API with the metamodel-based description in Fig. 3, you notice a strong and not surprising resemblance. Both examples describe the same part of the same API. The only difference is that in Xtend we cannot introduce our own keywords and have to use our annotations instead.

The example Xtend code that uses the generated library in the lower right of the same figure also shows strong resemblance to its Java counterpart (right of Fig. 3). In fact, the generated APIs are almost identical. But, since Xtend allows to access get-/set-methods like fields, omits empty parenthesis, and offers closures, we can express the same in a more compact form.

5   Related Work

Izquierdo and Cabot [11], Cánovas and Cabot [3], and Menkundle et al. [13] infer explicit schemas (e.g. in the form of Ecore-models) from the implicit schemas contained in example JSON data. These inferred descriptions are similar to our metamodel-based descriptions of complex data types. There is similar work based on metaprogramming side. The active Xtend annotation Jsonized [6] takes example JSON data and turns it into wrapper classes. JsonProvider [1] applies the same concept to type providers in F#.

Ed-Douibi et al. [5] build a server side REST framework for EMF-data. In a certain way, this can be interpreted as the opposite to our work. Instead of creating model-based descriptions of existing REST APIs, Ecore-models are interpreted as descriptions for new REST APIs. Gerhart et al. [10] is another example that represents EMF-data with JSON. With both works, JSON data can be processed safely via Java APIs generated from Ecore-models. But, in both cases the mapping between implicit JSON schema and Java API is fix and you cannot use unconventional names or custom representations of primitive data.

There are also metamodel-based frameworks for generating server-side code for new REST APIs [12,14,17]. The used metamodels are all similar to each other and ours and a single description could be used for both server and client code. Unfortunately, most service providers have not adopted such approaches yet, and no formal descriptions of the examined APIs exist.

Our idea of metaprogramming with active annotations is only one way; reflection is another: Jackson [7] uses regular Java annotations and runtime-introspection to facilitate type-safe JSON data bindings. Type providers in F# are a different metaprogramming mechanism from the .NET world.

6   Discussion and Conclusions

When comparing the two presented approaches metamodeling and metaprogramming the general known arguments from comparing external with internal DSLs apply [9]: no syntactical limitations, closed language, specialized tools for external DSLs and language integration, existing/stronger tool support, and easier to (co-)evolve for internal DSLs.

Based on REST APIs as a specific application, further arguments in favor of external DSLs can be made. First, metamodeling is programming language independent and code generators for multiple languages and with different semantics can be used. In principle, we could derive client libraries for multiple languages, server-side code, and API documentation from the same description. Secondly, metamodels can define standards and metamodel-based descriptions can be used interoperably by different parties. During this work, we often wished that web-service providers would publish their APIs in such a formal manner. Even with an MBD-based description language for client libraries, we still have to gather descriptions from informal artifacts like API documentation. For some vendors, we even decided to develop specialized HTML-parsers to automatically translate online API documentation. The work of Izquierdo and Cabot [11], Cánovas and Cabot [3], and Menkudle et al. [13] presents a different approach by inferring explicit schema information from actual application data.

In favor of internal DSLs, we can state that a metaprogramming mechanism like active annotations in Xtend drastically eXtends the possibilities to use a host language more specifically and elevates Xtend internal DSLs further from just being regular libraries. Now, we can introduce different static and dynamic semantics to existing language constructs without having to provide our own language tools. This is particularly ideal for applications that require to describe structures that consist of classes, features, and types like REST APIs, because similar concepts already exist in object-oriented host languages.

We stated three problems that arise when creating client libraries for one or multiple REST APIs in Sect. 2. First, not all names are allowed in all programming languages. In a metamodel-based description, we can use all names, since the metamodel is programming language independent. The code generator however has to identify non conforming names and has to change them accordingly. In an annotation based description, the names we want to use are already the names of Java/Xtend classes and fields. Consequently, we cannot always use the indented name. In general, we can also use implicit name conversions, but without further information, this can only be the same for all names (e.g. we could always convert camelCase names to snake_case names). This does not work for all non conforming names. Therefore, we often need to provide two names: one for the Xtend class or member, and one that is used to communicate with the server. We can provide the latter one with an annotation (example in Fig. 4 id_str vs id). In summary, we can solve this in both approaches, but for metaprogramming the description is less concise.

Secondly, programming language types are more specific than JSON types. Does a JSON string just mean a JSON string, or something that has a more specific type in a programming language, like a date or a color. Since this lays in the semantics of what is described and not within the syntax of it, it also does not matter whether we describe the API based on a metamodel or a set of annotations. In both cases, we have to provide conversion rules for features with primitive types. We allow users to program such conversions by implementing a given interface (refer to Fig. 4, left side and the end). In the metamodel, we can use an additional field in Feature to enable users to refer to converters by name; in an annotation-based description, developers can use an additional annotation WithConverter to add a specific converter to a feature (as done in Fig. 4: created_at). In Xtend, this referencing has good tool support, because we simply refer to a converter class written in Xtend/Java. With an external DSL, the same level of tool support is much harder to achieve.

Thirdly, different APIs implement common concepts differently. This problem lays within the semantics of the web applications themselves and has nothing to do with their APIs. REST APIs just provide a common way to access data, how a web-service decides to organize and structure this data is beyond the interface. Consequently, we can't do anything about it by means of describing REST APIs, neither with metamodels nor annotations. To identify common concepts and homogenize different APIs, we would need to create a common API and translate calls to the common API into calls for the individual specific existing APIs. This is a different topic and is beyond the scope of this paper.

Due to space restrictions, we had to leave out several aspects. We could not explain the use of constraints for request parameters and inheritance for complex data types (i.e. JSON data). The former is useful to enforce semantic conformance with APIs. The latter also for more concise descriptions. Rate-limits, authentication, and authorization are particularly challenging to integrate into client libraries homogeneously.

To summarize, both approaches, in principle, allow to describe REST APIs and allow to generate client libraries. The problems we identified are either solved in a similar fashion and cannot be solved by both approaches. In the end, general considerations, similar to those of external vs internal DSLs, decide. If you need to create libraries for a range of programming languages, or even want to create server side code, you should opt for a metamodel-based approach. If the goal is to quickly develop a library for the Java world, Xtend and the presented active annotations allow to develop this API quickly and with existing tool support. In general, our experiences have shown that active annotations provide a meaningful addition to an internal DSL host language that allows to apply semantic variations to existing language constructs.

References

1. F# data: Json type provider. http://fsharp.github.io/FSharp.Data/library/JsonProvider.html
2. Betten, S.: Richardson maturity model. Technical report, Fachgebiet Software Engineering, Universität Hannover (2011)
3. Cánovas Izquierdo, J.L., Cabot, J.: Discovering implicit schemas in JSON data. In: Daniel, F., Dolog, P., Li, Q. (eds.) ICWE 2013. LNCS, vol. 7977, pp. 68–83. Springer, Heidelberg (2013)
4. Eclipse.org: Xtend. http://www.eclipse.org/xtend/
5. Ed-Douibi, H., Izquierdo, J.L.C., Gómez, A., Tisi, M., Cabot, J.: EMF-REST: generation of restful apis from models. CoRR (2015)
6. Efftinge, S.: Jsonized. http://github.com/svenefftinge/jsonized
7. FasterXML: Jackson json processor wiki. http://wiki.fasterxml.com/JacksonHome
8. Fielding, R.T.: Architectural Styles and the Design of Network-based Software Architectures. Ph.D. thesis (2000)
9. Fowler, M.: Domain Specific Languages, 1st edn. Addison-Wesley Professional, Boston (2010)
10. Gerhart, M., Bayer, J., Höfner, J.M., Boger, M.: Approach to define highly scalable metamodels based on JSON. In: BigMDE 2015, p. 11 (2015)
11. Izquierdo, J.L.C., Cabot, J.: Composing JSON-based web APIs. In: Casteleyn, S., Rossi, G., Winckler, M. (eds.) ICWE 2014. LNCS, vol. 8541, pp. 390–399. Springer, Heidelberg (2014)
12. Maximilien, E.M., Wilkinson, H., Desai, N., Tai, S.: A domain-specific language for web APIs and services mashups. In: Krämer, B.J., Lin, K.-J., Narasimhan, P. (eds.) ICSOC 2007. LNCS, vol. 4749, pp. 13–26. Springer, Heidelberg (2007)
13. Menkudle, A., Sonawane, S., Jagtap, A.: Extracting application model from restful web services for client stub generation. Int. J. Comput. Technol. Appl. (IJCTA) 5(1), 226–232 (2014)
14. Rivero, J.M., Heil, S., Grigera, J., Gaedke, M., Rossi, G.: MockAPI: an agile approach supporting API-first web application development. In: Daniel, F., Dolog, P., Li, Q. (eds.) ICWE 2013. LNCS, vol. 7977, pp. 7–21. Springer, Heidelberg (2013)
15. Scheidgen, M.: XRAW-Easy development of REST API client libraries with Xtend. http://github.com/markus1978/xraw
16. Sheard, T.: Accomplishments and research challenges in meta-programming. In: Taha, W. (ed.) SAIG 2001. LNCS, vol. 2196, pp. 2–44. Springer, Heidelberg (2001)
17. Tavares, N., Vale, S., Luis, S., Brazil, M.: Towards interoperability to the implementation of RESTful web services: a model driven approach. In: International Conference on Systems (ICONS), pp. 234–240 (2014)
18. Tilkov, S.: REST und HTTP: Einsatz der Architektur des Web für Integrationsszenarien. dpunkt, Heidelberg (2009)

Experiences with Model-Driven Engineering in Neurorobotics

Georg Hinkel$^{(\boxtimes)}$, Oliver Denninger, Sebastian Krach, and Henning Groenda

Software Engineering, Forschungszentrum Informatik (FZI),
Haid-und-Neu-Straße 10-14,
Karlsruhe, Germany
{hinkel,denninger,krach,groenda}@fzi.de

Abstract. Model-driven engineering (MDE) has been successfully adopted in domains such as automation or embedded systems. However, in many other domains, MDE is rarely applied. In this paper, we describe our experiences of applying MDE techniques in the domain of neurorobotics – a combination of neuroscience and robotics, studying the embodiment of autonomous neural systems. In particular, we participated in the development of the Neurorobotics Platform (NRP) – an online platform for describing and running neurorobotic experiments by coupling brain and robot simulations. We explain why MDE was chosen and discuss conceptual and technical challenges, such as inconsistent understanding of models, focus of the development and platform-barriers.

1 Introduction

The field of neurorobotics uses insights from neuroscience to build robot controllers using neural networks. Of particular interest is the combination of biologically plausible spiking neural networks with robots. This enables neurophysiologists to study how brains can be connected to bodies, neuroscientists to study brain models in the real world and robotic scientists to perform locomotion or perception tasks – which are hard to solve with classical robot controllers – using the neural networks' ability to learn and adapt.

Building spiking neural networks is increasingly understood by domain experts. Robotics has a long experience of modelling robots and building robot controllers. However, establishing a closed loop between both artifacts – this means transferring sensor information from a robot to a brain and control information from the brain back to the robot – is still an open question. Few scientists know both neural network simulation and robotics well enough in order to perform adequate experiments.

As a consequence, most existing experiments in neurorobotics are handcrafted simulation scripts, able to perform only a tightly defined experiment without variations. Such scripts may easily get obsolete when the interface of the components from either domain changes.

Therefore, it is necessary to abstract from the technical implementation details and allow neuroscientists to describe the interconnection between neural

A. Wąsowski and H. Lönn (Eds.): ECMFA 2016, LNCS 9764, pp. 217–228, 2016.
DOI: 10.1007/978-3-319-42061-5_14

networks and robots in a formal model. The simulations gain flexibility as common operations such as pausing, stopping, resetting or interacting with the simulation can be implemented once, based on the formal model. Flexibility in accessing the model is crucial as users want to build and run experiments interactively as well as non-interactively. The interactive style is well-known to robotics where experiments are built iteratively with visualization close to real-time. In contrast, neural network simulation experiments are typically run as batch jobs.

Raising the abstraction level in order to limit the description of a system to domain concepts rather than implementation details is also one of the major goals of model-driven engineering (MDE). Hence, we have adopted MDE techniques in the development of the Neurorobotics-Platform (NRP), an integrated simulation platform to allow neuroscientists to specify a neurorobotics simulation on a high level of abstraction.

In this paper, we present our experiences in applying model-driven techniques in the domain of neurorobotics that we gained during the development of the NRP. We observed inconsistencies in the understanding of models that imply communication problems bringing together experts of the involved matters. A lack of good test concepts for the code generators has made us shift functionality towards the target platform and keep code generators as small as necessary. For the choice of generators or any other tools, we faced a platform barrier. Our agile Scrum development process seemed incompatible with the upfront initial effort implied by the model-driven software development approach we took.

The remainder of this paper is structured as follows: Sect. 2 briefly introduces the NRP. Section 3 discusses the potential advantages offered by MDE in neurorobotics. Section 4 details on the lessons learned during the development of the NRP. Finally, Sect. 5 concludes the paper.

2   The Neurorobotics Platform in a Nutshell

The Neurorobotics Platform (NRP) is developed as part of the Human Brain Project[1] to run coupled neuronal and robotics simulations in an interactive platform. Whereas there are multiple neuronal simulators (e.g. Neuron [1], NEST [2]), robotics and world simulations (e.g. Gazebo [3]), the NRP aims to offer a platform uniting the two fields. A core part of the NRP is the Closed-Loop-Engine (CLE) that allows to specify the data exchange between the brain simulation and the robot in a programmatic manner and orchestrates the simulations.

The key concept of the NRP is offering scientists an easy access to a simulation platform using a state-of-the-art web interface. Scientists are relieved from the burdensome installation process of scientific simulation software and are able to leverage large-scale computing resources. Furthermore, support for monitoring and visualizing the spiking activity of the neurons or joint states of the robot is offered as well as the camera image perceived by the robot.

---

[1] https://www.humanbrainproject.eu/.

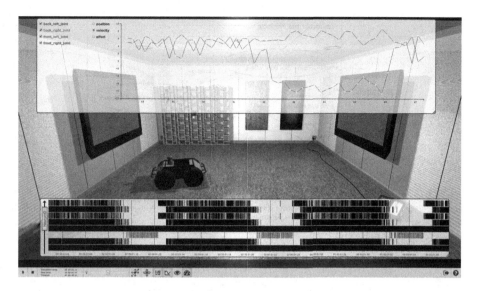

Fig. 1. Screenshot showing a Braitenberg vehicle inspired experiment in the Neurorobotics Platform (NRP). Upon perception of red color in the camera image, the robot moves forward, otherwise it keeps turning on the spot. A plot at the top shows velocity of the robot wheels while a plot at the bottom shows spiking activity of neurons. (Color figure online)

To give an impression on how the platform looks like, a screenshot of an experiment inspired by Braitenberg vehicles [4] using a Husky[2] robot is depicted in Fig. 1.

The different users of the NRP are depicted in Fig. 2. The NRP basically targets three science communities with overlapping fields of interest: *neuroscientists*, *neurophysicists* and *roboticists*. Neuroscientists are able to visualize brain models through embodiment. Neurophysiologists leverage the coupling mechanism of both simulations to analyze or validate models on signal transmission between perception, brain activity and motor control. Roboticists are able to validate and compare the performance of neuronal control compared to classic robot control approaches.

The platform aims to be usable by scientists with little programming knowledge. Based on templates, users can instantiate new experiments and adapt them at runtime using techniques familiar to the respective communities. Data interchange between a simulated brain and a robot is transcribed as so-called *Transfer Functions* using an internal Python-based DSL [5]. We use the Python programming language as it is generally accepted by neuroscientists and actively used for specifying brain models.

Figure 3 depicts the Closed-Loop-Engine which implements the core of the NRP. The CLE controls the neuronal and the world simulation, and realizes

---

[2] http://www.clearpathrobotics.com/husky/.

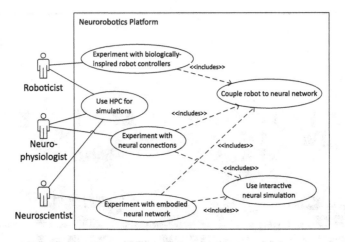

Fig. 2. The actors and their intentions of using the NRP

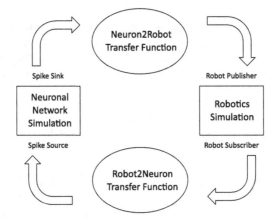

Fig. 3. A closed loop between a robotics simulation and a neural network

a lightweight simulation data interchange mechanism. Neuronal and robotics simulation are iteratively run in parallel for the same amount of time, after which the transfer functions are executed periodically. Communication with the brain is realized through recording and injecting spike data. Interfacing with the robot simulation is done using the middleware (ROS [6]). In order to ensure reproducibility, data exchange is conducted in a deterministic fashion.

Complex brain simulations require large scale computing resources and often exceed the capacities researchers have at hand. Furthermore, effectively leveraging computing resources provided by data centers is only available to neuroscientists with the appropriate competences or support from the computer scientific domain. The NRP provides a unified access to high-performance computing resources of different institutions. The shared infrastructure in particular offers the possibility to run simulations using specifically designed neuromorphic hardware, which is currently not widely available.

Neuronal simulation in data centers are usually run as non-interactive batch jobs whose execution is scheduled once and runs to completion before reporting results to the neuroscientist. The scientist has no means of influencing the simulation after the job has been scheduled and errors can only be detected by analyzing the results. The NRP is designed to enable interactive manipulations of the neuronal network, the simulated environment or the robot. Thus, erroneous behavior can be detected very quickly.

3 The Potential of Model-Driven Engineering in Neurorobotics

In this section, we discuss why MDE is a suitable approach for developing a simulation platform such as the NRP. As the NRP aims to support the specification of data transfers between neural networks and robots accessible also by users with little programming expertise, the process of assembling the simulation code and its goals are very similar to model-driven software development. While a frequent rationale of model-driven software development (MDSD) is to reduce the development effort, we regard the higher abstraction level even as an enabling technology for users with little programming experience.

The artifacts for a model-driven software development process as introduced by Völter and Stahl [7] are depicted in Fig. 4.

The idea of model-driven software development is to divide the code of an application into three parts, (i) the platform, (ii) schematic repetitive code and (iii) individual code. From the repetitive code, a metamodel is extracted. Application models are then created as instances of this metamodel through a domain-specific language (DSL) and are transformed to the repetitive code by means of a model transformation.

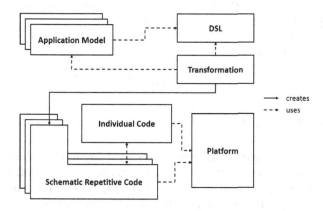

Fig. 4. Artifacts of model-driven software development as defined by Völter and Stahl [7]

The advantage is that the application model is very focused on domain concepts whereas technical implementation details are encoded in either the platform, the model transformation or the individual code. A goal of MDSD is clearly to keep the individual code as small as possible. The application models are thus usually specified in DSLs, either textual or graphical.

Understanding an experiment as an application, this model is also well suited to describe neurorobotics simulations of these experiments. Here, the ability to describe simulations in terms of domain concepts independent of technical implementation details allows also neuroscientists without a strong experience in programming languages to design and run experiments. At the same time, the technical implementation details can be exchanged in order to support new simulators. This is important as there is currently a multitude of neural network simulators available.

Another important aspect is the validation of experiments. As the involved neural networks become large, neurorobotics simulations require a large amount of resources. Additionally, especially in a web-based simulation platform accessible through the internet, simulations are run with an identity of the service host rather than the user. This raises security concerns in order to avoid the NRP to execute malicious code. Here, formal models can help by validating the models, whereas the code ultimately executed is generated and therefore can be trusted.

Finally, especially in neurorobotics, large assets of the experiments are likely to be reused. Hardly any neuroscientist will create both the robot, the neural network and its connection but rather reuse existing robots and potentially also neural networks and couple them in an experiment. This requires an introspection of both neural networks and robots for the neuroscientists to understand details of these artifacts such as e.g. the topology of the network or the kinematic of the robot.

These analyses, validations for security and potential mistakes as well as introspection, can be done independently of a running simulator if the experiment is available as a formal model. In this sense, the problems are similar to embedded systems, where formal models allow a verification, before a transformation converts them to integrated circuits.

We applied techniques and tools from model-driven engineering. In particular, we created formal metamodels to specify the connection between neural networks and robots, designed a DSL for it and created a transformation to generate the code to simulate an experiment [5].

4   Lessons Learned

In this section, we summarize our experiences applying model-driven techniques to the development of the NRP. These descriptions cover the domain analysis, development, tools, development process and project-internal communication. The selection of experiences presented here are the outcome of a brainstorming session reflecting on our experiences that we though could be interesting for others.

4.1   Inconsistent Understanding of Models

Though the notion of models has been clearly defined as early as 1973 by Stachowiak [8] and models are omnipresent in both robotics and neuroscience, there is a diversity of opinions how models should be implemented. Furthermore, as models always have a purpose, modeling standards of the same physical entities exist that incorporate abstractions for different usage scenarios.

In robotics, many modeling standards have been established. In the NRP, we came along Collada to describe the robots' appearance as a 3D-mesh, SDF, used in the Gazebo robotics simulator and the Unified Robot Description Format (URDF), used in the middleware ROS. While all of these standards are based on XML, neither of them complies to the XMI standard usually used in MDE. This has the consequence that tools such as generated parsers based on the XML Schema are not usable as the implied object-oriented class structure does not properly reflect the model. The framing XML language at least allows to reuse some functionality when writing parsers and allows some degree of validation.

Reusing these existing modeling standards seems appealing as this means that existing models can be easily reused, raising acceptance among users. However, one has to be very careful selecting the right model as it is hard to revoke this decision once the modeling standard used turns out to miss important aspects. For example, the SDF standard is used for simulation only and does not allow to inspect a robot model in terms of how it can be controlled. This is because the model contains references to packages that encapsulate the control channels offered to a potential neural control architecture. From such a description, it is close to impossible to restore a mapping of joints to robot topics, as this information is buried in controllers, only available in compiled form.

In the domain of neuroscience, the situation is very different. Here, an important question is the level of abstraction, a neuron is interpreted. While some approaches investigate the connection of entire regions of a neuronal network consisting each of hundreds or thousands of neurons, other approaches investigate the compartments inside a single neuron. Existing formal approaches to model neuronal networks such as NineML [9] or NeuroML [10] try to combine these diverse levels of abstraction and provide a uniform format to catalog knowledge. However, this makes them unusable for simulation purposes as there is no simulator that spans all these levels of abstraction. Most simulators we have been facing in the development of the NRP simulate neural networks at the level of point-neurons, meaning that each neuron is considered to be an opaque box whose behavior is described by a set of differential equations. These neuron models can be modeled in a formal way [11].

When it comes to simulating neural networks, the common format to pass in a model of a neural network to a simulator is a Python script that creates the model inside the simulator. To raise the compatibility between the simulators, there is an abstraction layer PyNN [12] which provides an interface that can be used to create the neural network independently of the used simulator, such that network scripts can be used with multiple simulators with only few modifications.

This very low degree of formalization implies some challenges as it makes it very hard to inspect neural networks without loading them into a simulator. This applies even to very simple analyses such as checking whether a given neuron or population exists at all. One of the reasons is that currently there are many neural networks that use a multitude of control structures and loops when creating the network. Hence, any formal model that does not allow such control structures has a risk of a low acceptance. If control structures are supported, there is a risk to end up with a formal metamodel that does not add much to the Python syntax. Furthermore, because Python scripts are so popular, this raises expectations that any new approach also supports them. As a result and to avoid an enforced language adoption [13], we created an internal DSL in Python [5], allowing to specify the coupling between a neural network and a robot in Python, but without the requirement that a simulator is already loaded. A formal metamodel on top of this internal DSL has not yet gained acceptance. We hope this will change when we can provide a graphical editor for it.

These very different understandings of models imply a communication challenge when bringing together experts of different fields. While for some in the team, the term model implicitly means the robots mesh, the term is bound to Python scripts or neuron models when speaking to others. Especially in the neuroscience domain, the level of formalization is currently very low, which makes it very hard to establish formal modeling standards.

As a possible reason, both in robotics and in neuroscience, models are often validated through simulation or even execution. A model is considered valid if its execution completes without failures and produces the intended behavior. However, it is difficult to specify when such a behavior is valid. This is different for the coupled simulation of both a robot and a neural network where one would like to ensure that for a given connection between the simulators, both the involved neurons or neuron populations as well as the involved sensors and actuators exist and have the expected format.

4.2   Focus the Platform, Not the Generator

Following a model-driven approach as depicted in Fig. 4, a very important question is whether a given functionality should be implemented in the target platform or the generator, if both are developed in the same team. Applying the approach of Völter and Stahl [7], we started with creating a reference simulation script after creating an initial version of the platform. We then extracted a code generator that would generate exactly this simulation script based on a given reference model.

However, this soon turned out to cause problems in the quality assurance. Generators are very hard to test in terms of unit testing. While an integration test is desirable, the resources necessary to run these makes it infeasible to cover large parts of the code through integration tests and make unit tests inevitably required, but ensuring that the produced simulation scripts are correct is complex and far beyond a usual unit test. Furthermore, we lack the tools to measure whether the code generator complied to our goal of 90 % coverage by unit tests.

Therefore, we only tested the generated output for a few example models by comparing with a predefined expectation and further created usual unit tests for any functionality called from the generator. However, this leads to highly fragile unit tests. Many changes in the target platform had an influence onto the code generator and as a result, the test cases had to be adjusted. Thus, developers started to simply copying all the generated output for the changed generator to the test oracle and peer-reviewers spent less attention as the code was only generated.

Therefore, we eventually decided to minimize the amount of code that is being generated and tried to drag as much code as we could into the target platform as Python modules. As a result, this code is subject to our continuous integration infrastructure and thus, many code checks are automatically performed by static code analysis that would otherwise have to be done by tests. The generator now only generates artifacts that are very hard to create by non-generating approaches such as expressions composed from model elements. While this could also be done through model interpretation at runtime, it would mean a less clear syntax (which is made visible to the user and therefore important) and degrade the performance.

An artifact that has helped a lot minimizing the generated code is our internal Python DSL PyTF [5]. Despite a syntax familiar to Python developers (which is why we created the language in the first place), it also helped us minimize the code generator transforming our formal model into PyTF. PyTF itself can then be executed directly.

4.3   Model-Driven Tooling Based on Java Platform

As of today, many of the tools available to support model-driven engineering are still based on Java, more specifically on the Eclipse Modelling Framework. The components that we used in the NRP are based on C++ and Python. As we also decided to create a Python interface for users to specify their connection between selected neural networks and robots, the simulation backend is also based on Python to avoid inter-process communication.

However, this decision puts a platform barrier that hampers the adoption of model-driven techniques since most available tools cannot be used, unless the involved developers install a Java IDE next to their Python or C++ environment. As suggested by Meyerovich [13], many developers do not like the idea of adopting a new language which yields a strong argument against the introduction of such tools. Indeed, our experience was that many developers tried to avoid Java as much as they could.

Therefore, the more pragmatic solution for us was to use XML technology. That is, we created the formal metamodel as an XML Schema. Though this has the drawback that XML has no direct support for typed cross-references (only ID and IDREF), this can be circumvented by designing the metamodel appropriately. In favor of XML, like most languages, Python includes tools to generate parsers based on a XML schema so that we can easily load and save models. Furthermore, XML Schema allows a basic validation of instance documents.

This validation is not as powerful as OCL and harder to specify but suffices for many applications. More advanced validation, such as checks whether a reference to a particular neuron or robot sensor is valid, has to be done separately anyhow since the data is not available in a formal model (cf. Sect. 4.1).

A promising approach was to use EMF tools to generate the XML Schema from an Ecore metamodel, but this turned out to be not a long-term solution. EMF by far does not export all validations done on models into the XML Schema. As we tend to include as much validation as we can, this quickly meant that we maintained the XML Schema manually. However, as long as the Schema complies to the XMI standard, the interoperability to modeling frameworks such as EMF is still given as these frameworks also use XMI.

This interoperability is important, as it allows to use editor technologies such as e.g. XText[3] or Sirius[4] and consume the created models in other languages. However, in our case, this is difficult as we need our editors to be web-based.

To generate code, we used Jinja2[5], normally used to generate HTML pages, though we generate Python code. This allows to use template-based code generation without additional effort. Nevertheless, these templates do not comply with static code analysis and as a result, the acceptance of these code generators among the developers is low. As a result, we have reduced the code generation to a minimum, meaning that we do not generate anything else than our Python DSL.

4.4   Customer Value of Model-Driven Artifacts in a Scrum Process

Though set up as a research project, the NRP is developed according to a distributed Scrum process in sprints of three weeks length. Model-driven software development introduces a high initial effort to set up the metamodel, transformations and editors. This seemingly contradicts the idea of Scrum where all items of the backlog should be user stories that add some value to the user.

On the other hand, it is the user that specifies models of a simulation in the final platform. Therefore, the typical development artifacts of a classical model-driven project are in fact parts of the ready-made platform and therefore do add a value to the user, hence fit into the format of a user story. For example, metamodels are created with a user story similar to "As a user, I want to have a clear specification how x is defined". This gives the developer one sprint to create an initial metamodel and possibly generate a visualization of it to show that to the (expert) user. Further documentation of the metamodel, accessible also to the non-expert user as well as other artifacts such as a DSL on top, generators or editors are then developed in subsequent sprints.

Slightly more problematic are evolution scenarios as there is a risk that new features are not introduced into all artifacts simultaneously. Therefore, the metamodel may diverge from subsequent artifacts such as the DSL. As there are few

---

[3] https://eclipse.org/Xtext/.

[4] http://www.eclipse.org/sirius/.

[5] http://jinja.pocoo.org/.

tools to detect this in a dynamic language such as Python, we rely on code-reviews. Though such evolution scenarios appear more often in agile methods, this problem is not limited to them as it is unlikely to have an optimal metamodel at the first attempt.

Overall, we think that the agile Scrum methodology met our needs creating a model-driven platform very well.

4.5   Missing Baseline for MDE Benefits

Although we already noted the multitude of potential benefits brought by MDE in Sect. 3, quite a number of people in the project are still skeptical on MDE. This is partially due to problems we discussed in the earlier sections, but also because the benefits are not obvious. We see having a formal representation of domain concepts used in the NRP as the key benefit. But as we are developing both the formal metamodel and the target platform on which it is executed in parallel and in the same team, it is hard to distinguish whether the metamodel has influenced the platform development or vice versa.

As a consequence, it is easy to claim that the formal metamodel just formalizes the concepts implemented in the platform anyway. After all, abstractions can also be employed without MDE techniques in place. It is hard to proof this wrong as the usage of proper abstractions does not strictly require MDE. We believe that even if some of the models are supplied very informally, attempts to formalize these models still improved our domain understanding and helped us to ask domain experts the right questions. However, further research is required to analyze and show potential advantages and disadvantages.

5   Conclusion

In this paper, we reported our experience applying MDE in the development of the Neurorobotics Platform, a web-based simulation platform to run experiments coupling spiking neural networks with robots. Though we identified large potential given the overlap of defining and running such an experiment on the one side and model-driven software development on the other, there are a couple of challenges and obstacles that make the application difficult.

We expect that our lessons learned of these challenges can help others who want to apply model-driven techniques in the area of neurorobotics and help to identify obstacles in the future development of the model-driven approach as a whole. An inconsistent understanding of models means that few assumptions can be made on how a model is specified and many models are only available rather informal. Especially in neuroscience, people are used to Python, making it infeasible to use model-driven tools, often based on Java. As the support for validating generated Python code is limited, we limited code generation to the places where it is absolutely necessary. The compatibility with the Scrum process we are following could be solved. However, the overall benefit of MDE was not as clear for other developers, making arguments in favor of it difficult.

Acknowledgment. The research leading to these results has received funding from the European Union Seventh Framework Programme (FP7/2007-2013) under grant agreements no. 604102 (Human Brain Project) and 610711 (Cactos).

References

1. Hines, M.L., Carnevale, N.T.: The NEURON simulation environment. Neural Comput. **9**(6), 1179–1209 (1997)
2. Gewaltig, M.-O., Diesmann, M.: NEST (NEural Simulation Tool). Scholarpedia **2**(4), 1430 (2007)
3. Koenig, N., Howard, A.: Design and use paradigms for gazebo, an opensource multi-robot simulator. In: Proceedings of the IEEE/RSJ International Conference on Intelligent Robots and Systems (IROS), vol. 3, pp. 2149–2154. IEEE (2004)
4. Braitenberg, V.: Vehicles: Experiments in Synthetic Psychology. MIT press, Cambridge (1986)
5. Hinkel, G., Groenda, H., Vannucci, L. et al.: A domain-specific language (DSL) for integrating neuronal networks in robot control. In: Joint MORSE/VAO Workshop on Model-Driven Robot Software Engineering and View-based Software-Engineering (2015)
6. Quigley, M., Conley, K., Gerkey, B. et al.: ROS: an open-source Robot Operating System. In: ICRA Workshop on Open Source Software, vol. 3, p. 5 (2009)
7. Völter, M., Stahl, T.: Model-Driven Software Development. Wiley, New York (2006)
8. Stachowiak, H.: Allgemeine Modelltheorie. Springer, Heidelberg (1973)
9. Raikov, I., Cannon, R., Clewley, R., et al.: NineML: the network interchange for neuroscience modeling language. BMC Neurosci. **12**(Suppl 1), 330 (2011)
10. Gleeson, P., Crook, S., Cannon, R.C., et al.: NeuroML: a language for describing data driven models of neurons and networks with a high degree of biological detail. PLoS Comput. Biol. **6**(6), e1000815 (2010)
11. Plotnikov, D., Blundell, I., Ippen, T. et al.: NESTML: a modeling language for spiking neurons. In: Modellierung (2016, to appear)
12. Davison, A.P., Brüderle, D., Eppler, J.M., et al.: PyNN: a common interface for neuronal network simulators. Front. Neuroinformatics **2**(11), 1–10 (2009)
13. Meyerovich L.A., Rabkin, A.S.: Empirical analysis of programming language adoption. In: Proceedings of the ACM SIGPLAN International Conference on Object Oriented Programming Systems Languages & Applications, pp. 1–18. ACM (2013)

Variability and Uncertainty

Supporting Variability Exploration and Resolution During Model Migration

Davide Di Ruscio[1], Juergen Etzlstorfer[2(✉)], Ludovico Iovino[3],
Alfonso Pierantonio[1], and Wieland Schwinger[2]

[1] Department of Information Engineering, Computer Science and Mathematics,
Università degli Studi dell'Aquila, L'Aquila, Italy
{davide.diruscio,alfonso.pierantonio}@univaq.it
[2] Department of Cooperative Information Systems,
Johannes Kepler University Linz, Linz, Austria
{juergen.etzlstorfer,wieland.schwinger}@jku.at
[3] Gran Sasso Science Institute, L'Aquila, Italy
ludovico.iovino@gssi.infn.it

Abstract. In Model-Driven Engineering (MDE) metamodels are pivotal entities that underpin the definition of models. Similarly to any software artifact, metamodels evolve over time due to evolutionary pressure. However, whenever a metamodel is modified, related models may become invalid and adaptations are required to restore their validity. Generally, when adapting a model in response to metamodel changes, more than one migration strategy is possible. Unfortunately, inspecting all of them, which greatly overlap one with another, can be prone to errors. In this paper, we present an approach supporting the identification of variability during model migration and selection of migration alternatives by generating an *intensional* and thus concise representation of all migration alternatives by including also an explicit visualization of conflicting solutions.

1 Introduction

In Model-Driven Engineering [24] (MDE) metamodels are often considered a pivotal concept used for formalizing and describing application domains. A wide range of artifacts, tools and applications are defined upon one or more metamodels that altogether form a modeling ecosystem [6]. Generic modeling platforms (e.g., ADOxx[1], EMF[2], and Metaedit[3]) enable the development of full-fledged modeling environments that are specifically tailored around organization needs [8,14]. Similarly to any other software artifact, metamodels are prone to evolution during their routinely use, to cope with improvements, extensions, and corrections [18]. However, any change to a metamodel can endanger the integrity and consistency of the modeling ecosystem as models, transformations, or even editors might become

---

[1] http://www.adoxx.org.
[2] http://eclipse.org/modeling/emf/.
[3] http://www.metacase.com/products.html.

© Springer International Publishing Switzerland 2016
A. Wąsowski and H. Lönn (Eds.): ECMFA 2016, LNCS 9764, pp. 231–246, 2016.
DOI: 10.1007/978-3-319-42061-5_15

invalid [7]. The metamodel co-evolution (or coupled evolution) problem concerns the process of recovering the relationship between evolving metamodels and the dependent artifacts in the modeling ecosystem [7]. In this paper, we focus on the *model co-evolution* problem, i.e., on the process of migrating a model to restore the conformance relation between evolving metamodels and those models affected by the metamodel changes.

Over the last decade, numerous approaches for co-evolution of metamodels and models have been proposed. Most of them can be distinguished by falling into the groups of *inductive* and *prescriptive* ones: the former ones (e.g., [4,12]) automatically derive a model migration procedure from the metamodel differences, while in the course of the latter ones models are programmatically migrated by means of predefined procedures (e.g., [13,21,29]). An aspect that has been largely neglected so far is the following: when migrating a model in response to a metamodel change there might be multiple alternatives to restore its conformance. For instance, if the multiplicity of an association in a metamodel is decreased, there are many ways of selecting the exceeding associations to be removed from the instance models. Identifying the right migration alternative is a challenging task as it should consider also aspects that go beyond the mere conformance recovering, such as information erosion [25] and reducing the number of model changes. Recently, an approach has been proposed to mitigate such difficulties by generating *all* possible migrations at once [25]. Then, the responsibility of identifying the *right* model migration is shifted from the implementer of the migration program to the modeler, who can then inspect the solution space and identify the most adequate solution. Unfortunately, already little changes in the metamodel usually give place to a multitude of possible model migrations that are difficult to inspect as they greatly overlap one with another.

In this paper, we present an approach to alleviate the consequences of dealing with the multitude of model migrations that can restore model conformance. The purpose of the approach is to help the modeler in finding the co-evolution for models by supporting the modeler with a proper visualization of potential conflicting solutions. Instead of *extensionally* [20] generating all migrated model as done in [25], an *intensional* representation of them is given. In essence, the approach permits to represent different solutions as a model with *variability* that indicates which parts of the solution are different for each migration alternative and is able to indicate if there are conflicts between solutions. The overall solution space is represented by a feature model [1] to better navigate alternatives and identify the wanted migration alternative. In addition, traceability between the individual metamodel changes and the corresponding migration alternatives is also provided in order to record modeler decisions and avoid to deal with already resolved variability.

Outline. In Sect. 2 a motivating example is given to illustrate how migration strategies can proliferate. Section 3 introduces the approach by presenting the variability metamodel for the intensional representation of the different solutions and illustrates it on the motivating example. The approach is critically

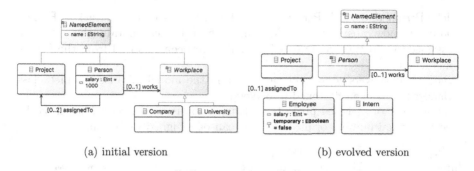

(a) initial version   (b) evolved version

Fig. 1. The simple workplace metamodel (SWMM)

discussed in Sect. 4. In Sect. 5 related work is considered and, Sect. 6 draws some conclusions and outlines future plans.

2   Motivating Example

In order to satisfy unforeseen requirements or to better represent the considered application domain, metamodels can be subject to modifications as for instance in the case of the Simple Workplace MetaModel (SWMM) shown in Fig. 1a[4]. In particular, let us suppose that a number of changes have been performed on the SWMM metamodel leading to the evolved version shown in Fig. 1b. More specifically, the performed changes (or refactorings) shall be the following:

R1. Introduce subclasses: the metaclasses Employee and Intern have been added as subtype of Person that becomes abstract.

R2. Push down attribute: the attribute salary has been pushed down in the hierarchy, from Person to Employee.

R3. Add mandatory attribute: the mandatory attribute temporary has been added to the metaclass Employee.

R4. Restrict reference cardinality: the multiplicity of reference assignedTo has been restricted from [0..2] to [0..1].

R5. Flatten hierarchy: the metaclasses Company and University have been removed, flattening the hierarchy of Workplace.

A simple workplace model conforming to the initial version of SWMM is shown in Fig. 2. The model specifies an instance of the metaclass Person named John: he works at the University of L'Aquila and is employed in two projects, namely LearnPad and MDEForge. Such a model is no longer conforming to the newer version of the SWMM metamodel, therefore it has to be migrated in order to re-establish the lost conformance relationship. In particular, the following elements violate the conformance relationship:

---

[4] For the sake of clarity, abstract classes are depicted in gray.

– John:Person and Adele:Person cannot be instances of the metaclass Person, which is now abstract; in addition, such instances contain the reference assignedTo and the attribute salary that have been removed from the Person metaclass;
– the Univaq:University element cannot be in the model because the metaclass University has been flattened into Workplace;
– the number of assigned projects to John:Person is higher than 1 which is the new maximal number of projects that can be assigned to Person.

In general, various migration procedures to recover the conformance are possible, each providing a different solution. Thus, it is of utmost importance to inspect the different alternatives for detecting the one, which fits modeler's needs best. However, because the alternatives largely overlap each other and might present conflicts among them, the procedure can be tedious and prone to errors if executed without (semi) auto-

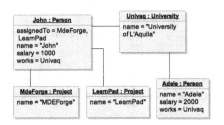

Fig. 2. A simple workplace model

mated support. For instance, because of the SWMM metamodel refactoring the simple workplace model in Fig. 2 can be migrated by means of several *model migrations* as reported in Table 1 and explained in the following[5]:

R1. Introduce subclasses: this metamodel change involving the metaclass Person can be resolved by means of any of the following alternatives:

– *R1a1:* all instances of Person are removed;
– *R1a2, R1a3:* all instances of the abstract superclass Person are re-typed into either Employee (*R1a2*) or Intern (*R1a3*);
– *R1a4:* a non-empty set of instances is re-typed to Employee while another non-empty set of instances is re-typed to Intern; the decision criteria about which instances are retyped to one or the other type has to be provided by the user in form of, e.g., OCL expressions.

R2. Push down attribute: this change, which pushed down the attribute salary from Person to Employee, can be resolved by operating one of the following model migrations:

– *R2a1:* retain the value of the pushed attribute;
– *R2a2:* delete the value of the pushed attribute;

R3. Add mandatory attribute: the addition of the mandatory attribute temporary can be resolved by setting its value either to *true* (*R3a1*), or to *false* (*R3a2*). This should be decided by the user.

R4. Restrict reference cardinality: this change operated on the reference assignedTo can be resolved applying one of the following migration alternatives:

---

[5] Please note that each migration alternative is identified by a term like *R1a1* where *a1* is one of the possible migration alternative related to the metamodel change *R1*.

Table 1. Possible model migration alternatives for the motivating example

Metamodel change	Possible migration alternatives
R1. Introduce subclasses	*R1a1.* Remove the existing instances of type **Person**
	R1a2. Re-type the existing instances from **Person** to **Employee**
	R1a3. Re-type the existing instances from **Person** to **Intern**
	R1a4. Re-type the existing instances from **Person** to **Employee** or **Intern** with different (non-empty) combinations
R2. Push down attribute	*R2a1.* Maintain the attribute value of **salary** in the re-typed instance
	R2a2. Remove the attribute value of **salary**
R3. Add mandatory attribute	*R3a1.* Set the attribute value of **Employee.temporary** to true
	R3a2. Set the attribute value of **Employee.temporary** to false
R4. Restrict reference cardinality	*R4a1.* Remove one of link to the project assigned to a **Person**[a]
	R4a2. Remove all the links of project related to a **Person**
	R4a3. Re-assign one of the project to other persons[a]
	R4a4. Re-assign all the project to other persons[a]
R5. Flatten hierarchy	*R5a1.* Re-type all the instance with the corresponding flattened subclasses with the supertype
	R5a2. Remove all instances of **Workplace**

[a]The selection criteria can be decided by the generation process, e.g. first, last, random.

- *R4a1:* unassign one of the two **Projects** from a **Person**;
- *R4a2:* unassign all **Projects** to allow for a complete reassignment;
- *R4a3, R4a4:* reassign one **Project** instance (R4a3) or all instances of **Project** (R4a4) to another instance of **Person**.

R5. Flatten hierarchy: this modification, which affected **Workplace**, **Company**, and **University**, can be resolved by re-typing all the instances of **University** or **Company** to the superclass **Workplace** (*R5a1*) or by deleting all of them (*R5a2*).

A *migration solution* consists of a combination of selected migration alternatives, one for each metamodel refactoring, which are not in conflict to each other. However, alternatives can be combined in different manners by exponentially increasing the number of migration solutions and thus the complexity of the problem. For instance, by considering the 5 changes operated on the initial SWMM metamodel of the previous example, the total number of possible migration solutions for the sample workplace model are 128 ($= 4 \times 2 \times 2 \times 4 \times 2$), although this might be an over-approximation because conflicts might occur between migration alternatives as discussed later on the paper. However, if user-specified decision criteria are allowed, the number might be even higher.

3   Approach

In this section, we present an approach to represent, explore, and select migration alternatives in response to metamodel changes. The approach allows to *intentionally* represent multiple solutions for the model migration problem at hand. In particular, instead of *extensionally* represent all the possible solutions as typically done by existing techniques (e.g., [25]), a single model with *variability* is employed to precisely denote which parts of the solution are different for each migration alternative. The proposed approach also permits to highlight aspects that are not evident with classical approaches, such as conflicting alternatives.

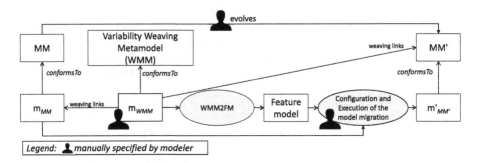

Fig. 3. Proposed approach

Figure 3 shows the main artifacts and activities of the proposed approach. The main concepts are represented by the Variability Weaving Metamodel (WMM), which employes model weaving [2] (see m_{WMM}) by linking different models to represent all possible migration solutions that can be alternatively applied on the initial model m_{WMM} in order to obtain models conforming to the evolved metamodel (MM'). In particular, for each metamodel change the weaving model represents corresponding migration alternatives for m_{WMM}. Some of those alternatives might be in conflict with others, e.g., the deletion of an element is in conflict with other operations consuming it. In order to make the visualization of alternatives and their conflicts easier to be analyzed, a model transformation is applied on the source model m_{WMM} to generate a target feature model [1]. The generated feature model can be inspected by the user in order to chose a valid combination of migration alternatives, to finally obtain a model m' conforming to MM'.

In the remaining of the section all the parts of the approach shown in Fig. 3 are described.

3.1   Variability Metamodel for Representing Different Migration Solutions

The variability metamodel WMM previously mentioned is shown in Fig. 4 and has been constructed by building upon our previous work on difference

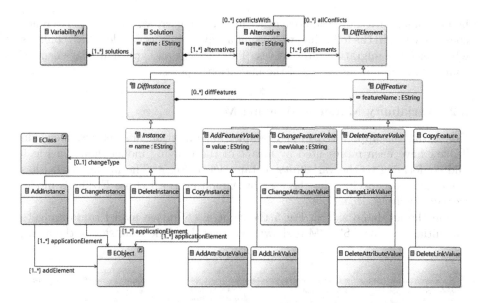

Fig. 4. Variability weaving metamodel (WMM)

representation for metamodels [3], but shifting the concepts from the M2 level of the OMG modeling stack to the M1 level [16]. Since we employ the Eclipse technology stack, Ecore serves as meta-metamodel of the proposed variability metamodel.

The metamodel consists of the root metaclass VariabilityModel that serves as a container for all migration Solutions, each of which is performed on the affected model to restore its conformance with respect to the newer metamodel version. In order to express all the possible migration strategies, each Solution consists of one or more disjunct Alternatives. Each alternative (as those illustrated in Table 1) is represented in terms of effects on the model to be migrated. To this end, the DiffInstance and DiffFeature metaclasses have been introduced: the former identifies the model element affected by the metamodel refactoring, whereas the latter identifies the corresponding structural features. The metamodel is capable of describing all added, deleted, and changed metamodel instances along with their added, deleted, and changed features. Additionally, instances that remain the same, i.e., migration is not needed, can be specified (cf. CopyInstance). Thus, all possible migration alternatives can be represented. Please note that applicationElement is the reference to an element subject to change in m. The properties name and featureName, value, newValue represent the changed/new values in changed/new instances and features, respectively.

As already mentioned above, migration alternatives might also be in conflict with each other. For example, considering a deletion of an element as a possible alternative, this alternative is in conflict with all other alternatives that still depend on the existence of this element. As shown in Fig. 4, an Alternative might be in conflict with more than one other migration alternatives (see the reference conflictsWith). In the following, we present a way how users can deal with conflicts when selecting migration alternatives. This enables an explicit management of conflicts in subsequent stages of the migration process.

3.2 Variability Model as Weaving Model

Employing the approach to our example, all migration alternatives shown in Table 1 have been represented by means of the weaving model shown in Fig. 5 and conforming to the variability metamodel in Fig. 4. The model m_{WMM} has been manually specified by the user by exploiting the Eclipse Epsilon's model weaving facilities *ModeLink*[6].

On the left-hand side of Fig. 5 the sample workplace model conforming to the initial version of SWMM is shown, whereas the right-hand side of the figure

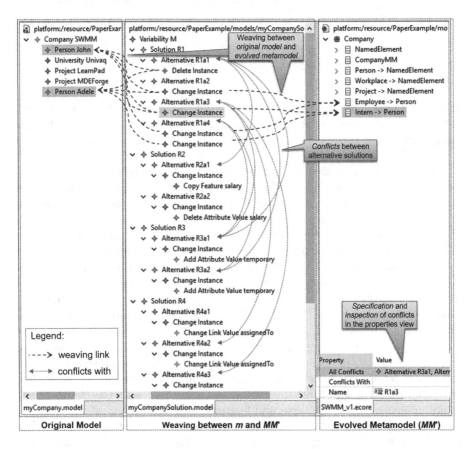

Fig. 5. Sample weaving model represented by means of epsilon ModeLink

---

[6] https://www.eclipse.org/epsilon/doc/modelink/.

shows the evolved version of SWMM. In the middle, all the weaving elements representing the possible migration alternatives of the sample workplace model are shown. In particular, the weaving model consists of links (annotated by dashed lines) relating model elements that have to be migrated (see the left-hand side of the figure), with metaclasses in the newer metamodel (see the right-hand side of the figure). Weaving links are organized in solutions, each consisting of migration alternatives. For instance, the solution for the metamodel change *R1 - Introduce subclasses* applied to the metaclass Person consists of four alternatives (R1a1–R1a4), each representing the corresponding model migration. In particular,

– the alternative R1a1 contains a Delete Instance that refers to John and Adele, meaning that this choice deletes both instances.
– the alternative R1a3 links the instances John and Adele to the class Intern of the new SWMM via a Changed Instance element, meaning that they are re-typed to be instances of Intern during migration.

Since not all migration alternatives might be compatible with each other, WMM also allows to specify conflicts to declare disjunct alternatives. For instance, the property view on the lower right-hand side of Fig. 5 shows the specified conflicts for R1a3, which is in conflict with the alternative R3a1. In particular, R1a3 retypes all the instances of Person to Interns, whereas in R3a1 the attribute temporary, which is not existing in the Intern, is set to true. Conflicts are annotated in Fig. 5 by means of (vertical) dotted lines connecting the weaving model elements.

Please note that for the sake of clarity not all weaving links and conflicts are shown in Fig. 5, nevertheless all weaving links and conflicts regarding the R1 alternatives are shown.

3.3   Variability Model as Feature Model

Feature models [1] are a compact representation of different configurations for a system, e.g., software product lines. In our approach, we employ feature models to provide a suitable representation of all Solutions along with their migration Alternatives, to support the user in identifying the right migration alternative. Therefore, Solutions are represented as mandatory features (since for each change a solution has to be chosen), while migration Alternatives are disjunct subfeatures of Solutions, thus the user can only decide for one concrete alternative at a time. However, since alternatives might be in conflict among them, we exploit constraints as part of the feature model to define these conflicts.

For instance, in order to provide a convenient representation for the solution and alternatives illustrated in Fig. 5, the feature model in Fig. 6 can be used. It can be automatically generated from the weaving model using the model transformation shown in Listing 1.1. The generated feature model consists of mandatory elements R1–R5 representing the different solutions that have to be considered to migrate the simple workplace model. Each of them consists of

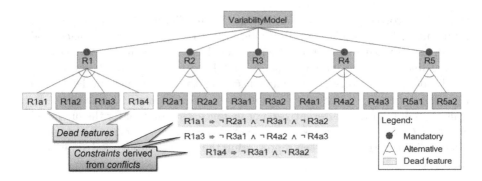

Fig. 6. Feature model related to the running example

several disjunct alternatives that represent the concrete migration actions to be undertaken. If conflicts have been specified, they are denoted in the feature model by means of constraints, e.g., by $R1a1 \Rightarrow \neg R2a1 \wedge \neg R3a1 \wedge \neg R4a2$, thus, excluding specific alternative combinations. Interestingly, the presence of constraints in mandatory alternatives might reveal "dead features", which means that in order to apply all solutions, some choices might not be valid. In the example, R1a1 and R1a4 are detected as dead features, since they either delete the instance John or retype it to Intern, thereby hindering all subsequent migration actions that rely on the instance itself or features of Employee. Besides dead features, all other conflicts lead to constraints that might restrict some solutions. For example, the choice of R1a3 will prevent the modeler from choosing also R3a1, R4a2, and R4a3.

3.4   The *WMM2FM* transformation

Feature models like the one in Fig. 6 can be automatically generated from a weaving model by means of a model transformation. Listing 1.1 provides such a transformation, which has been developed with the Epsilon Generation Language (EGL) [22]. Please note that this transformation is actually a model-to-text transformation, since the employed feature model representation is technically based on XML, thus, XML code is produced. In line 1–3 all solutions of the model are queried, while in line 9–15 we iterate over these solutions and create a feature for each solution containing all of its alternatives as possible subfeatures (line 11–13). Thus, alternatives belonging to the same Solution are disjunct by default. In order to automatically derive conflicts between migration alternatives belonging to different Solutions, in line 20–36 we create a rule for each migration that is in conflict with another migration alternative. More specifically, a conflict between Alternatives implies that those alternatives are not compatible to each other (line 27–29). The generated constraints correspond to the following expression, which states that selection of a implies that $a_1, \ldots , a_n$ are not valid anymore, i.e., they are in conflict with a, more formally:

$$a \Rightarrow \neg a_1 \wedge \neg a_2 \wedge \ldots \wedge \neg a_n$$

Once the feature model is generated, it can be loaded, displayed and edited by the FeatureIDE plugin [27] for Eclipse.

Listing 1.1. Fragment of the *WMM2FM* transformation

```
1    [%
2    var solutionModel := SolutionM.allInstances().at(0);
3    var allSolutions := solutionModel.solutions; %]
4    <?xml version="1.0" encoding="UTF-8" standalone="no"?>
5    <featureModel chosenLayoutAlgorithm="1">
6      <struct>
7        <and abstract="false" mandatory="true" name="SolutionModel">
8    [%
9    for (s in allSolutions) { %]
10         <alt mandatory="true" name="[%=s.name%]">
11           [% for (a in s.alternatives) { %]
12             <feature mandatory="true" name="[%=a.name%]" />
13           [% } %]
14         </alt>
15   [% } %]
16       </and>
17     </struct>
18     <constraints>
19   [%
20   for (s in allSolutions) {
21     for (a in s.alternatives) {
22       if (a.allConflicts.size() > 0) { %]
23       <rule>
24         <imp>
25           <var>[%=a.name%]</var>
26           <conj>
27           [% for (conflict in a.allConflicts) { %]
28             <not><var>[%=conflict.name%]</var></not>
29           [% } %]
30           </conj>
31         </imp>
32       </rule>
33       [%
34       }
35     }
36   } %]
37     </constraints>
38     ...
39   </featureModel>
```

The feature model represents all possible configurations (i.e., migration solutions) for model migration. However, in order to create one specific m' a single configuration in the feature model must be selected. Since configurations can also be executed with FeatureIDE, it is possible to automatically migrate m to m' by attaching the needed migration actions for model migration directly to the alternatives in the feature model.

3.5   Configuration and Execution of Model Migration

As aforementioned, the modeler has to ultimately decide on a combination of valid options in the feature model, i.e., a configuration, to define a migration. In this process, the user is supported by the provision of constraints that restrict the number of valid solutions. In Fig. 7a a concrete but not yet finalized configuration taken by the user is shown. It is highlighted in the picture that the decision for R2 is not made yet, i.e., the modeler can still choose among the two available configurations (empty boxes shown in green). Once the user decides for a valid configuration (cf. Fig. 7b), this configuration can be executed. This means that all migration actions attached to the alternatives can be applied. Please note that discussing the actual migration process is outside the scope of this paper, however migration actions elaborated in our previous work [17] are adequate to be reused in this approach. As shown in Fig. 7c an exemplary execution log is provided to show the potential of this approach when executed.

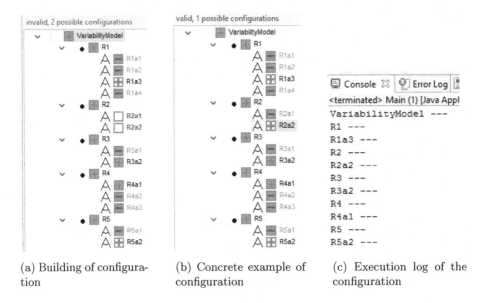

(a) Building of configuration

(b) Concrete example of configuration

(c) Execution log of the configuration

Fig. 7. Configuration and execution of model migration

4   Discussion

Although the approach has been validated by considering representative examples only, early feedback provides interesting elements for outlining benefits and potential drawbacks. The idea of using feature models for representing the various alternatives simplifies the representation of explicit and relevant knowledge to be conveyed to the modeler. A manifest representation of alternatives, their conflicts, and how traceability cross-links them to the metamodel refactoring is a useful instrument for assisting the modeler in meeting her migration design decisions. On the contrary, model migration has always been based on individual and spontaneous processes prone to errors and inconsistencies. Therefore, shifting the responsibility of deciding which migration best fits the requirements from the migration program implementer to the modeler is greatly beneficial if properly supported.

To the best of our understanding, the major drawback of the approach is represented by the manual creation of the weaving model and the conflict representation. Although the automated generation of such artifacts is outside the scope of this paper, both the weaving model and the conflict representation we are confident that it can be obtained in an automated manner. In particular, we plan to revise our work from [25] (in which a corrupted conformance relationship is re-established by applying so-called repair actions that generate multiple solutions) to generate the weaving model instead of the concrete solutions. For identification of conflicts, starting from our work on dependent metamodel changes [3], we intend to generate admissible scheduling of migration actions. Both extensions are desirable and seem viable as no major technical obstacle is evident at this stage.

5   Related Work

There has been only little research on the unified management of multiple migration strategies in the modeling community so far. Thus, in the following, first more close approaches are compared to our approach, while in the latter approaches from other engineering domains are discussed.

The closest work to our approach has been proposed recently in [11], in which the authors propose a Variable Metamodel (VMM) during metamodel evolution. This metamodel unifies the concepts of different metamodel evolutions in a way that all models that need to be migrated conform to the VMM. In fact, a model is not migrated but matches the VMM in each evolution of the metamodel, which is in contrast to our approach since we provide possibilities to explore different migration alternatives how the model can conform to the latest version of the metamodel.

In [25] the authors introduce an approach to re-establish the conformance relationship between models and metamodels by manipulating the non-conforming model according to specific rules. Thus, multiple valid m' are being generated that are sorted and presented to the user according to quality criteria. However, each solution is presented as its own model in contrast to the approach proposed in this paper, which attempts to present variability in model migration in one single model to better cope with overlapping solutions.

In [15] variability is tackled by the provision of multiple alternative repair actions in order to repair a violated, i.e., non-conforming, model. However, the user has to decide on the lower level of repair actions, while in our approach the user decides on the level of models.

An approach which allows to define custom migration actions while still satisfying quality criteria, and thus tackles variability by user involvement, has been proposed in [19]. However, exploration of the different possibilities for migration is not part of their work.

In [9] the consistency restoration between different UML models, e.g., class and sequence diagrams, is addressed. To ensure consistency, an approach to automatically generated choices to repair inconsistent UML models is proposed.

The tool lets the user explore alternative ways to fix inconsistencies in a UML model. However, the tool is limited to generate resolutions that only involve a change at a single location at a time.

The necessity of dealing with multiple alternatives arised also in other fields, including model merging and versioning and requirement engineering. In [5] the authors propose an approach to automatically merge different versions of a model according to user-definable consistency constraints. In fact, in case of inconsistencies the approach is able to inform the modeler about which model elements have to be changed. However, the approach focuses on merging different model versions into one model, while our approach is able to highlight different migration alternatives in one variability model.

Wieland et al. [30] present an approach for optimistic model versioning, meaning that conflicts do not have to be resolved immediately but rather when a decision can be made how to resolve them. The approach is able to accept conflicts and resolve them later in the process, by having the conflicted model elements annotated to reflect the modifications. However, the approach focuses on the simultaneous editing of models and arising conflicts, in contrast to our approach which deals with different strategies on how to migrate a model.

In [26] the authors propose an approach merge similar algebraic graph transformation (AGT) rules and generate a single rule with variability. Doing so, rule variants can be expressed in a compact manner.

In [10] partial models are introduced in order to let the designer to specify uncertain information by means of a base model enriched with annotations and first-order logic, which highlights the need for variability also in other engineering domains. In [23] the authors stress the need for uncertainty since the requirements engineering field it is common to have uncertainty in both the content and structure of the models. However, they do not cope with uncertainty by providing a number of different possible choices to resolve uncertainty.

In goal-oriented methodologies such as KAOS or i* [28] intentionality and variability aspects are also treated, but they are more widely used in early phases of a project, while the models considered in this paper are the central artifacts in the development process.

6   Conclusion and Future Work

In this paper, an approach for representing and visualizing different solutions for model migration in presence of metamodel changes has been proposed. Besides the capability to represent all possible alternatives in an intensional fashion, the approach permits the explicit representation of conflicts that easily arise in the migration process. In particular, the different options are represented in a weaving model between the model to migrate and the evolved version of the metamodel. In addition, it has been shown how to transform the weaving model into a feature diagram, a commonplace notation that can be used out-of-the-box. Among the advantages of the approach there is the traceability between the metamodel refactorings and the migrations alternatives, which provides a useful way to better grasp the rationale behind the migration actions.

The presented approach suggests further developments. In particular, the idea of automating the generation of the weaving models seems viable according to our previous work [25]. The generation of conflicts is also another aspect we intend to investigate starting from our previous work on the management of dependent changes [3]: an opportunity to harness is given by analyzing how dependencies among metamodel changes can give place to scheduling of model migration actions.

References

1. Batory, D.: Feature models, grammars, and propositional formulas. In: Obbink, H., Pohl, K. (eds.) SPLC 2005. LNCS, vol. 3714, pp. 7–20. Springer, Heidelberg (2005)
2. Bézivin, J., Jouault, F., Rosenthal, P., Valduriez, P.: Modeling in the large and modeling in the small. In: Aßmann, U., Akşit, M., Rensink, A. (eds.) MDAFA 2003. LNCS, vol. 3599, pp. 33–46. Springer, Heidelberg (2005)
3. Cicchetti, A., Di Ruscio, D., Pierantonio, A.: Managing dependent changes in coupled evolution. In: Paige, R.F. (ed.) ICMT 2009. LNCS, vol. 5563, pp. 35–51. Springer, Heidelberg (2009)
4. Cicchetti, A., Di Ruscio, D., Eramo, R., Pierantonio, A.: Automating co-evolution in model-driven engineering. In: Proceedings of EDOC, pp. 222–231. IEEE (2008)
5. Dam, H.K., Egyed, A., Winikoff, M., Reder, A., Lopez-Herrejon, R.E.: Consistent merging of model versions. J. Syst. Softw. **112**, 137–155 (2015)
6. Di Ruscio, D., Iovino, L., Pierantonio, A.: Coupled evolution in model-driven engineering. IEEE Softw. **29**(6), 78–84 (2012)
7. Di Ruscio, D., Iovino, L., Pierantonio, A.: Evolutionary togetherness: how to manage coupled evolution in metamodeling ecosystems. In: Ehrig, H., Engels, G., Kreowski, H.-J., Rozenberg, G. (eds.) ICGT 2012. LNCS, vol. 7562, pp. 20–37. Springer, Heidelberg (2012)
8. Di Ruscio, D., Paige, R.F., Pierantonio, A.: Guest editorial to the special issue on success stories in model driven engineering. Sci. Comput. Program. **89**, 69–70 (2014)
9. Egyed, A., Letier, E., Finkelstein, A.: Generating and evaluating choices for fixing inconsistencies in UML design models. In: 23rd IEEE/ACM International Conference on Automated Software Engineering, pp. 99–108, September 2008
10. Famelis, M., Salay, R., Chechik, M.: Partial models: towards modeling and reasoning with uncertainty. In: Proceedings of ICSE, pp. 573–583, June 2012
11. Font, J., Arcega, L., Haugen, O., Cetina, C.: Addressing metamodel revisions in model-based software product lines. In: Proceedings of the 2015 ACM SIGPLAN International Conference on GPCE, pp. 161–170. ACM (2015)
12. Garcés, K., Jouault, F., Cointe, P., Bézivin, J.: Managing model adaptation by precise detection of metamodel changes. In: Paige, R.F., Hartman, A., Rensink, A. (eds.) ECMDA-FA 2009. LNCS, vol. 5562, pp. 34–49. Springer, Heidelberg (2009)
13. Herrmannsdoerfer, M.: COPE – a workbench for the coupled evolution of metamodels and models. In: Malloy, B., Staab, S., van den Brand, M. (eds.) SLE 2010. LNCS, vol. 6563, pp. 286–295. Springer, Heidelberg (2011)
14. Hutchinson, J., Whittle, J., Rouncefield, M., Kristoffersen, S.: Empirical assessment of MDE in industry. In: Proceedings of the ICSE, pp. 471–480. ACM (2011)

15. Körtgen, A.T.: New strategies to resolve inconsistencies between models of decoupled tools. In: 3rd Workshop on Living with Inconsistencies in Software Development, Bd, vol. 661, pp. 21–31 (2010)
16. Kurtev, I., Bzivin, J., Aksit, M.: Technological spaces: an initial appraisal. In: CoopIS, DOA'2002 Federated Conferences, Industrial Track (2002)
17. Kusel, A., Etzlstorfer, J., Kapsammer, E., Retschitzegger, W., Schwinger, W., Schönböck, J.: Consistent co-evolution of models and transformations. In: Proceedings of the 18th International Conference on Model Driven Engineering Languages and Systems (MODELS). IEEE, Ottawa, Canada (2015)
18. Lientz, B.P., Swanson, E.B.: Software Maintenance Management. Addison-Wesley, Reading (1980)
19. Mantz, F., Taentzer, G., Lamo, Y.: Well-formed model co-evolution with customizable model migration. In: Electronic Communications of the EASST, vol. 58 (2013)
20. Parsons, J., Wand, Y.: Using objects for systems analysis. Commun. ACM **40**(12), 104–110 (1997)
21. Rose, L.M., Kolovos, D.S., Paige, R.F., Polack, F.A.C.: Model migration with epsilon flock. In: Tratt, L., Gogolla, M. (eds.) ICMT 2010. LNCS, vol. 6142, pp. 184–198. Springer, Heidelberg (2010)
22. Rose, L.M., Paige, R.F., Kolovos, D.S., Polack, F.A.C.: The epsilon generation language. In: Schieferdecker, I., Hartman, A. (eds.) ECMDA-FA 2008. LNCS, vol. 5095, pp. 1–16. Springer, Heidelberg (2008)
23. Salay, R., Chechik, M., Horkoff, J., Di Sandro, A.: Managing requirements uncertainty with partial models. Requirements Eng. **18**(2), 107–128 (2013)
24. Schmidt, D.C.: Guest editor's introduction: model-driven engineering. Computer **39**(2), 25–31 (2006)
25. Schönböck, J., Kusel, A., Etzlstorfer, J., Kapsammer, E., Schwinger, W., Wimmer, M., Wischenbart, M.: CARE - a constraint-based approach for re-establishing conformance-relationships. In: Proceedings of the APCCM (2014)
26. Strüber, D., Rubin, J., Arendt, T., Chechik, M., Taentzer, G., Plöger, J.: RuleMerger: automatic construction of variability-based model transformation rules. In: Stevens, P., Wasowski, A. (eds.) FASE 2016. LNCS, vol. 9633, pp. 122–140. Springer, Heidelberg (2016). doi:10.1007/978-3-662-49665-7_8
27. Thüm, T., Kästner, C., Benduhn, F., Meinicke, J., Saake, G., Leich, T.: FeatureIDE: an extensible framework for feature-oriented software development. Sci. Comput. Program. **79**, 70–85 (2014)
28. Van Lamsweerde, A.: Goal-oriented requirements engineering: a guided tour. In: Fifth IEEE International Symposium on Requirements Engineering, pp. 249–262. IEEE (2001)
29. Wagelaar, D., Iovino, L., Di Ruscio, D., Pierantonio, A.: Translational semantics of a co-evolution specific language with the EMF transformation virtual machine. In: Hu, Z., de Lara, J. (eds.) ICMT 2012. LNCS, vol. 7307, pp. 192–207. Springer, Heidelberg (2012)
30. Wieland, K., Langer, P., Seidl, M., Wimmer, M., Kappel, G.: Turning conflicts into collaboration. Comput. Support. Coop. Work **22**(2–3), 181–240 (2013)

Understanding Uncertainty in Cyber-Physical Systems: A Conceptual Model

Man Zhang[1]([✉]), Bran Selic[1], Shaukat Ali[1], Tao Yue[1,2],
Oscar Okariz[3], and Roland Norgren[4]

[1] Simula Research Laboratory, Oslo, Norway
{manzhang, bselic, shaukat, tao}@simula.no
[2] University of Oslo, Oslo, Norway
[3] ULMA Handling Systems, Oñati, Spain
ookariz@manutencion.ulma.es
[4] Future Position X, Gävle, Sweden
roland.norgren@fpx.se

Abstract. Uncertainty is intrinsic in most technical systems, including Cyber-Physical Systems (CPS). Therefore, handling uncertainty in a graceful manner during the real operation of CPS is critical. Since designing, developing, and testing modern and highly sophisticated CPS is an expanding field, a step towards dealing with uncertainty is to identify, define, and classify uncertainties at various levels of CPS. This will help develop a systematic and comprehensive understanding of uncertainty. To that end, we propose a conceptual model for uncertainty specifically designed for CPS. Since the study of uncertainty in CPS development and testing is still irrelatively unexplored, this conceptual model was derived in a large part by reviewing existing work on uncertainty in other fields, including philosophy, physics, statistics, and healthcare. The conceptual model is mapped to the three logical levels of CPS: Application, Infrastructure, and Integration. It is captured using UML class diagrams, including relevant OCL constraints. To validate the conceptual model, we identified, classified, and specified uncertainties in two distinct industrial case studies.

Keywords: Uncertainty · Cyber-Physical systems · Conceptual model

1 Introduction

Cyber-Physical Systems (CPS) are present in a variety of safety/mission critical domains [2–4]. Given the pervasiveness of CPS and their criticality to the daily functioning of society, it is vital for such systems to operate in a reliable manner. However, since they generally function in an inherently complex and unpredictable physical environment, a major difficulty with these systems is that they must be designed and operated in the presence of uncertainty. By *uncertainty* we mean here the

---

This work is funded by the U-Test H2020 Project (www.u-test.eu).

A. Wąsowski and H. Lönn (Eds.): ECMFA 2016, LNCS 9764, pp. 247–264, 2016.
DOI: 10.1007/978-3-319-42061-5_16

lack of certainty (i.e., knowledge) about the timing and nature of inputs, the state of a system, a future outcome, as well as other relevant factors.

As a first crucial step in such an investigation, we feel that it is necessary to understand the phenomenon of uncertainty and all its relevant manifestations. This means to systematically identify, classify and specify uncertainties that might arise at any of the three levels of CPS: *Application*, *Infrastructure*, and *Integration*. Based on studying and analyzing existing uncertainty models developed in other fields, including philosophy, physics, statistics and healthcare [5–8], we have defined an uncertainty conceptual model for CPS (*U-Model*) with the following objectives: (1) provide a unified and comprehensive description of uncertainties to both researchers and practitioners, (2) classify uncertainties with the aim of identifying common representational patterns when modeling uncertain behaviors, (3) provide a reference model for systematically collecting uncertainty requirements, (4) serve as a methodological baseline for modeling uncertain behaviors in CPS, and, last but not least, (5) provide a basis for standardization of the conceptual model leading to its broader application in practice.

To verify the completeness and validity of the *U-Model*, we validated it using uncertainty requirements[1] collected from two industrial case studies from two different domains: (1) Automated Warehouses developed by ULMA Handling Systems (www.ulmahandling.com/en/), Spain, (2) GeoSports (fpx.se/geo-sports/) developed by Future Position X, Sweden. This empirical validation was systematically performed in several stages and, as a result, several revisions of the *U-Model* were obtained in addition to a refined set of uncertainty requirements. The version of the *U-Model* that emerged from this work is presented in this paper. Based on the results of this validation, we discovered 61.5 % (averaged across the two case studies) additional uncertainties not identified in the initial specifications. The rest of this paper is organized as follows: Sect. 2 presents the background and a running example. Section 3 presents the *U-Model*. Section 4 presents evaluation and discussion. Section 5 discusses related work and we conclude the paper in Sect. 6.

2 Background and Running Example

A CPS is defined in [1] as: *"A set of heterogeneous physical units (e.g., sensors, control modules) communicating via heterogeneous networks (using networking equipment) and potentially interacting with applications deployed on cloud infrastructures and/or humans to achieve a common goal"* and is conceptually shown in Fig. 1. As defined in [1], uncertainty can occur at the following three levels (Fig. 1): (1) *Application level:* Due to events/data originating from the application of the CPS; (2) *Infrastructure level*: Due to interactions including events/data among physical units, networking infrastructure, and/or cloud infrastructure, (3) *Integration level:* Due to either interaction among uncertainties at the first two levels or due to interactions between application and infrastructure levels.

---

[1] Use cases containing scenarios having uncertainty.

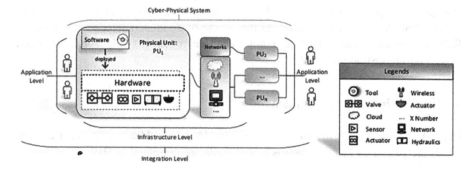

Fig. 1. Conceptual model of a Cyber-Physical System [1]

Due to confidentiality constraints, the actual industrial CPS case studies that we used to evaluate the *U-Model* (Sect. 4) cannot be described in detail. Instead, we chose a Videoconferencing Systems (VCS) developed by Cisco, Norway, as an example to illustrate the conceptual model that has been used in our previous projects.

A typical VCS sends and receives audio/video streams to other VCS in a video-conference including dedicated hardware-based VCS, software-based VCS for PCs, and cloud-based VCS solutions (e.g., WebEx) as shown in Fig. 2 (inspired from [9] and our existing collaboration with Cisco). To support videoconferences a complex infrastructure is provided by Cisco (Fig. 2) comprising of a variety of hardware such as gateways (e.g., Expressway) and dedicated servers (e.g., Telepresence and unified Call Management servers). In Fig. 2, we also show the various levels at which the uncertainties can occur in the context of our running example. For example, as shown in Fig. 2, at Site 2, the interactions of *Application level* uncertainties in VCS 2 and uncertainties in the Telepresence Servers are shown as *Integration level* uncertainties.

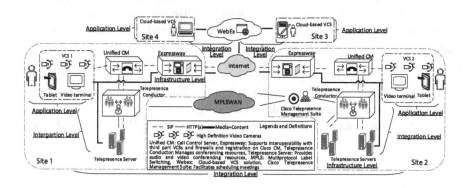

Fig. 2. Running example – Videoconferencing System (VCS)

To facilitate the understanding of concepts, a VCS represents aspects of the physical world in a somewhat simplified form. Among other functions, the VCS controls the movement of a set of cameras that are directly attached to it via wired/wireless media.

This can also be performed via a cloud-based VCS application (i.e., WebEx) in addition to dedicated hardware-based solutions. In the course of a videoconference, a number of different uncertainties exist due to the complex and heterogeneous collection of networks, cloud-based infrastructures, and VCSs.

3   Uncertainty Conceptual Model

The *U-Model* includes *Belief Model, Uncertainty Model* and *Measure Model*. Their key details are presented below, whereas more details are presented in [10].

3.1   Belief Model

The *U-Model* takes a subjective approach to representing *uncertainty*. This means that uncertainty is modeled as a *state* (i.e., worldview) of some agent or agency – henceforth referred to as a BeliefAgent – that, for whatever reason, is incapable of possessing complete and fully accurate knowledge about some subject of interest. Since it lacks perfect knowledge, a BeliefAgent possesses a set of subjective Beliefs about the subject. These may be *valid*, if the beliefs accurately represent facts, or *invalid*, if they do not[2]. A Belief is an abstract concept, but can be expressed in concrete form via one or more explicit BeliefStatements. Different BeliefAgents may hold different views about a given subject, which is why each BeliefStatement is associated with a particular BeliefAgent. Note that a BeliefAgent does not necessarily represent a human individual; it could constitute a community of individuals, some non-human organism, or even some technological system, such as a computer system[3].

These and other core concepts of the *U-Model* are represented as a class diagram in Fig. 3, where *subjective* concepts are represented by the grey-filled boxes and *objective* concepts as the unfilled boxes in Fig. 3. Subjective concepts are manifestations of the imperfect knowledge of a BeliefAgent. Conversely, objective concepts reflect objective reality and are, therefore, independent of BeliefAgents and their imperfections. One significant characteristic of the subjective concepts is that they can vary over time, as might occur, e.g., when more information becomes available[4].

Uncertainty (lack of confidence) represents *a state of affairs whereby a* BeliefAgent *does not have full confidence in a* Belief *that it holds*. This may be due to various factors: lack of information, inherent variability in the subject matter, ignorance, or even due to physical phenomena, e.g., the Heisenberg uncertainty principle. While Uncertainty is an

---

[2] Such a strictly binary categorization may not be always realistic, since *Beliefs* could be characterized by degrees of validity. However, in this model, we choose to ignore such subtleties. Specifically, a BeliefStatement is deemed to be valid if it is a sufficient approximation of the truth for the purpose on hand.

[3] In this case, the Beliefs would be reflected in the rules that are programmed into the system.

[4] However, more information does not necessarily imply a decrease in uncertainty.

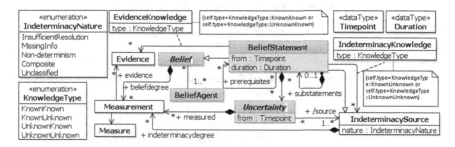

Fig. 3. The Core Belief Model

abstract concept, it can be represented by a corresponding Measurement expressing in some concrete form the *subjective degree* of uncertainty held by the agent to a BeliefStatement. Since the latter is a subjective notion, a Measurement should not be confused with the degree of validity of a BeliefStatement. Instead, it indicates the level of confidence that the agent has in a statement[5].

Finally, note that this model is intentionally made very general, which allows it to be extended and customized for a variety of purposes, e.g., uncertainty model-based testing of CPS in the context of our project. Figure 3 does not show the complete model, e.g., to reduce visual clutter, some of the OCL constraints have been removed. The complete model is described in [10]. In the remainder of this section, we examine key concepts of the core model in more detail and illustrate some of them using the running VCS example (see Table 1).

Belief, BeliefAgent and BeliefStatement. A Belief is an *implicit* subjective explanation or description of some phenomena or notions[6] held by a BeliefAgent. This is an abstract concept whose only concrete manifestation is as a BeliefStatement. In our running example, a test engineer at Cisco may have his/her own Beliefs about how a VCS works. When coding test cases, he/she concretizes his/her Beliefs as executable test scripts that may or may not correspond to the actual implementation the VCS. A BeliefStatement in this context could be manifested as one executable test case file and in other contexts it may correspond to other artifacts, e.g., source code.

A BeliefAgent is a physical entity[7] owning one or more Beliefs about phenomena/notion. A BeliefAgent can take actions based on its Beliefs. In our example of CPS testing, BeliefAgents include: (1) *Application level*: software test engineers focusing on testing new versions of the VCS software, and (2) *Infrastructure level*: Network engineers focusing on testing a VCS under diverse network situations.

---

[5] E.g, many people in the past were absolutely certain that the Earth was flat.

[6] "Phenomena" here is intended to cover aspects of objective reality, whereas "notion" covers abstract concepts, such those encountered in mathematics or philosophy.

[7] We exclude here from this definition "virtual" BeliefAgents, such as those that might occur in virtual reality systems and computer games.

Table 1. Running example – *Dial* of VCS

Package	Concept	Explanation
Belief Model	Level	*Application*
	BeliefAgent	Software testing engineers
	BeliefStatement	The VCS successfully dials to another VCS 70 % of the time.
	Indeterminacy Source	Improper human behavior where he/she enters an incomplete name/number of VCS to dial `IndeterminacyNature:: Non-determinism`, and `IndeterminacyKnowledge.type= KnowledgeType::KnownUnknown`
	Evidence	Execution of 100 test cases on the VCS in the past week involving the dial command `EvidenceKnowledge.type =KnowledgeType::KnownKnown`
	Uncertainty	Uncertainty in whether the dial to another VCS will be successful or not. This concept may depend on (see self-association of Uncertainty in Fig. 4) another uncertainty composed by another BeliefStatement specified by the network engineer, e.g. "The Expressway gateway is 99 % of the time successful in connecting Cisco's VCS with third party VCS."
Uncertainty Model	Type	Occurrence
	Lifetime	Difference of time that the dial was initiated and response from the system was received
	Locality	Invocation of the dial API of VCS
	Pattern	Derived pattern from the collection of values of lifetime of the uncertainty
	Risk	Low or even can be ignored
Measure Model	Measurement	70 % of the time, derived from Evidence based on test execution history
	Measure	Probability

A BeliefStatement is a concrete and explicit specification of some Belief held by a BeliefAgent about possible phenomena or notions belonging to a given subject area. A BeliefStatement can be an aggregate of two or more component BeliefStatements, or it may require one or more prerequisite BeliefStatements.

The concrete form of a BeliefStatement can vary, and may represent informal pronouncements made by individuals or groups, documented textual specifications expressed in either natural or formal languages, formal or informal diagrams, etc.

Due to the complex nature of objective reality and our human and technical limitations, it may not always be possible to determine whether or not a BeliefStatement is valid. Furthermore, the validity of a statement may only be meaningfully defined within a given context or purpose at a given point of time. Thus, the statement that "the Earth can be represented as a perfect sphere" may be perfectly valid for some purposes but invalid or only partly valid for others. For our needs, we are more interested in analyzing uncertainties in a BeliefStatement rather than studying its validity.

In our example, we define the following BeliefStatements: (1) *Application level*: The VCS will successfully connect to another VCS 70 % of the time (see Table 1); (2) *Infrastructure level*: The Expressway gateway is successful 99 % of the time in connecting a Cisco VCS with a third party VCS (see Table 1); and (3) *Integration level*: A VCS communicates with the Expressway gateway with a 90 %–95 % success rate.

Evidence, EvidenceKnowledge, IndeterminacySource and IndeterminacyKnowledge. Evidence is either an observation or a record of a real-world event occurrence or, alternatively, the conclusion of some formalized chain of logical inference that provides information that can contribute to determining the validity (i.e., truthfulness) of a BeliefStatement. Evidence is inherently an objective phenomenon, representing *something that actually happened.* This means that we exclude here the possibility of counterfeit or invented evidence. Nevertheless, although Evidence represents objective reality, it needs not be conclusive in the sense that it removes all doubt (Uncertainty) about a BeliefStatement. In our example of an *Application level* BeliefStatement, i.e., "The VCS successfully dials to another VCS 70 % of the time". The Evidence of the 70 % of success rate of dial may be obtained from the execution of 100 test cases on the VCS in the past week (see Evidence Table 1).

EvidenceKnowledge expresses an objective relationship between a BeliefStatement and relevant Evidence. It identifies whether the corresponding BeliefAgent is aware of the appropriate Evidence. Thus, an agent may be either aware that it knows something (KnownKnown), or it may be completely unaware of Evidence (UnknownKnown). This is formally expressed by the two constraints attached to EvidenceKnowledge (Fig. 3). An example is provided in Table 1.

Indeterminacy is a situation whereby the full knowledge necessary to determine the required factual state of some phenomena/notions is unavailable[8]. This is an abstract concept whose only concrete manifestation is in the form of an IndeterminacySource. As noted earlier, this may be due either to subjective reasons (e.g., agent ignorance) or to objective reasons (e.g., the Heisenberg uncertainty). It is also useful to explicitly identify factors that lead to Uncertainty referred to as IndeterminacySources. This represents a situation whereby the information required to ascertain the validity of a BeliefStatement is indeterminate in some way, resulting in Uncertainty being associated with that statement. One possible source of indeterminacy can be another BeliefStatement, which is why the latter is a specialization of IndeterminacySource (Fig. 3). For example, for the following BeliefStatement: "The VCS successfully dials to another VCS 70 % of the time", for which there might be several IndeterminacySources. A possibility is incorrect operator behavior, where an incomplete name of the target VCS specified (IndeterminacySource entry in Table 1).

---

[8] Care should be taken to distinguish between indeterminacy and non-determinism. The latter is only one possible source of indeterminacy.

IndeterminacyNature represents the specific kind of indeterminacy and can be one of the following: (1) InsufficientResolution – The information available about the phenomenon in question is not sufficiently precise; (2) MissingInfo – The full set of information about the phenomenon in question is unavailable at the time when the statement is made; (3) Non-determinism – The phenomenon in question is either practically or inherently non-deterministic; (4) Composite – A combination of more than one kinds of indeterminacy; (5) Unclassified – Indeterminate indeterminacy.

IndeterminacyKnowledge expresses an objective relationship between an IndeterminacySource and the awareness that the BeliefAgent has of that source. So, even though it is agent specific, it is still an objective concept since it does not represent something that is declared by the agent. For instance, an agent may be aware that it does not know something about a possible source (KnownUnknown), or the agent may be completely unaware of a possible source of indeterminacy (UnknownUnknown).

KnowledgeType (represented as enumeration) has four values: (1) KnownKnown indicates that an associated BeliefAgent is consciously aware of some relevant aspect; (2) KnownUnknown (*Conscious Ignorance*) indicates that an associated BeliefAgent understands that it is ignorant of some aspect; (3) UnknownKnown (*Tacit Knowledge*) indicates that an associated BeliefAgent is not explicitly aware of some relevant aspect, but may be able to exploit in some way; (4) UnknownUnknown (*Meta Ignorance*) indicates that an associated BeliefAgent is unaware of some relevant aspect.

At a given point in time, a BeliefAgent always makes a statement based on a KnownKnown Evidence and a KnownUnknown IndeterminacySource. Splitting EvidenceKnowledge and IndeterminacyKnowledge provides the flexibility to enable transitions among different knowledge types (e.g., from UnknownKnown to KnownKnown), based on the evolution of EvidenceKnowledge and IndeterminacyKnowledge related to the associated BeliefAgent. For the following BeliefStatement: "The VCS successfully dials to another VCS 70 % of the time" and an IndeterminacySource is improper operator behavior, the KnowledgeType of IndeterminacyKnowledge is KnownUnknown.

Measurement and Measure. Measurement when associated with a given IndeterminacySource represents the optional quantification (or qualification) that specifies the degree of indeterminacy of the IndeterminacySource. For example, in the case of a Non-determinism IndeterminacySource, its measurement could be expressed by a probability or a probability density function. For the example presented in Table 1, '70 %' is the measurement of the IndeterminacySource improper operator behavior.

Measurement when associated with Uncertainty is a subjective concept representing the actual measured value of an uncertainty defined by a BeliefAgent. It may be possible to specify a Measurement that quantifies in some way (e.g., as a probability) the degree of the uncertainty that a BeliefAgent associates with a BeliefStatement. Measurement when associated with Belief represents sets of measured values of all the uncertainties contained by a BeliefStatement defined by a BeliefAgent. Several constraints on Measurement ensure that each Measurement owned by either Belief, Uncertainty or IndeterminacySource has a unique Measure. Currently, we modeled three different measures, i.e., Probability, Ambiguity and Vagueness that are discussed in the *Measure Model* (Sect. 3.3). In the future, we will provide UML model libraries for Measurement when implementing *U-Model* as a UML profile. Measure is an objective concept specifying method of measuring uncertainty. More details are presented in Sect. 3.3.

3.2 Uncertainty Model

This model (Fig. 4) was inspired by concepts defined in the literature on uncertainty [11–15] and is an adjunct to the *Core Belief Model* (Sect. 3.1). The uncertainty model expands on Uncertainty from several different viewpoints and introduces related abstractions. Notice that Uncertainty has a self-association. This self-association facilitates: (1) relating different *Application level* uncertainties to each other, (2) relating different *Infrastructure level* uncertainties to each other, (3) relating *Application level* and *Infrastructure level* uncertainties to each other, (4) relating *Integration level* uncertainties to each other, and (5) relating *Application, Integration*, and *Infrastructure level* uncertainties. This self-association can be specialized into different types of relationships such as ordering and dependencies. Here, we intentionally did not specialize it to keep the model general, so that it can be specialized for various purposes and contexts. In the rest of the section, we discuss each subtype of Uncertainty and its associated concepts.

Uncertainty, Lifetime and Pattern. Uncertainty represents a situation whereby a BeliefAgent lacks confidence in a BeliefStatement. Figure 4 shows a conceptual model for different types of Uncertainty inspired from the concepts reported in [12, 14, 15]. Uncertainty is specialized into the following types: (1) Content – represents a situation, whereby a BeliefAgent lacks confidence in content existing in a BeliefStatement; (2) Environment – represents a situation whereby a BeliefAgent lacks confidence in the surroundings of a physical system existing in a BeliefStatement; (3) GeographicalLocation – represents a situation whereby a BeliefAgent lacks confidence in geographical location existing in a BeliefStatement; (4) Occurrence – represents a situation whereby a BeliefAgent lacks confidence in the occurrence of events existing in a BeliefStatement; (5) Time – represents a situation whereby a BeliefAgent lacks confidence in time existing in a BeliefStatement. For example, for the BeliefStatement: "The VCS successfully calls another VCS 70 % of the time", the

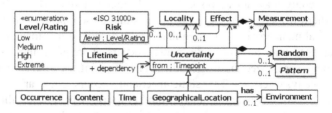

Fig. 4. The core uncertainty model

Uncertainty is whether the dialing to another VCS will be successful or not and classified as Occurrence uncertainty. In case of the BeliefStatement: "The Expressway gateway is successful 99 % of the time in connecting a Cisco VCS with a third party VCS", the Uncertainty is in the connection of the gateway with the third party VCS, and type of uncertainty is again Occurrence (see type of Uncertainty in Table 1).

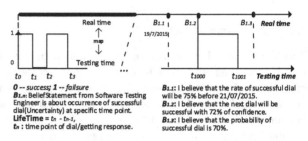

Lifetime represents an interval of time, during which an Uncertainty exists. That is, an Uncertainty may appear temporarily and then disappear. On the other

Fig. 5. Example of Lifetime and Pattern of Uncertainty

hand, an Uncertainty could be persistent, i.e., it remains until appropriate actions are taken to resolve it. An example of Lifetime is shown in Table 1. We show two types of time in Fig. 5: (1) *Real Time* showing the actual passing of the time, (2) *Testing Time*, i.e., a time point in real time, where a testing activity was performed, e.g., a call attempt to establish a videoconference (stimulus to the system under test) or a response from the system was received about success or failure of the call (test result). Time points t_n are shown on *Testing Time* in Fig. 5. A BeliefStatement can be made at any point in the real time, for example, three versions of BeliefStatement B_1 ($B_{1.1}$, $B_{1.2}$, and $B_{1.3}$) can be made at different points of time as shown in Fig. 5. Lifetime of Uncertainty (the occurrence of successful dial) in BeliefStatement B_1 should be $t_n - t_{n-1}$: difference of time that the dial was initiated and response from the system was received for $B_{1.3}$.

Figure 6 shows a conceptual model for the *occurrence Pattern of Uncertainty* inspired from concepts reported in [14, 16, 17]. Notice that in this section, patterns presented are by no means the representation of a complete set of patterns that may exist for an Uncertainty. Rather, we only present the most common patterns.

Periodic uncertainty occurs at regular intervals of time, whereas Persistent uncertainty is the one that lasts forever. The definition of "forever" varies; e.g., an uncertainty may exist permanently until appropriate actions are taken. On the other hand, an uncertainty may not be resolvable and remains forever. Both Periodic and Persistent inherit from Systematic, which means that these types of patterns occur in some methodical manners, i.e., a pattern that can be described in a mathematical way.

An uncertainty with an Aperiodic pattern occurs at irregular intervals of time, which is further specialized into Sporadic and Transient. A Sporadic uncertainty occurs occasionally, whereas a Transient uncertainty occurs temporarily. Systematic and Aperiodic uncertainty patterns inherit from Temporal, which means that they both inherently have the notion of time. If an uncertainty occurs without a definite method, purpose or conscious decision, the type of the pattern it follows is referred to as

Random. For example, when looking at Fig. 5, a pattern of the Uncertainty (the occurrence of a successful call attempt) can be derived after collecting values of Lifetime of the Uncertainty (see Pattern in Table 1).

Locality and Risk. Locality (see Fig. 4) is a particular place or a position where an Uncertainty occurs in a BeliefStatement. For example, for the BeliefStatement: "The VCS successfully dials to another VCS 70 % of the time", the Locality of the Uncertainty (whether the call attempt to another VCS will be successful or not) is in the invocation (position) of dial API of VCS (see Locality in Table 1).

An uncertainty may have an associated Risk and high-risk uncertainties deserve special attention. As shown in Fig. 4, an Uncertainty might or might not associated to Risk, whose level can be classified into four levels according to the ISO 31000 – Risk Management standard [18]. Level/Rating is derived from Measurement owned by Uncertainty (e.g., Probability of the Occurrence of an Uncertainty) and Measurement owned by Effect (e.g., high impact using the risk matrix in [19] or any other matrix). For example, for the BeliefStatement: "The VCS successfully calls another VCS 70 % of the time", the Risk associated with the Uncertainty in this BeliefStatement is low or the risk could be even ignored (see Risk in Table 1).

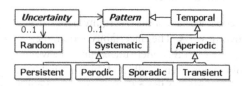

Fig. 6. The Patterns of Uncertainty

3.3 Measure Model

Figure 7 shows the *Measure Model* of the *U-Model*, inspired from concepts reported in [12–14] and by no means complete. Depending on the type of Uncertainty, a variety of measures could be applied and new ones can also be proposed when needed. We aim to give a high-level introduction to commonly known measures.

An uncertainty may be described ambiguously (Ambiguity). For example, in statement "The camera is down", the ambiguity is in the measurement, i.e., the camera is either facing down or disconnected. Interested readers may consult [20] for various measures of Ambiguity. Another common way of measuring Uncertainty is in a vague manner (i.e., Vagueness), which can be further classified into Fuzziness and NonSpecificity. Regarding Fuzziness, an uncertainty may be measured using fuzzy methods. More details can be referred to the fuzzy logic literature such as [20]. In certain cases, it may not be possible to measure an uncertainty using quantitative measurements and instead qualitative measurements can be used. Such qualitative measurements are classified under NonSpecificity methods. Finally, a common way of measuring uncertainty is via Probability. For example, for the BeliefStatement: "The VCS successfully calls another VCS 70 % of the time", the Uncertainty is measured by Probability (see Measure in Table 1).

4 Evaluation

This section presents the results of the industrial case studies that we conducted to evaluate the *U-Model* and collect uncertainty requirements. First case study is about Automated Warehouse (AW) provided by ULMA Handling Systems and the second case study is about Geo Sports (GS) by Future Position X (further details in [10]).

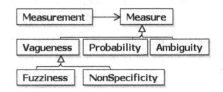

Fig. 7. Measure Model

4.1 Development and Validation of Uncertainty Requirements and U-Model

We collected uncertainty requirements from the two industrial case studies in the following ways. The uncertainty requirements were collected as part of an EU project on testing CPS under uncertainty (www.u-test.eu). An initial set of uncertainty requirements were collected by the industrial partners themselves and were later classified into the three CPS levels: *Application*, *Infrastructure*, and *Integration*. Later on, the researchers of Simula Research Laboratory conducted one workshop per partner to further refine the requirements. For AW, the onsite workshop took around three days, whereas in case of GS, a one-day onsite workshop was organized.

The validation procedure is summarized in Fig. 8 and comprises two parallel validation processes. The first validation process is related to the validation of the *U-Model* and was mainly conducted by the researchers. The second validation process focuses on the validation of uncertainty requirements and was mainly performed by the industrial partners.

The validation was developed incrementally (Activities A1 and A2 in Fig. 8), based on existing models in the literature and other related published works (see Sect. 5 for details). The Simula team validated the conceptual model using two types of examples shown as inputs to A2 in Fig. 8: (1) Examples of uncertainties from domains other than CPS, and (2) A subset of VCS requirements. As a result an initial version of the *U-Model* was produced referred as *U-Model* V.1 in Fig. 8.

In parallel, initial uncertainty requirements (Reqs V.1) were provided (Activity B1 in Fig. 8) by the industrial partners based on their domain knowledge, existing requirements of their CPS, and some information from the real operation of the CPS. These initial uncertainty requirements were used as input for A3, focusing on further refining the *U-Model*. In addition, the researchers inspected the collected uncertainty requirements using a requirements inspection checklist provided in [21] and provided a set of comments for the industrial partners on how to improve their requirements. There were two key outputs of the A3 activity: *U-Model* V.2 and comments to refine the requirements. These comments were used by the industrial partners to produce a second version of requirements (Reqs V.2) in B2.

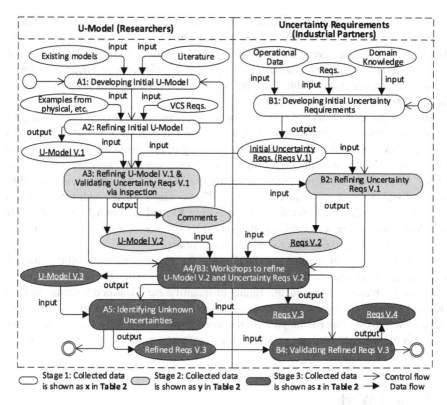

Fig. 8. Development and validation of uncertainty requirement and U-Model

4.2 Evaluation Results

For each of the industrial case studies, we mapped the three versions of uncertainty requirements (Reqs V.1, Reqs V.2, and Reqs V.4) to the three versions of *U-Model* (V.1 to V.3). The number of the instances of the concepts are shown in columns x (for mapping Reqs V.1 to *U-Model* V.1), y (for mapping Reqs. V.2 to *U-Model* V.2), and z (for mapping Reqs V.4 to *U-Model* V.3) of Table 2, respectively. Notice that Reqs V.3 was the result of the onsite workshops together with *U-Model* V.3 and thus these requirements are not mapped to the model since both the conceptual model and requirements were refined together. We analyzed in total 20 use cases for *AW* and 18 use cases for *GS*. Notice that, the number of use cases for each case study did not change during the requirements collection and the *U-Model* validation process. They were selected at the beginning of the process to capture and specify the key functionalities of the CPS.

Based on the final version of requirements, we can see from Table 2 that most common types of identified uncertainties are Content uncertainties having 91 instances (the last column in Table 2) and Occurrence uncertainties having 205 instances. On the other hand, a relatively lower number of Time uncertainties (50), Environment uncertainties (32), and GeographicalLocation uncertainties (31) were found in the case studies. Most of the time, uncertainties are due to InsufficientResolution (42 instances), MissingInfo (31 instances) or Non-determinism (89 instances). In terms of Measure, our analysis revealed that 76 of the uncertainties across the case studies may be measured with the Fuzziness measures, 119 with NonSpecificity, whereas 148 with Probability. Notice that in Table 2, we do not show the concepts that have no instances identified from any of the case studies.

In Table 2, the $R1 = y/x - 1$ column represents the increased percentage of mapping of concepts explicitly captured in Reqs V.2 as compared to Reqs V.1. The $R2 = z/y - 1$ column shows the increased percentage of mapping of concepts explicitly captured in Reqs V.4, i.e., including unknown uncertainties that weren't explicitly specified in Reqs V.2. As can be seen from Table 2, in case of AW for $R1$, on average, we identified an additional 1.43 of uncertainties and in $R2$ we identified an additional 0.51 of uncertainties. For GS, these percentages are 2.39 in $R1$, and 0.72 in $R2$, respectively. In total, in $R1$ on average we identified additional 1.91 of uncertainties, whereas in R2 we identified on average 0.615 of unknown uncertainties.

In Table 2, one can see that we didn't have exact data (e.g., probability) and risk information available at the moment. Such data will be collected using questionnaire-based surveys in the future to quantify the identified uncertainties. In addition, we didn't observe any pattern for the occurrences of the identified uncertainties. Moreover, the Belief part of the conceptual model (e.g., concepts Belief, BeliefAgent) was derived to understand Uncertainty and is not relevant for the validation.

5 Related Work

Uncertainty is a term that has been used in various fields such as philosophy, physics, statistics and engineering to describe a state of having limited knowledge where it is impossible to exactly tell the existing state, a future outcome or more than one possible outcome [18]. Various uncertainty models have been proposed in the literature from different perspectives for various domains. For instance, from an ethics perspective, uncertainties are classified as objective uncertainty and subjective uncertainty, both of which are further classified into subcategories to support decision-making [5]. In healthcare, uncertainty has often been defined as "the inability to determine the meaning of illness-related events" [6] and comprehensive domain-specific uncertainty models (e.g., [7]) have been proposed, as discussed in [8].

Uncertainty is receiving more and more attention in recent years in both system and software engineering, especially for CPS, which are required to be more and more context aware [22–24]. Moreover, CPS inherently involves tight interactions between various engineering disciplines, information technology, and computer science. This magnifies uncertainties. Therefore, adequate treatment of uncertainty becomes increasingly more relevant for any non-trivial CPS. However, to the best of our knowledge, there is no comprehensive uncertainty conceptual model existing in literature that focused specifically on CPS design or on system/software engineering in general. In the remainder of the section, we discuss how the concepts uncovered during the literature review align with our proposed conceptual model.

Table 2. Evaluation results of uncertainty requirements and *U-Model*

Concept		AW					GS					Freq
		x	y	z	$R1^*$	$R2^*$	x	y	z	$R1$	$R2$	$Total^+$
Uncertainty	*Content*	14	36	55	1.57	0.53	16	20	36	0.25	0.80	91
	Time	6	16	28	1.67	0.75	5	11	22	1.20	1.00	50
	Occurrence	27	81	126	2.00	0.56	6	50	79	7.33	0.58	205
	Environment	13	15	22	0.15	0.47	4	6	10	0.50	0.67	32
	Geographical Location	4	11	14	1.75	0.27	3	11	17	2.67	0.55	31
Sum for x, y, z/Average for R1, R2		**64**	**159**	**245**	**1.43**	**0.51**	**34**	**98**	**164**	**2.39**	**0.72**	**409**
Indeterminacy	*Insufficient Resolution*	7	18	24	1.57	0.33	11	14	18	0.27	0.29	42
	Non-determinism	7	45	52	5.43	0.16	11	20	37	0.82	0.85	89
	MissingInfo	2	19	24	8.50	0.26	0	5	7	N/A	0.40	31
Sum for x, y, z/Average for R1, R2		**16**	**82**	**100**	**2.67**	**0.43**	**22**	**39**	**62**	**0.55**	**0.57**	**162**
Measure	*Fuzziness*	6	22	51	2.67	1.32	6	15	25	1.50	0.67	76
	NonSpecificity	16	40	73	1.50	0.83	12	26	46	1.17	0.77	119
	Probability	18	56	98	2.11	0.75	4	37	50	8.25	0.35	148
Sum for x, y, z/Average for R1, R2		**40**	**118**	**222**	**2.09**	**0.96**	**22**	**78**	**121**	**3.64**	**0.60**	**343**

$^*R1 = y/x - 1$ $^*R2 = z/y - 1$ $^+Total = AW(z)+GS(z)$ *Freq is Frequency*

The *U-Model* concepts BeliefAgent, BeliefStatement, and Belief of the Belief model were adapted from [12]. The author of [12] postulates that uncertainty involves a statement whose truth is expected by a person, and therefore the truth might differ for different persons (defined as BeliefAgent in our model). However, as we discussed in Sect. 3.1, we assigned a broader meaning to BeliefAgent: which can be an individual, a community of individuals, or a technology. The *U-Model* concepts Environment and Locality were adapted from [12, 25–27], and we related them to the other *U-Model* concepts.

Our knowledge conceptual model aligns well with the model of knowledge reported in [28]. Here the authors looked at how to manage different types of known and unknown knowledge to distinguish what is known from what is not known. Knowledge is also classified from a different perspective: something that everyone knows, tacit knowledge, conscious ignorance and meta-ignorance. Their objective is to better understand ignorance. The author of [29] also studied unknowns and provided a taxonomy particularly focusing on ignorance (named as KnownUnknown and UnknownUnknown in our conceptual model). In our conceptual model, we further elaborate these concepts and captured them as KnowledgeType, which is associated to Evidence and IndeterminacySource via EvidenceKnowledge and IndeterminacyKnowledge.

We classified uncertainties into various types including Content, Time and Occurrence. In [12], a chapter was dedicated to the discussion of content uncertainty and its measurement. The other two types of uncertainties were mentioned in [12, 14, 15], with examples but with no clear definitions provided. We adopted the measurements in our conceptual model. Different types of sources of uncertainty for various purposes have been identified in the literature. In [30], the authors captured sources of uncertainty by considering risk and reliability analyses, based on which they classified uncertainty. The authors of [15, 31] identified sources of uncertainty in active systems. In [23, 32], the authors described the sources of uncertainty in software engineering in general. We however proposed the *U-Model* concepts IndeterminacySource and IndeterminacyNature to capture sources of uncertainty.

Aleatory and *Epistemic* uncertainties are the two generic categories of uncertainties discussed in many works [30, 33]. According to the work reported in [30], Aleatory is due to the inherent randomness of phenomena, whereas the Epistemic uncertainty is mainly due to the lack of knowledge. These two types are also covered in the *U-Model*. For example, the Non-determinism (nature of indeterminacy in *U-Model*) represents the randomness as in Aleatory, and Epistemic is covered by MissingInfo — nature of indeterminacy.

In [34], the author noted that uncertainty can occur in a random or systematic manner. In the Pattern part of the *U-Model*, we further elaborated the "systematic" concept by introducing Pattern and its sub categories. In literature, uncertainty is often related to Risk. The acquisition project team of the US Air Force Electronic System Center (ESC) has proposed a risk matrix for evaluating risks [19]. They introduced the concepts of Risk, impact, likelihood of occurrence, and rate of Risk and also identified their relations. We reused these concepts and linked them with Uncertainty.

6 Conclusion

Cyber-Physical Systems (CPS) often consist of heterogeneous physical units (e.g., sensors, control modules) communicating via various networking equipment, interacting with applications and humans. Thus, uncertainty is inherent in CPS due to tight interactions between hardware, software and humans, and the need for them to be increasingly context aware. To understand uncertainty in the context of CPS, unified and comprehensive uncertainty conceptual model should be derived. The *U-Model* is such a conceptual model developed in an EU project, based on a thorough literature review of existing uncertainty models from various domains (e.g., philosophy, healthcare), and refined and validated with two industrial CPS case studies of various domains. Based on the results of several stages validation, we obtained the current version of the conceptual model in addition to refined uncertainty requirements. On average, we managed to learn 61.5 % of unknown uncertainties that weren't explicitly specified in the uncertainty requirements collected from the two case studies.

References

1. Ali, S., Yue, T.: U-test: evolving, modelling and testing realistic uncertain behaviours of cyber-physical systems. In: Software Testing, Verification and Validation (ICST), pp. 1–2. IEEE (2015)

2. Broy, M.: Engineering cyber-physical systems: challenges and foundations. In: Proceedings of Complex Systems Design & Management, CSD&M, pp. 1–13 (2013)
3. Huang, H.-M., Tidwell, T., Gill, C., Lu, C., Gao, X., Dyke, S.: Cyber-physical systems for real-time hybrid structural testing: a case study. In: Proceedings of the 1st ACM/IEEE International Conference on Cyber-Physical Systems, pp. 69–78 (2010)
4. Tidwell, T., Gao, X., Huang, H.-M., Lu, C., Dyke, S., Gil, C.: Towards configurable real-time hybrid structural testing: a cyber physical systems approach. In: Proceedings of Object/Component/Service-Oriented Real-Time Distributed Computing, pp. 37–44 (2009)
5. Tannert, C., Elvers, H.D., Jandrig, B.: The ethics of uncertainty. EMBO reports 8 (2007)
6. Mishel, M.H.: Uncertainty in illness. Image: J. Nurs. Scholarsh. 20, 225–232 (1988)
7. Babrow, A.S., Kasch, C.R., Ford, L.A.: The many meanings of uncertainty in illness: toward a systematic accounting. Health Commun. 10, 1–23 (1998)
8. Han, P.K., Klein, W.M., Arora, N.K.: Varieties of uncertainty in health care a conceptual taxonomy. Med. Decis. Making 31, 828–838 (2011)
9. Cisco: Cisco Preferred Architecture for Video - Design Overview (2015)
10. Zhang, M., Selic, B., Ali, S., Yue, T., Okariz, O., Norgren, R.: Understanding uncertainty in cyber-physical systems: a conceptual model. Simula Laboratory Research (2016)
11. Bammer, G., Smithson, M.: Uncertainty and Risk: Multidisciplinary Perspectives. Routledge, New York (2012)
12. Lindley, D.V.: Understanding uncertainty (revised edn.). Wiley, Hoboken (2014)
13. Potter, K., Rosen, P., Johnson, C.R.: From quantification to visualization: a taxonomy of uncertainty visualization approaches. In: Dienstfrey, A.M., Boisvert, R.F. (eds.) Uncertainty Quantification in Scientific Computing. IFIP AICT, vol. 377, pp. 226–249. Springer, Heidelberg (2012)
14. Taylor, B.N.: Guidelines for Evaluating and Expressing the Uncertainty of NIST Measurement Results (rev. DIANE Publishing 2009)
15. Wasserkrug, S., Gal, A., Etzion, O.: A taxonomy and representation of sources of uncertainty in active systems. In: Etzion, O., Kuflik, T., Motro, A. (eds.) NGITS 2006. LNCS, vol. 4032, pp. 174–185. Springer, Heidelberg (2006)
16. Cimatti, A., Micheli, A., Roveri, M.: Timelines with Temporal Uncertainty. In: AAAI (2013)
17. Sprunt, B., Sha, L., Lehoczky, J.: Scheduling sporadic and aperiodic events in a hard real-time system. DTIC Document (1989)
18. ISO: ISO 31000: Risk management (2009)
19. Garvey, P.R., Lansdowne, Z.F.: Risk matrix: an approach for identifying, assessing, and ranking program risks. Air Force J. Logistics 22, 18–21 (1998)
20. Klir, G.: Facets of Systems Science. Springer Science & Business Media, New York (2013)
21. Yue, T., Briand, L.C., Labiche, Y.: Facilitating the transition from use case models to analysis models: approach and experiments. ACM Trans. Softw. Eng. Methodol. (TOSEM) 22, Article No. 5, 1–38 (2013)
22. Rajkumar, R.R., Lee, I., Sha, L., Stankovic, J.: Cyber-physical systems: the next computing revolution. In: Proceedings of the 47th Design Automation Conference. ACM (2010)
23. Conti, M., Das, S.K., Bisdikian, C., Kumar, M., Ni, L.M., Passarella, A., Roussos, G., Tröster, G., Tsudik, G., Zambonelli, F.: Looking ahead in pervasive computing: Challenges and opportunities in the era of cyber–physical convergence. Pervasive Mob. Comput. 8, 2–21 (2012)
24. Garlan, D.: Software engineering in an uncertain world. In: Proceedings of the FSE/SDP Workshop on Future of Software Engineering Research, pp. 125–128. ACM (2010)
25. Hu, F.: Cyber-Physical Systems: Integrated Computing and Engineering Design. CRC Press, Boca Raton (2013)

26. Cheng, B.H., Sawyer, P., Bencomo, N., Whittle, J.: A goal-based modeling approach to develop requirements of an adaptive system with environmental uncertainty. In: Schürr, A., Selic, B. (eds.) MODELS 2009. LNCS, vol. 5795, pp. 468–483. Springer, Heidelberg (2009)
27. Wan, K., Man, K.L., Hughes, D.: Specification, analyzing challenges and approaches for cyber-physical systems (CPS). Eng. Lett. **18**, 308 (2010)
28. Kerwin, A.: None too solid medical ignorance. Sci. Commun. **15**, 166–185 (1993)
29. Smithson, M.: Ignorance and Uncertainty: Emerging Paradigms. Springer, New York (1989)
30. Der Kiureghian, A., Ditlevsen, O.: Aleatory or epistemic? Does it matter? Struct. Saf. **31**, 105–112 (2009)
31. Esfahani, N., Malek, S.: Uncertainty in self-adaptive software systems. In: De Lemos, R., Giese, H., Müller, H.A., Shaw, M. (eds.) Self-Adaptive Systems. LNCS, vol. 7475, pp 214–238. Springer, Heidelberg (2013)
32. Ziv, H., Richardson, D., Klösch, R.: The uncertainty principle in software engineering. In: Proceedings of the 19th International Conference on Software Engineering (1997)
33. Matthies, H.G.: Quantifying uncertainty: modern computational representation of probability and applications. In: Extreme Man-Made and Natural Hazards in Dynamics of Structures, pp. 105–135. Springer, The Netherlands (2007)
34. Bell, S.: A Beginner's Guide to Uncertainty of Measurement. National Physical Laboratory Teddington, Middlesex (2001)

Author Index

Printed in the United States
By Bookmasters